TOEFL iBT® TEST ライティングのエッセンス

TOEFL is a registered trademark of ETS. This publication is not endorsed or approved by ETS.

論理性×表現力を高めるトレーニング

Ｚ会編集部 編

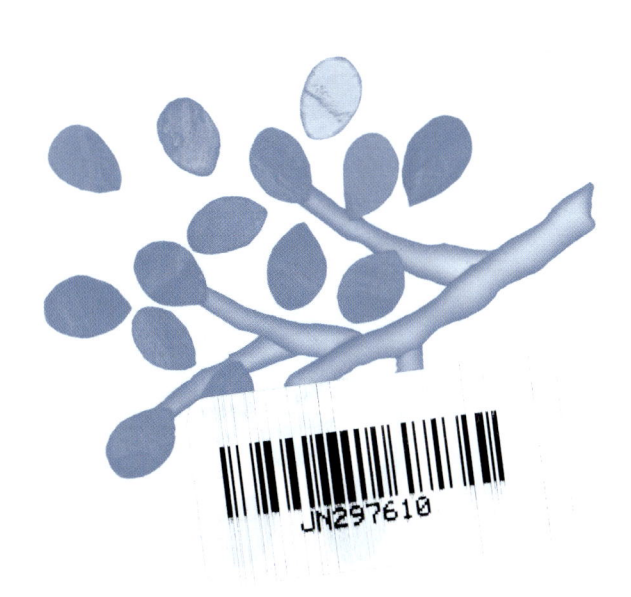

Ｚ会

はじめに

　TOEFL®テストは，英語を母国語としない人の英語力を，「読む」「聞く」「話す」「書く」の4つの面から測定するテストです。主に英語圏への留学を希望する学生の英語力の指標として活用されており，日本では大学院入試や企業内の試験にも取り入れられています。また，英語教育が大きく変わろうとしている中で，大学入試への活用も検討されており，英語4技能を総合的に評価することのできるTOEFLは，今非常に大きな注目を集めています。

　また，TOEFLでは，英語の運用能力だけでなく，「情報を正確に理解する」，「問われていることに的確に答える」，「自分の意見を論理的に伝える」といった力が問われます。つまり，TOEFLでは，単なる英語の知識や運用能力といった「英語を使う力」ではなく，「英語で伝える力」が問われているのです。したがって，TOEFLでハイスコアを獲得するには，そもそもの思考のベースとなる論理性を身につける必要があるのです。これは Critical Thinking（批判的思考力）と呼ばれるスキルであり，本書では，英語の表現力と同時に，一貫してこれを身につけることを目指します。

　そこで本書は，ライティングセクションの各設問について，解答の考え方・取り組み方を学ぶ「解答のエッセンス」，実践的な問題演習を積む「集中トレーニング」，本番前のシミュレーションを行う「確認テスト」を設けています。この一冊で，基礎になる考え方を学び，それを本番で使える力へと磨き上げることができるようになっています。「ライティングが苦手」「何をどのように書けばよいのかわからない」「ライティングセクションの得点がなかなか伸びない」といった悩みを持つ方は，本書で論理的に考えて書く力を鍛えると同時に，豊かな表現力を身につけ，ライティングセクションでハイスコアを獲得しましょう。

　本書が，皆さんの夢や目標を達成するための学習の一助となることができれば幸いです。皆さんが，真の英語力を身につけ，さまざまな場でご活躍されることを心よりお祈り申し上げます。

2015年11月　Z会編集部

目次

はじめに ………………………………………………………………… 3
本書の構成と利用法 …………………………………………………… 6
TOEFL iBT® とは ……………………………………………………… 9
TOEFL ライティングの対策を行うにあたって〜「論理的に書く」とは〜 … 12

各設問の対策と実戦演習

Integrated Task Question 1 の概要とポイント ……………… 18
Question 1　解答のエッセンス ………………………………… 20
　　　　　　例題 ……………………………………………… 22
　　　　　　演習問題【1】 ………………………………… 32
　　　　　　演習問題【2】 ………………………………… 39
　　　　集中トレーニング ………………………………… 46
　　　　　　問題 1 ………………………………………… 46
　　　　　　問題 2 ………………………………………… 51
　　　　　　問題 3 ………………………………………… 55
　　　　　　問題 4 ………………………………………… 60
　　　　　　問題 5 ………………………………………… 65
　　　　　　問題 6 ………………………………………… 69
　　　　　　問題 7 ………………………………………… 73
　　　　　　問題 8 ………………………………………… 77
　　　　　　問題 9 ………………………………………… 81
　　　　　　問題 10 ……………………………………… 86
　　　　　　問題 11 ……………………………………… 90
　　　　　　問題 12 ……………………………………… 95
　　　　　　問題 13 ……………………………………… 100
　　　　　　問題 14 ……………………………………… 104
　　　　　　問題 15 ……………………………………… 108

Independent Task Question 2 の概要とポイント ……… 112
Question 2　解答のエッセンス ………………………… 114
　　　例題 ………………………………………………… 115
　　　演習問題【1】……………………………………… 123
　　　演習問題【2】……………………………………… 127
　　集中トレーニング ……………………………………… 132
　　　問題 1 ……………………………………………… 132
　　　問題 2 ……………………………………………… 138
　　　問題 3 ……………………………………………… 144
　　　問題 4 ……………………………………………… 150
　　　問題 5 ……………………………………………… 156
　　　問題 6 ……………………………………………… 162
　　　問題 7 ……………………………………………… 168
　　　問題 8 ……………………………………………… 174
　　　問題 9 ……………………………………………… 180
　　　問題 10 …………………………………………… 186
　　　問題 11 …………………………………………… 192
　　　問題 12 …………………………………………… 198
　　　問題 13 …………………………………………… 204
　　　問題 14 …………………………………………… 210
　　　問題 15 …………………………………………… 216

確認テスト 第1回
　問題 ……………………………………………………… 224
　解説 ……………………………………………………… 226

確認テスト 第2回
　問題 ……………………………………………………… 234
　解説 ……………………………………………………… 236

本書の構成と利用法

　本書は，TOEFL iBT®テストのライティングセクションの各設問に対し，以下のステップで効果的な学習ができるよう構成されています。以下に示す利用法を参考にして取り組みましょう。

[1] Integrated Task，Independent Task の概要とポイント

　ライティングセクションには2種類の設問があり，その出題形式によって Integrated Task（統合型問題／Question 1 が該当）と Independent Task（独立型問題／Question 2 が該当）とに分類されます。各設問の形式の特徴と，実際のテストでの評価基準をまとめていますので，学習に入る前に必ず確認しましょう。

[2] 解答のエッセンス

　各 Question に論理的に解答するためのポイントを解説したページです。本書では，解答をまとめるにあたり「論理マップ」という図にアイディアや情報をまとめる方法を紹介しています。

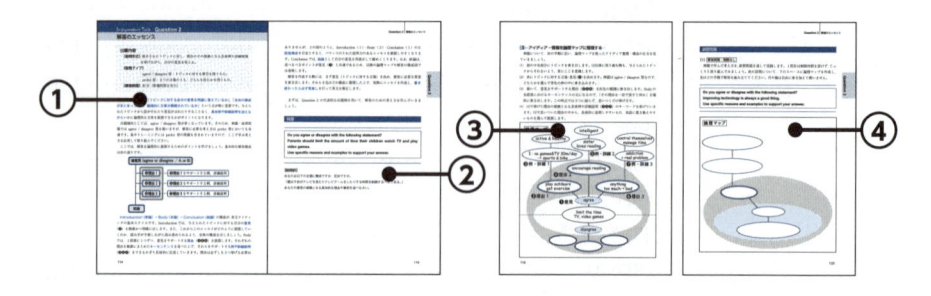

① Question の出題内容と解答の構成

　各 Question の出題形式を確認した上で，解答の代表的な構成例を知り，イメージをつかみましょう。

② 例題

　各 Question の例題を示しています。ここでは「Ⅰ アイディア・情報を論理マップに整理する」，「Ⅱ 解答を組み立てる」の2ステップで解答をまとめていきます。

③ 論理マップ

　Ⅰでアイディア・情報を整理する際に活用します。次の「論理マップのポイント」は，この時に注意すべき点をまとめていますので，参考にしながら考えてみましょう。ここでアイディア・情報が整理できたら，Ⅱでそれを解答の形に仕上げていきます。

④ 演習問題

　例題で学んだことを実践して定着させるための問題を各 Question に2問ずつ設けています。1問目には書き込み用の論理マップを掲載していますので，ぜひ実際に活用してください。

[3] 集中トレーニング

各設問について，本番に即した実戦形式の問題で集中的に演習を積みましょう。

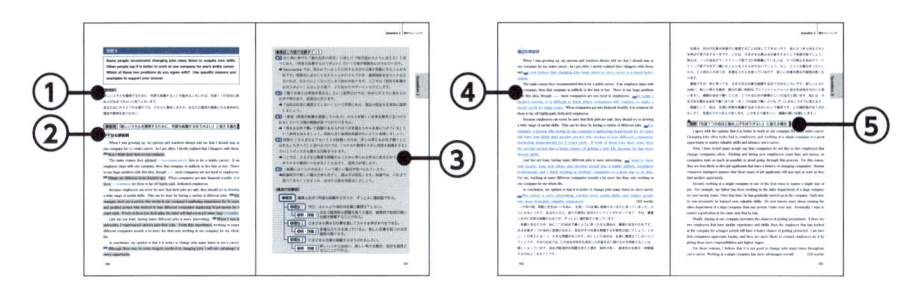

① 問題
本番と同様の出題形式の問題となっています。課題文を読む時間や解答時間については，自分で時間を計って取り組んでください。

② 不十分な解答例
学習者が陥りやすいミスを再現した解答です。修正が必要な箇所にはグレーの網掛けがしてあります。英文中にある★1などの番号は，その後に続く解説「構成と内容の改善ポイント」の項目と一致しています。なお，全体の構成や内容に関わらない文法ミス（時制，名詞の数など）は，英文中に青字で修正内容を示してあります。

③ 構成と内容の改善ポイント・構成の改善例
解答全体の構成や内容をどう改善すればよいかという視点から解説を加えています。さらに，構成の改善例を，論理マップと対応する図で示しています。

④ 適切な解答例
②③のコメント箇所を中心に内容を改善し，全体を構成し直した模範解答です。この英文中の★1などの番号も，②③の項目と一致しています。なお，特別に改善すべき点として取り上げていなかった部分でも，よりよい表現になるよう変更を加えている箇所があります。

⑤ 別解　※ Question 2 のみ
Independent Task である Question 2 は，④の解答例とは異なる立場の解答例として，別解を示しています。

[4] 確認テスト

ライティングセクション全体の模擬問題を2回分収録しています。解答時間を守りながら2問続けて取り組み，本番のシミュレーションを行いましょう。

■付属ＣＤ／音声ダウンロードサイトについて

・CD に収録されている内容は，下記 Web サイトより音声ファイルをダウンロードすることができます。
　※ダウンロードは無料です。

　　　　　　　　http://www.zkai.co.jp/books/toeflsw/

・問題を解くための音声のトラック番号は，以下のように確認してください。
　［例］　●01　→CD：トラック番号 01 という意味です。
　　　　　　　　音声ファイル：toeflw01 というファイルが該当します。

TOEFL iBT® とは

TOEFL® テスト (Test of English as a Foreign Language) は，英語を母語としない人々の英語力を測るためのテストです。英語圏の国（アメリカ，カナダ，イギリス，オーストラリアなど）の高等教育機関（大学や大学院）への正規留学の際，入学審査基準の1つとして提出が求められます。日本では 2006 年 7 月より iBT 形式が導入されました。

1. 試験概要

リーディング，リスニング，スピーキング，ライティングの 4 つのセクションから構成されています。スピーキングセクションとライティングセクションにおいて，Integrated Task（統合型問題）が導入されたことが iBT の大きな特徴の 1 つと言えます。純粋にスピーキングやライティングの力を問うだけでなく，リーディングやリスニングを含む 4 技能が統合的に測定されます。なお，すべてのセクションでメモを取ることが可能です。試験時間はトータルで 4 ～ 4.5 時間と長時間に及ぶので，集中力をいかに保てるかが高得点獲得のための 1 つのカギと言えます。

【構成】

セクション	問題数	試験時間
リーディング	36 ～ 56 問	60 ～ 80 分*
リスニング	34 ～ 51 問	60 ～ 90 分*
スピーキング	6 問	20 分
ライティング	2 問	50 分

＊リスニングセクションとリーディングセクションは問題数により試験時間が変わります。

2. 解答方法

TOEFL iBT テストでは，コンピュータ上で問題に解答します。リーディングセクションとリスニングセクションでは，マウスを使って正解の選択肢をクリックやドラッグして問題に解答します。スピーキングセクションでは，ヘッドセットのマイクに向かい問題に解答し，録音された音声がインターネットを通じて採点者に送られます。ライティングセクションでは，キーボードを使ってタイピングをします。スペリングや文法のチェック機能はついていませんが，CUT・COPY・PASTE の機能は使用できます。

【ライティングセクションの操作画面】
Question 1
①課題文が表示される。
　画面に課題文が表示されます。読む時間（Reading Time）として3分が与えられます。
②講義を聞くよう指示が流れる。
　講義の前に,「今読んだトピックについての講義を聞きなさい」という指示があります。
③講義が流れる。
　大学で行われる講義の一部が流れます。
④問題指示文が表示される。
　課題文と講義についての問題指示文が表示されます。
⑤解答を入力する。
　解答時間は20分です。残り時間が表示されます。解答中はヘッドホンを外しても構いません。また,課題文は常に読むことができます。

Question 2
①問題指示文が表示される。
　課題についての指示文が表示されます。
②解答を入力する。
　自分の意見や考えを画面に入力します。解答制限時間は30分です。Question 1・2とも,タイピングする欄の右上に使用語数がカウントされ表示されるので,解答時の目安にするとよいでしょう。

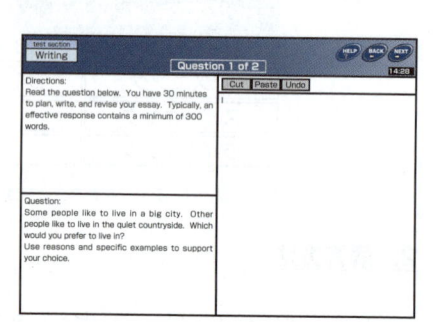

3. スコアについて

　4つのセクションはそれぞれ0～30点で採点され，トータルのスコアは0～120点です。スピーキングセクションとライティングセクションは，複数の採点者によって採点されます。スピーキングセクションは，各設問0～4の素点の平均点が，30点満点に変換されます。ライティングセクションについても同様に，0～5までの素点の平均点が30点満点に換算されます。

　出願の際，一般大学レベルは61～80点，難関大学・大学院レベルは80～100点，超難関校レベルは105点以上が目安になりますが，それぞれの大学や専門分野によって要求されるスコアが異なるので，志望する大学，大学院のホームページなどで必要なスコアを確認するようにしましょう。スコアは受験終了後，約1カ月後に送付されますが，受験日の約10日後からオンラインで確認することができます。スコアの有効期限は2年間です。

4. 申し込み方法

　TOEFL® Information Bulletin（受験要綱）を入手し，受験に関する情報を熟読してください。また，ETS（Educational Testing Service）やCIEE（国際教育交換協議会）のWebページに受験方法が詳しく記載されているので，確認してください。

TOEFL ライティングの対策を行うにあたって
～「論理的に書く」とは～

日本人が陥りがちなミスとは

　英語で文章を書くのは難しいと思っている日本人は多いようですが，具体的にどんなところが難しいのでしょうか。例えば，文法的に正しく書けない，または正しく書けているかどうか自信がない，適切な単語が思いつかない，単語を正しく使いこなせない，などが考えられます。文法を正しく理解し語彙を増やすことは，語学学習において大変重要なポイントですね。

　ところが，それ以前に何をどう書いたらよいのかわからない，考えがまとまらない，そもそも考えが浮かばないという場合も多いようです。あるいは，それらをクリアし，適切な長さで語法や文法のミスのない英文が書けたとしても，第三者が読むと，意見が明確に伝わらないケースが多いのも実情です。これは，内容に一貫性がない，文章全体が漠然としている，具体例や裏づけがなく説得力に欠けている，といった原因が考えられます。自分ではよく書けたつもりでも，TOEFL のスコアが思ったほどよくなかったという場合は，このような理由で減点された可能性があります。文章を書く目的は，第三者に自分の意見や主張を正確に理解してもらうことですので，常に読み手を意識し，独りよがりの文章にならないように書かなければなりません。

論理的で説得力のある文章を書くには

　つまり，ライティングセクションでハイスコアを獲得するためには，誰が読んでも納得してもらえるような説得力のある文章を，制限時間内に書く必要があるということです。そのためには，思いついたことをやみくもに書き連ねるのではなく，「論理的に考えて書く」ことが大切です。そこで身につけるべきものが「Critical Thinking（批判的思考力）」です。ここでの Critical（批判的）とは分析的，合理的という意味合いで，物事を論理的にとらえ，問われたことや自分の意見を相手に伝わりやすく，かつ説得力をもって表現するという一連の思考の流れを表しています。本書ではこの力を身につけるための方法として，「論理マップ」にアイデアや情報を整理する手法を提案しています。

　さて，説得力のある文章を書くための具体的な方法について考える前に，多くの人に共通する悩みの原因について考えてみましょう。前述の通り，英文を書くことが難しい理由の1つに，そもそも考えが浮かばないというのがあります。それはなぜでしょうか。その理由の1つとして，日頃から何かを吟味し，確固たる自分の意見を持つ機会が少ないことが挙げられます。また，何か意見があったとしても，それを周りの人に伝えなければ，論理的にまとめる機会にはなりません。そもそも，自分の意見を主張するのに抵抗があったり，周りの人の意見に合わせてしまう人もいるかもしれません。それらは文化的背景の影響もあるかもしれませんが，日頃からそのような機会が少ないことが原因の1つと言えるでしょう。

それでは逆に，多くの英語のネイティブスピーカーが，小さな子供でさえも，自分の意見を理由を添えて明確に述べることができるのは，なぜでしょうか。彼らも自然にそのような能力が身についたわけではないようです。彼らは小学生の頃から，自分の意見を持ち，相手に対して論理的に説明することを求められ，練習を繰り返してきているのです。

　つまり，私たち日本人もそのような訓練をすることで，アイディアを膨らませ，説得力のある論理的な文章を書く力をつけることができるのです。そのために必要なCritical Thinking を身につける手法について，もう少し具体的に考えてみましょう。

「論理的な英文」の構成を知る

　普段英文を読む際にはあまり意識していないかもしれませんが，英語の文章構成には，基本となる大原則があります。基本的な構成を知ることで，正しく内容を把握し，素早く要点を拾うことができるようになりますので，まずはそれを確認しましょう。

　英語の文章は，Introduction・Body・Conclusion という3つのパートから成っています。Introduction は文章の導入の役割を果たしており，これから展開されるトピックと筆者の主張の要点が述べられます。また，読み手が内容を予測しながら読むことができるように，全体の構成が示されます。Body は内容を具体的に展開する部分です。1つの段落に1つの理由や根拠が置かれ，筆者の主張を裏づけるための論証がなされます。説得力のある議論を展開するため，通常3つ以上の段落が置かれます。Conclusion では，文章の締めくくりとして，Introduction とは異なる表現で再度要点が簡潔にまとめられます。

　これらの段落はそれぞれ，キーセンテンスと，サポートセンテンスから成り立っています。キーセンテンスは，筆者がその段落で最も言いたいことを表し，多くの場合，その段落の第1文に書かれています。サポートセンテンスは，より具体的な情報を述べることでキーセンテンスの裏づけ・説明をしたり，次の段落への展開を促したりします。これは筆者独自の考えではなく，誰でも納得のできる内容であることが大切です。以下に例を示します。

例）　　　　　　　　　　　　　　　　　　本書 p.51 Question 1 集中トレーニング問題2課題文より

① The introduction of the assembly line revolutionized manufacturing and led to great cost cuttings. ② The idea was to assign people individual tasks, which they could repeat quickly instead of using workers who did a whole series of tasks one after another. ③ If the tasks themselves were unchanged, why was it more efficient to use the assembly line?

それぞれの段落は以下のような構成になっています。

> ①キーセンテンス（トピックの提示）
> 組立てラインの導入は製造過程に革命を起こし，大幅なコスト削減をもたらしました。
>> ②サポートセンテンス（キーセンテンスの補足）
>> その考えは，人々に個別の仕事を割り当てるというもので，それは，一連の作業全体をすべてこなしていく作業員を使う代わりに，素早く仕事を繰り返せるというものでした。
>>
>> ③サポートセンテンス（次の段落への展開）
>> 作業自体が変わらないのであれば，なぜ組立ラインの方が効率的なのでしょうか。

また，各段落は単独でバラバラに書かれているわけではなく，いくつかの段落が結びついて1つの文章を構成しています。その段落をつなぐ役割をするのがディスコース・マーカーです。ディスコース・マーカーは，論理の流れを明確にするための接続表現のことで，英文と英文，段落と段落をつなぐ役割を持っているため，これらに注目することで段落の関係を理解しやすくなります。逆に自分が英文を発信する際にも，これらを上手に利用することで，相手に自分の意図が伝わりやすくなります。

「論理的でない文章」とは

上記のような構成で論理的に文章を書くのが理想ですが，最初から上手に書ける人は少ないようです。以下はZ会の講座で学ぶ学習者の中にもたびたび見受けられる問題点です。心当たりがある人や，知らず知らずこのようなエッセイを書いてしまっている人もいるかもしれませんね。問題点を知っておくことで，注意して書くことができますので，よくある事例を確認しておきましょう。

【主張に一貫性がない】
・Introduction で反対の立場を表明したにもかかわらず，「しかしこのような長所もある」などと書き進め，最終的に Conclusion で「長所もあるので完全に反対とは言えない」と述べてしまう。
・「賛成である」と自分の意見を述べた後に，「ところが反対意見の人も多い」と反対意見について深く議論を進めてしまい，読み手を混乱させる。

【全体の構成にまとまりがない】
・話があちこちに飛んでいる。トピックとは関係のないことが書かれている。
・自分の意見・立場をはっきり示す一文がないまま理由や具体例から書き始めており，最後まで読まなければどのような意見なのかわからない。
・ディスコース・マーカーが使われておらず，それぞれの段落や文の役割がわかりにくい。

【段落の役割が正しく理解できていない】
・要点を示すべき Introduction が冗長で，具体的な情報で意見を膨らませるべき Body の内容が薄く，説得力に欠けている。
・まとめの段落である Conclusion で，新しい意見を付け加えている。

【段落内の構成にまとまりがない】
・具体的な情報から書き始めており，最後まで読まなければ何が言いたいのかわからない。
・1つの段落に2つ以上のトピックが書かれている。

TOEFL ライティングでハイスコアを獲得するために

　エッセイライティングでは，以上のような問題点に気をつけ，相手に伝えるという点を常に意識しなければなりません。また，「論理的な文章を書く」というスキルに加え，「短時間で情報を読み取って整理する」，「問いに対する考えをまとめて表現する」といった TOEFL で試されるスキルはすべて，Critical Thinking の観点を持っているかが問われています。つまり，TOEFL ライティングセクションで，一読しただけで採点者に自分の主張を理解してもらうエッセイを書くには，Critical Thinking を身につける学習をする必要があるのです。

　そこで，本書では，論理マップを用いた学習を提案しています。論理マップにアイディアや情報を整理する練習を繰り返すことで，自分の意見を論理的にまとめ，それを相手に説得力をもって伝えることができるようになります。また同時に，見聞きした情報を速く正確に整理する力も身につけることができます。説得力があり筋の通った文章が書けるよう，本書を通して Critical Thinking を効果的に鍛えるトレーニングを積みましょう。

MEMO

各設問の対策と実戦演習

Integrated Task

Question 1 の概要とポイント

■ Integrated Task の特徴

ライティングセクションの Question1 は，課題文を読み，さらに講義を聞いた上で解答する「**統合型問題 (Integrated Task)**」です。すなわち，ライティングの力だけでなく，リーディングとリスニングの力も試される問題です。

リーディングとリスニングの最中には，鉛筆とメモ用紙を使ってメモをとることができます。メモは試験後に回収されますが，それが採点対象になることはありません。

■ 設問形式

試験は以下のプロセスで進みます。

① リーディング（制限時間：3 分）

アカデミックなトピックについての，250 語前後の課題文を読みます。課題文にはタイトルがついていません。課題文はリスニングが始まると画面から消えます。

② リスニング（約 2 分）

課題文に関連する内容の講義を聞きます。講義の長さは 230 ～ 300 語です。

③ ライティング（解答時間：20 分）

リスニングが終了すると，問題指示文が表示されます。また，課題文が再び現れ，解答時間中，表示され続けます。適切とされる解答の語数は **150 ～ 225 語**です。残り時間と使用語数はコンピュータ画面に表示されます。

■ Integrated Task の評価基準

解答は，最低 2 名の採点者が，以下の 3 つの観点から，0 ～ 5 点まで段階的に採点します。
① 講義の重要な論点を正確に要約し，その情報と課題文の関係を明示しているか。
② 内容に一貫性があるか，全体の構成が整っているか。
③ 文法・語彙・表現に誤りはないか。

設問の指示の中心は「**講義の要約**」であるため，解答は，講義の内容を中心にまとめます。課題文は，解答時間中画面に表示され続けていますが，センテンスをそっくりそのまま書き写した場合，大きな減点の対象となりますので気をつけましょう。

また，高得点をとることのできる適切な解答には，最低ラインの 150 語を超えることが必要不可欠です。逆に，適切とされる語数の上限である 225 語以上を書いても減点の対象とはなりませんので，**解答で示すべきポイントを漏れなく挙げる**ことを心がけましょう。

以下が，ETS の採点者が解答を評価する際に用いる基準の概略です。

評価	評価の基準
5	このレベルの解答は，講義から重要な情報を選び出し，その情報と課題文の関連情報との関係を明確に提示できている。構成が優れており，ところどころに語彙や文法上の誤りがあるものの，意味の正確な伝達を妨げるものではない。
4	このレベルの解答は，概して講義から重要な情報を選び出し，その情報と課題文の関連情報との関係を明確に提示できているが，講義の内容や課題文の論点との関係に関して，わずかな不正確さ，曖昧さ，漏れが見られる。語彙や文法上の誤りがあるものの，それは明確さや議論の流れをところどころで阻害する程度のものでしかない。
3	このレベルの解答は，講義の重要な情報をある程度盛り込み，課題文の情報との関連性をある程度示しているものの，以下の点のうち1つかそれ以上に当てはまる。 ・講義と課題文の論点との関係の示し方が曖昧，不明瞭，あるいは若干不正確である。 ・講義の中の重要な論点の1つが盛り込まれていない。 ・講義または課題文の中の論点のいくつかが不完全，または不正確である。 ・語彙や文法上の誤りがさらに多い，または，曖昧な表現や，意味の伝達の阻害へとつながる誤りがある。
2	このレベルの解答は，講義に関する情報をある程度盛り込んでいるが，重大な漏れや誤りがあり，以下のうちの1つかそれ以上が認められる。 ・講義と課題文の全体的な関係にまったく触れていない，または完全に誤って提示している。 ・講義の重要な論点の多くを盛り込んでいない，または著しい誤りがある。 ・重要箇所において意味の伝達を阻害する語彙，文法上の誤りがある。
1	このレベルの解答は，以下のうちの1つかそれ以上が認められる。 ・講義で示された意味のある内容，または適切な内容を，ほとんど，あるいはまったく盛り込んでいない。 ・言語レベルが非常に低く，意味を理解することが困難である。
0	課題文の文章を丸写ししているだけ，またはトピックに無関係である。英語以外の言語で書かれている。ただキーを押しただけ，あるいは白紙のままである。

Integrated Task　Question 1

解答のエッセンス

> **出題内容**
> 《設問形式》アカデミックなトピックに関する課題文を3分間で読んだ後，同じトピックについての2分ほどの講義を聞き，課題文の情報と関連付けながら講義を要約する。
> 《設問タイプ》
> 反論型：講義が課題文に対してどのように反論しているか，あるいは疑問を呈しているかを説明するもの。
> サポート型：講義が課題文をどのように補足・強化しているかを説明するもの。
> 《解答時間》20分（リーディング・リスニングの時間を除く）

　Question 1では特に，**「講義のポイントを的確に要約しているか」**，**「講義のポイントと課題文のポイントの関係を明示しているか」**が問われます。この2つを確実にするためには，課題文と講義のポイントを正確に理解し，整理した上で，論理的な文章を展開しなければなりません。そのために，リーディング・リスニングの取り組み方や，情報整理のポイント，論理的な解答の展開の仕方を学んでいきましょう。

　出題傾向としては，**反論型が圧倒的に多く**，概して捉えるべき**ポイントは3つ**です。つまり，Question 1のほとんどは，「講義が，課題文の3つのポイントに対してどのように反論しているのか」を論理的に伝えるエッセイを書く課題であると言えます。そのため，例題・演習問題ではこの反論型について扱いますが，集中トレーニングにはサポート型の問題も含まれています。**解答に必要な考え方は，サポート型においても共通**ですので，ここで解答のエッセンスを定着させ，サポート型にも応用しましょう。

　初めに，解答の基本的な構成を紹介します。

- **❶【L】講義の立場**
    - **❷【L】ポイント1：講義のポイント1つ目**
      （【R】ポイント1：❷に対応する課題文のポイント）
    - **❸【L】ポイント2：講義のポイント2つ目**
      （【R】ポイント2：❸に対応する課題文のポイント）
    - **❹【L】ポイント3：講義のポイント3つ目**
      （【R】ポイント3：❹に対応する課題文のポイント）
- (結論)

Question 2 にも共通しますが，エッセイライティングでは，**Introduction（序論）→ Body（本論）→ Conclusion（結論）** という構成が基本です。Question 1 の解答では，まず Introduction で，教授が課題文に対してどのような立場をとっているのか（反論またはサポート）を明示します。その後，Body の各段落で，講義の3つのポイントそれぞれについて，課題文のポイントと対比しながら説明します。最後に，Conclusion で改めて教授の立場や講義のまとめを提示し，締めくくります。なお，結論で述べるべき内容は❶【L】講義の立場と共通であるため，以降の論理マップや解答の構成図では省略します。また，比較的短いエッセイであるため，結論は省略しても構いません。

　では，次に，課題文の情報と講義の情報の整理の仕方と，その組み立て方を学んでいきます。

Question 1 の代表的な出題例を用いて，解答のポイントを押さえましょう．

例題

Reading Time: 3 minutes

The sad fact is that the California water shortage shows no signs of stopping. California is a naturally dry environment, and the 20th century was an unusually wet period for the state. Now, scientists warn, the area is turning back into a dry, desert landscape, making the water crisis worse than ever. Luckily, there are plenty of options available for solving it.

One option is to change nature itself. For example, with a technique referred to as cloud seeding, scientists can actually produce artificial rain. In fact, using cloud seeding, China produces over 50 billion tons of artificial rain per year. Furthermore, scientists are currently researching cloud ionization —— a process of forming rainclouds using ion-emitting towers.

Another method for increasing the water supply is via water desalination plants, which pull water from the ocean and remove its salt and minerals. These plants are capable of producing millions of gallons of drinkable water per day. California government bodies are already funding some of the world's largest desalination facilities. Increasing the number of such facilities may solve the water crisis permanently.

The obvious solution, of course, is to simply decrease individual water consumption. Americans consume more water than anyone else on the planet. Per person, the United States uses more than twice the world average. Recent years have seen an increased number of people pushing water conservation, with more and more people cutting back on their daily water usage, but what the state really needs is a focused, organized water conservation movement.

Now listen to part of a lecture on the topic you just read about. ● CD 01

Summarize the points made in the lecture you just heard, being sure to explain how they challenge specific arguments made in the reading passage.

Response Time: 20 minutes

【設問訳】
今聞いた講義の論点を要約しなさい。その際，課題文で挙げられているどの論点にどのように反論しているかを必ず説明しなさい。

課題文訳，スクリプト ➡ p.28

Ⅰ ▶ アイディア・情報を論理マップに整理する

例題について，解答の骨組みとなる情報を論理マップに整理していきます。

(1) まずは課題文を読んでトピックを把握し，課題文のポイント3点を，【R】ポイント1～3に書き込んでおきます。トピックは❶の中にあらかじめ記入しておくと，講義が聞きやすくなるでしょう。
(2) 次に講義を聞き，課題文のトピックに対し，教授がどのような立場をとっているかを把握して❶に記入します。
(3) 続いて，❶に関して講義で述べられているポイント3点を，【L】ポイント1～3（❷～❹）にそれぞれ書き出して整理します。

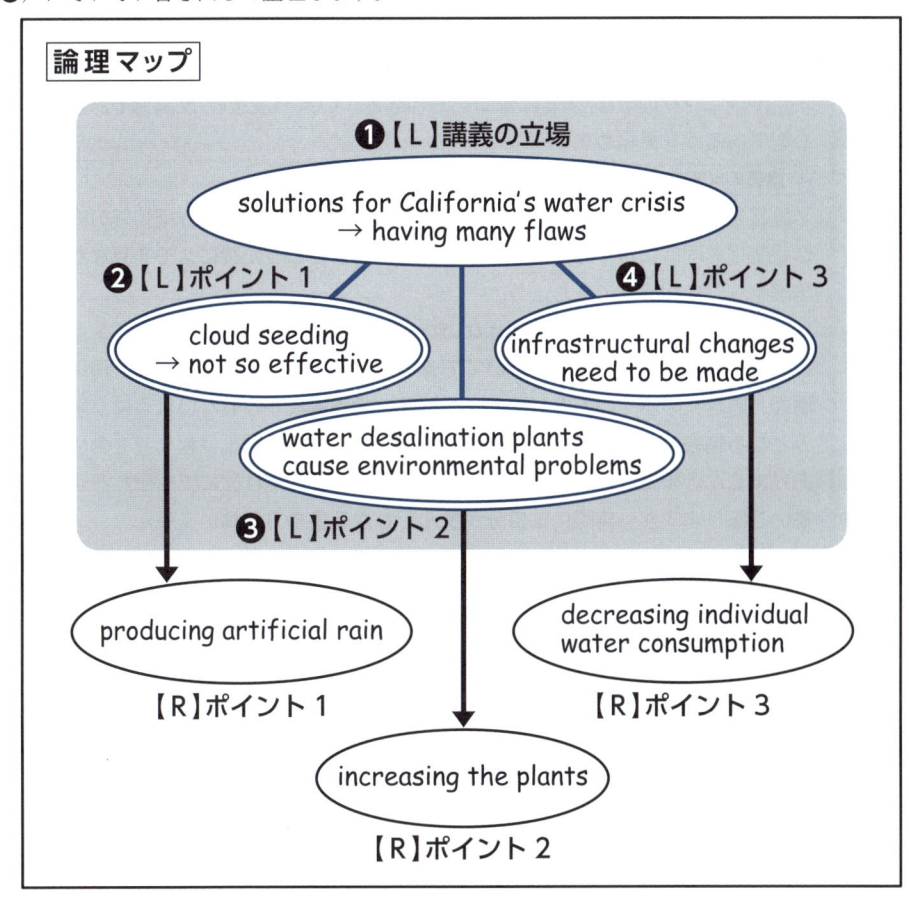

論理マップ

❶【L】講義の立場
solutions for California's water crisis
→ having many flaws

❷【L】ポイント1
cloud seeding
→ not so effective

❹【L】ポイント3
infrastructural changes need to be made

❸【L】ポイント2
water desalination plants cause environmental problems

producing artificial rain
【R】ポイント1

increasing the plants
【R】ポイント2

decreasing individual water consumption
【R】ポイント3

論理マップのポイント

☆**課題文で，トピック（主題）とポイント（論点）を素早く把握する**

課題文を読むために与えられた3分間で，トピックの把握とポイントの整理を行います。課題文は画面に表示され，下線などを引くことはできません。課題文は解答時間に再度表示されますが，**講義をスムーズに理解できるようにする**ためにも，この時間に論理マップに課題文のポイントを整理しておきます。逆に言えば，解答作成の際には課題文を参照することが可能なため，**細かい情報までメモする必要はありません**。課題文自体は**2分程度**で通読できるようにしておくとよいでしょう。

例題では，the California water shortage がトピックになっており，3つのポイントは，それぞれ**ディスコース・マーカー**（One option / Another method / The obvious solution）に導かれています。

☆**講義の冒頭で，課題文との関係性を把握する**

設問の指示にあるように，解答では，課題文と講義の関係性を示さなければなりません。英語の特徴として，**話者の主張（立場）は冒頭に述べられる**ことがほとんどです。リスニングの際は，まずは冒頭を聞き逃さないよう注意し，反論型であるかサポート型であるかを見極めます。

☆**講義のメモから，骨組みとなる情報を抜き出して整理する**

講義を聞きながら論理マップを作成できるとベストですが，詳細情報の聞き取りと情報整理を同時に行うのが難しい場合には，**聞き終わった後にメモを見ながら素早く論理マップを組み立て**ましょう。

講義は一度しか聞くことができないため，リスニングの最中は，ポイントをつかむと同時に**具体例や詳細情報についてできる限りメモ**をとります。逆に，論理マップは講義と課題文のポイントを対比させ，**解答の論理構成がぶれないように，解答の骨組みとなる情報を整理する**ものですので，課題文や講義の詳細情報までを含める必要はありません。また，本書に掲載している論理マップの例は誰にでも伝わるよう丁寧に書いてありますが，実際には**自分が読んでわかる書き方**で構いません。

▮ 解答を組み立てる

次に，Ⅰで整理された情報を，解答の形にまとめます。各要素のキーワードに必要な言葉を補い，キーセンテンスを書いてみましょう。

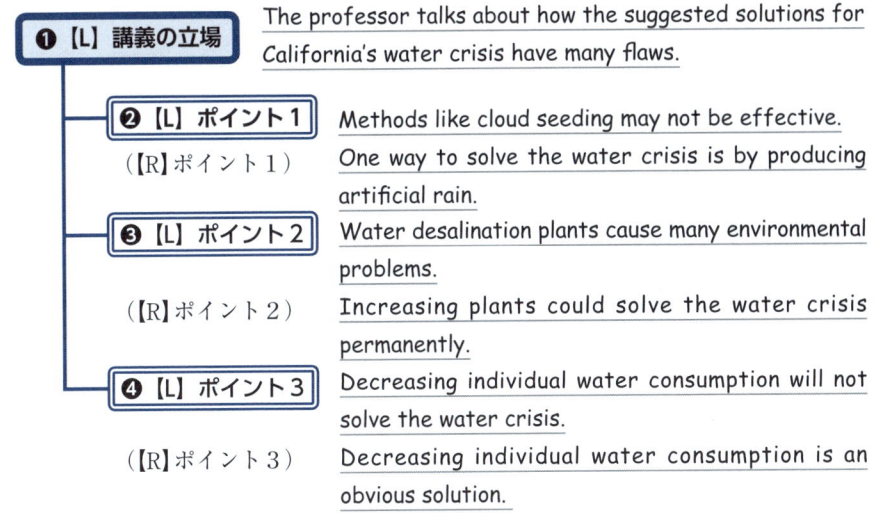

- ❶【L】講義の立場：The professor talks about how the suggested solutions for California's water crisis have many flaws.
  - ❷【L】ポイント1：Methods like cloud seeding may not be effective.
  - (【R】ポイント1)：One way to solve the water crisis is by producing artificial rain.
  - ❸【L】ポイント2：Water desalination plants cause many environmental problems.
  - (【R】ポイント2)：Increasing plants could solve the water crisis permanently.
  - ❹【L】ポイント3：Decreasing individual water consumption will not solve the water crisis.
  - (【R】ポイント3)：Decreasing individual water consumption is an obvious solution.

キーセンテンスが書けたら，以下のポイントに注意して，解答を仕上げていきましょう。

● Introduction（序論）では，講義の立場を明確に示す

まずは講義の立場・主張を示すキーセンテンスを配置します。解答例の Introduction はこの一文で終わっていますが，その後に講義の3つのポイントを示したり，課題文の立場に言及したりしてもよいでしょう。ただし，どちらの場合も，Introduction 全体が **2～3文程度** になるように簡潔にまとめましょう。

● Body（本論）では，作成した論理マップに従い，各ポイントについて講義と課題文を対比させる

すでに解答の骨組みはできていますので，具体例や詳細情報を交えて論を展開させていきます。学習者が陥りやすいミスとして，**課題文の情報を丸写しする，課題文との関係が示されていない**といったものがあります。あくまで「講義を要約する課題」ですので，講義の内容を中心にまとめ，課題文のポイントとの対比を漏れなく盛り込みましょう。

講義と課題文を対比するには，各段落において，「課題文では～と述べているが，教授は…と述べている」，あるいは「教授は…と述べている。これは～と述べる課題文に反論している（をサポートしている）。」などと展開することができます。こうした構成を基本とし，的確にポイントをまとめましょう。

なお，ポイントは3つであることが多いので，次のような**ディスコース・マーカー**を用

いて構成すると，伝わりやすい解答になります。

[役に立つ表現]
＊順序立てて書く
☐ First(ly)..... Second(ly)..... Third(ly).....「第1に，…。第2に，…。第3に，…。」
☐ First of all / To begin with「まず初めに」
☐ Next / Also / In addition / Moreover / Furthermore「次に，さらに，その上」
☐ Finally / Last(ly) / In the end「最後に」

●可能な限り多様な表現を用いる

　Integrated Task では明確に採点基準とはされていませんが，**表現の多様性**は，高評価を得るための大切な要素の1つです。同じ語が繰り返し登場すると，単調な印象を与えます。以下の表現も参考に可能な限り**パラフレーズ**（言い換え）を行い，洗練されたエッセイを目指しましょう。

[役に立つ表現]
＊意見を紹介する
☐ according to ～ / in the opinion of ～「～によると」
☐ as for ～ / regarding ～ / with respect to ～「～に関しては」
☐ mention / state / say / note that ...「…と述べる」
☐ think / believe / feel that ...「…と考える／感じる」
☐ claim / argue that ...「…と主張する」
☐ show / indicate / suggest that ...「…であることを示す／示唆する」
☐ explain / point out that ...「…と説明する，指摘する」
☐ talk about / discuss「～について論じる」

＊反論の立場を示す
☐ disagree with ～ / oppose / refute / contradict「～に反論する，～と意見が食い違う」
☐ challenge / question / doubt「～を疑う，～に疑問を持つ」
☐ have a different[contrary/opposing] view「～とは異なる／反対の意見を持つ」

＊サポートの立場を示す
☐ add that ...「…と付け加える」
☐ expand on ～「～についてさらに詳しく述べる」
☐ offer[provide/give] details about ～「～について詳細を述べる」
☐ give examples of ～「～の例を挙げる」

□ offer reasons for 〜「〜の理由を説明する」

＊逆接・譲歩・対比を示す
□ however / though / yet「しかしながら」　□ still / yet「それでもなお」
□ in spite of 〜 / despite 〜「〜にもかかわらず」
□ nevertheless「それにもかかわらず」
□ Although / Though / While 〜, ...「〜だけれども／ではあるが, …である。」
□ even if ...「たとえ…でも」
□ It is true that 〜, but ...「〜というのは確かだが, しかし…」
□ indeed「確かに」　　　　　　　　□ rather / instead「むしろ」
□ contrary to 〜「〜とは反対に」　□ in contrast to 〜「〜とは対照的に」
□ similarly / likewise / in the same way「同様に」

● Conclusion では，講義の立場・主張を再提示する

　比較的短いエッセイであるため，Conclusion は省略してもよいですが，最後に改めて全体をまとめ，エッセイを締めくくりましょう。

● 見直しの時間を確保する

　エッセイを書いたら，スペルや文法のミスがないか，講義と課題文のポイントを漏れなく説明しているかなどを必ず確認します。時間配分としては，論理マップの作成（3〜4分），解答作成（13〜15分），見直し・修正（2〜3分）を目安に，自分なりのペースをつかめるように練習しましょう。

【解答例】　　　：ディスコース・マーカー

　The professor talks about how the suggested solutions for California's water crisis have many flaws.

　First, methods like cloud seeding may not be effective. The technology for producing artificial rain has existed for over 100 years. However, some scientists doubt that it is effective. Also, ion-emitting towers do not create rain. Rather, they steal rain from other places. This refutes the reading passage, which states that one way to solve the water crisis is by producing artificial rain.

　Second, water desalination plants cause many environmental problems. The professor explains that these plants pollute ocean water by dumping large amount of salt and minerals into the sea, and this may cause problems for delicate ecosystems. In addition, the plants kill millions of fish each year. Also, they consume high amounts of energy. Again, this contradicts the reading passage, which states that increasing plants could solve the water crisis permanently.

Third, decreasing individual water consumption will not solve the water crisis. She explains that the real problem is not individuals using too much water. Rather, California's farms use too much water, because they produce a large amount of the country's fruits and vegetables. She suggests that infrastructural changes need to be made for water conservation to be effective. With this point, she opposes the reading's claim that decreasing individual water consumption is an obvious solution.

Thus, the professor believes that the options suggested in the reading passage don't address the California's water shortage.   (241 words)

（教授は，カリフォルニアの水の危機に対して提案されている解決策には，いかに多くの欠陥があるかについて話しています。

　第1に，人工降雨のような方法は効果的ではない可能性があります。人工的に雨を降らせる技術は，100年以上前から存在しています。しかし，その効果を疑わしく思っている科学者もいます。また，イオンを発生するタワーは雨を生み出しません。そうではなく，他の場所の雨を奪っているのです。このことは，水の危機を解決する方法の1つが人工雨を生成することであると述べている課題文に反論しています。

　第2に，海水淡水化工場は多くの環境問題を引き起こします。教授は，こうした工場は海に大量の塩分やミネラルを廃棄することによって海水を汚染し，繊細な生態系に問題を引き起こす可能性があると説明しています。さらに，工場は毎年何百万もの魚を殺しています。また，工場は多くのエネルギーを消費します。ここでも，海水淡水化工場を増やすことが水の危機を恒久的に解決し得ると述べている課題文と相違しています。

　第3に，個人の水の消費量を減らすことは，水の危機の解決にはなりません。教授は，真の問題は大量に水を消費する個人ではないと説明しています。むしろ，カリフォルニアの農場が，国内の果物と野菜の多くを生産するためにあまりに多くの水を使っているのです。教授は，節水を有効にするためには，インフラ面での変革がなされるべきだと提案しています。この点でも，教授は，個人の水の消費量を減らすことが明白な解決策であるという課題文の主張に反対しています。

　このように，教授は，課題文で示されている選択肢は，カリフォルニアの水不足を解決するものではないと考えています。）

【課題文訳】

　カリフォルニアの水不足に終わる気配がないことは，悲しい現実です。カリフォルニアはもともと乾燥した環境で，20世紀はこの州にとって，いつになく湿潤な期間でした。現在，科学者たちは，この地域が乾燥した砂漠のような風景に戻りつつあり，水の危機がこれまで以上に悪化すると警告しています。幸い，これを解決するのに使える選択肢はたくさんあります。

1つの選択肢は，自然そのものを変えることです。例えば，人工降雨と呼ばれる技術を使って，実際に科学者たちは人工的な雨を降らせることができます。事実，人工降雨を使って，中国は1年に500億トン以上の人工的な雨を生み出しています。さらに，科学者たちは現在，イオン化による人工雲の生成，すなわちイオンを発生するタワーを使って雨雲を形成するプロセスの研究をしています。

　水の供給を増やすもう1つの方法は，海水から水を引き揚げ，塩分とミネラルを除去する海水淡水化工場によるものです。こうした工場は，1日に何百万ガロンもの飲料水を生成することができます。カリフォルニア州政府機関は，すでに世界最大の海水淡水化施設のいくつかに出資しています。こうした施設を増やすことは，水の危機を恒久的に解決するかもしれません。

　もちろん，明らかな解決策は単純に個人の水の消費量を減らすことです。アメリカ人は，世界で一番水を消費しています。アメリカでは，1人あたり世界平均の2倍以上の水を消費しています。近年では，節水を推進する人々が増えており，ますます多くの人々が日々の水の使用量を減らしていますが，カリフォルニア州が本当に取り組むべきことは，集中的で体系化された節水運動です。

【リスニングスクリプト】

Now listen to part of a lecture on the topic you just read about.

　Let's look at some of the drawbacks to the "solutions" presented in the reading.

　The article talks about producing artificial rain, right? The technology behind creating rain has actually been around for about a hundred years... So why don't countries use this technique more often? Well, many scientists claim that cloud seeding isn't really effective at producing more rainfall... The introduction of these ion-emitting towers sounds promising to some, but experts have pointed out that these towers would simply 'steal' rainfall from other areas. They don't create rain; they just take it from someone else...

　So why not just take water from the ocean? As the author mentions, it appears that the use of water desalination plants cannot be avoided. But that does not necessarily make them a good solution... Environmentalists, in particular, have a lot of complaints about desalination facilities... The primary complaint is usually that these plants pollute oceans. You see, after they remove all of the salt and minerals from the water, they simply dump the leftovers back into the ocean. This could cause damage to sensitive ecosystems, and it's still not clear what negative effects they can have. On top of this, these facilities kill millions of fish and other marine life per year. Combined with the huge amounts of energy required to run these plants, they're essentially an environmental nightmare.

　The seemingly simple solution would be to reduce water usage, but that's not as easy as it sounds. For one thing, individual water consumption is not the real issue. Rather, California farms are using too much water, because they produce so much of the country's fruits and vegetables. The only conservation efforts capable of fixing this problem would be infrastructural changes to water systems, pipes, and food production.

【リスニングスクリプト訳】
今読んだトピックに関する講義の一部を聞きなさい。

　では，この読み物で提示された「解決策」の欠点についていくつか検証してみましょう。

　この記事は，人工雨の生成について話していますね。雨を降らせる背景にある技術は，実は100年ほど前からありました…。それならばなぜ，国々はこの技術をもっと頻繁に使わないのでしょうか。ええ，人工降雨は降雨量を増やすのにはあまり効果的でないと多くの科学者たちが主張しているのです…。イオンを発生するタワーの導入が有望に思える人もいるかもしれませんが，専門家たちはこうしたタワーは，単に他の地域の降雨を「盗んでいる」だけだと指摘しています。雨を生成しているのではなく，誰かの雨を奪っているだけなのです。

　それでは，海から取水するというのはだめでしょうか。この著者が述べているように，海水淡水化工場の使用は避けられないように思われます。しかし，それは必ずしもよい解決策にはなりません…。特に，環境保護活動家たちは海水淡水化施設についてたくさんの苦言を呈しています…。その主な内容は，多くが，これらの工場が海を汚染するということです。皆さんもおわかりのように，こうした工場は，海水から塩分とミネラルをすべて除去した後，その残留物を単純に海に廃棄しますよね。このことは，繊細な生態系にダメージを与える可能性がありますが，どのような負の影響を持ち得るのか，まだはっきりしていないのです。これだけでなく，こうした工場は，1年に何百万という魚や海洋生物を殺します。こうした工場を稼働するのに必要な大量のエネルギーと相まって，環境面からすると実質的には悪夢のようなものなのです。

　一見簡単に思える解決策は，水の使用量を減らすことですが，これもそれほど簡単なことではありません。まず，個人の水の消費量は真の問題ではありません。そうではなく，国内で果物と野菜をたくさん生産しているために，カリフォルニアの農場が水を使いすぎているのです。この問題を解決できる唯一の環境保全努力は，水道システムや送水管，食料生産に対するインフラ面での変革です。

✓ 重要表現チェック

課題文	□ shortage「不足」	□ (be) referred to as ～「～と呼ばれる」
	□ artificial「人工の」	□ ionization「イオン化」
	□ desalination「淡水化」	□ plant「工場，施設」
	□ facility「施設，設備」	□ permanently「永久に，恒久的に」
	□ cut back on ～「～を減らす」	
解答例	□ flaw「欠点」	□ address「～に対処する」
リスニングスクリプト	□ drawbacks「欠点，難点」	□ promising「有望な」
	□ steal「～を盗む」	□ complaint「不満，苦言」
	□ leftover「残留物，残り物」	□ seemingly「一見したところ」

仕上げ
☐ 課題文や講義の内容を見直し,自分の作成した論理マップについて,ポイントが的確に捉えられているかチェックし,必要があれば修正しましょう。
☐ 自分の作成した解答について,論理マップに基づいて修正しましょう。
☐ 解答例をパソコンで入力する練習をしてみましょう。その際,スペルチェック機能をオフにします。メモ帳ソフトを利用してもよいでしょう。

演習問題

【1】 解答時間：制限なし

例題で学んだ考え方を，演習問題を通して実践します。1問目は制限時間を設けず，じっくりと取り組みましょう。次の設問について論理マップを作成し，先ほどの手順で解答を組み立ててください。円や線は自由に書き加えて構いません。

Reading Time: 3 minutes

There are thousands of cases of laser eye surgery patients that have had horrible, negative side effects to LASIK surgery. For this reason, laser eye surgery procedures should be banned until further research can guarantee positive results for a majority of patients.

The biggest problem with laser eyes surgery is that patients are almost guaranteed to experience negative side effects. The most common side effect is dry eyes. In fact, up to 30% of patients are reported to suffer from dry eyes after LASIK treatment. One patient was quoted as saying, "I can't wear eye makeup anymore, because I have to put eye drops in multiple times per day, every day." This frequent usage of eye drops can lead to dependency, and serious cases of dry eyes can even result in blindness.

The worst part is that eye doctors are not honest with their patients about the likely side effects of laser eye surgery. Nearly two-thirds of patients that get LASIK surgery express disappointment upon learning that they still need to use glasses. In a recent independent study, over one-third of eye treatments clinics failed to describe the risks of laser eye surgery during a free consultation.

While the majority of laser eye surgery patients have improved vision in the weeks after the procedure, long-term side effects are a huge problem. Up to 75% of laser eye surgery patients will have worse vision at the end of ten years. This means that the majority of patients will still need glasses later in life, especially for activities such as driving at night. Some patients even experience severe vision loss years later and have to undergo major surgical operations such as corneal transplants.

Question 1 | 解答のエッセンス

Now listen to part of a lecture on the topic you just read about.　● CD 02

Summarize the points made in the lecture you just heard, being sure to explain how they challenge specific arguments made in the reading passage.

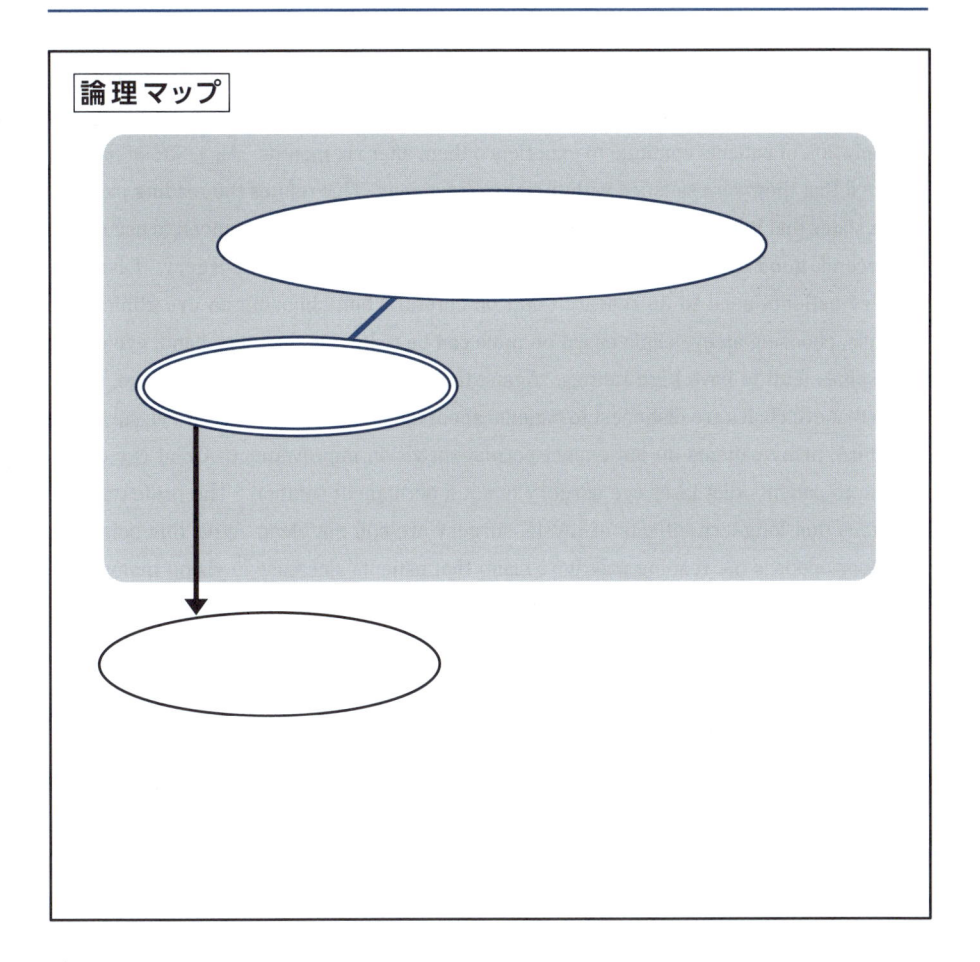

論理マップ

【設問訳】

今聞いた講義の論点を要約しなさい。その際，課題文で挙げられているどの論点にどのように反論しているかを必ず説明しなさい。

課題文訳，スクリプト ➡ p.36

【解答例】

　　The professor says that laser eye surgery still has some problems, but it is generally safe and effective.

　　First, most patients are happy with the results, and most side effects are not permanent. Although the professor acknowledges that side effects are quite common, he points out that only 20% of patients continue to experience them after six months. Also, 80% of patients reported that they were satisfied with their eye treatment. This refutes the reading passage, which states that it is a big problem negative side effects are almost guaranteed to occur.

　　Second, good eye clinics are honest about the risks of laser eye surgery. Laser eye surgery patients need to do research and be careful when choosing an eye clinic. For example, choosing an eye clinic based on price can be risky. On the other hand, eye clinics in hospitals tend to have high ratings. Again, this contradicts the reading passage, which states that eye clinics are dishonest to patients about the possible risks of laser eye surgery.

　　Third, many patients do not expect permanent vision improvement. Good eye clinics explain to patients that laser eye surgery is not a permanent solution. The professor also mentions that long-term effects of LASIK surgery are still not clear. With this point, the professor opposes the reading passage's claim that patients' decrease in vision many years after a procedure is a major concern. (234 words)

　　（教授は，レーザー眼科手術はいくつか問題点もあるものの，概して安全で効果的であると話しています。

　　第1に，ほとんどの患者はその結果に満足しており，副作用のほとんどは永遠に続くものではありません。教授は，副作用がかなり広く見られることは認めているものの，6カ月経ってからも副作用が続くのは患者の20パーセントしかいないと指摘しています。また，80パーセントの患者が目の治療に満足していると述べています。このことは，悪い副作用がほぼ確実に起こることは大きな問題だと述べている課題文に反論しています。

　　第2に，よい眼科クリニックはレーザー眼科手術のリスクについて誠実です。レーザー眼科手術の患者は，眼科クリニックを選ぶ際，下調べをして慎重になる必要があります。例えば，値段をもとに眼科クリニックを選ぶことは危険かもしれません。他方，病院内の眼科クリニックは評価が高い傾向にあります。ここでも，レーザー眼科手術で起こりうるリスクについて，眼科クリニックが患者に不誠実だと述べている課題文に反論しています。

　　第3に，多くの患者は永遠に視力がよくなることを期待しているわけではありません。よい眼科クリニックは，患者にレーザー眼科手術が恒久的な解決策ではないと説明します。教授は，レ

ーシック手術の長期的な副作用はいまだはっきりとはわかっていないとも述べています。この点で，教授は，術後何年も経過すると視力が低下することが大きな懸念事項だと述べている課題文の主張に反対しています。)

【解説】

教授が課題文のポイントにどのように反論しているかを説明する，反論型の問題です。課題文がレーザー眼科手術の3つの問題点を提示しているのに対し，教授はそれら1つ1つについて反論しながら，レーザー眼科手術の安全性を主張しています。解答の際は，まず Introduction でこの教授の立場を示し，それから Body で各ポイントについての教授の反論の内容を順に展開します。

解答例の Body の展開の仕方を見てみると，First / Second / Third で構成をわかりやすく示しています。ポイント1は副作用の存在です。教授は，「副作用が恒久的でないこと」と「患者の大半が満足していること」を挙げ，「副作用がほぼ確実に起こることは大きな問題だ」と主張する課題文に反論しています。これを補強する情報として，講義中で挙げられている具体的な数字にも言及できるとよいでしょう。ポイント2は，眼科医の誠実さについてです。教授は，「眼科医を選択する患者へのアドバイス」を含めながら，「誠実な眼科医の存在」を示すことで，「眼科クリニックはリスクについて患者に対して不誠実である」と主張する課題文に反論していますので，それらについて説明します。ポイント3は，課題文が指摘する「長年経つと視力が低下する」という問題点についてですが，この点への反論の中心となるのが「多くの患者は恒久的な視力の維持を期待してはいない」ということです。さらに，「レーシック手術の長期的な影響は不明だ」という説明も加えることができます。

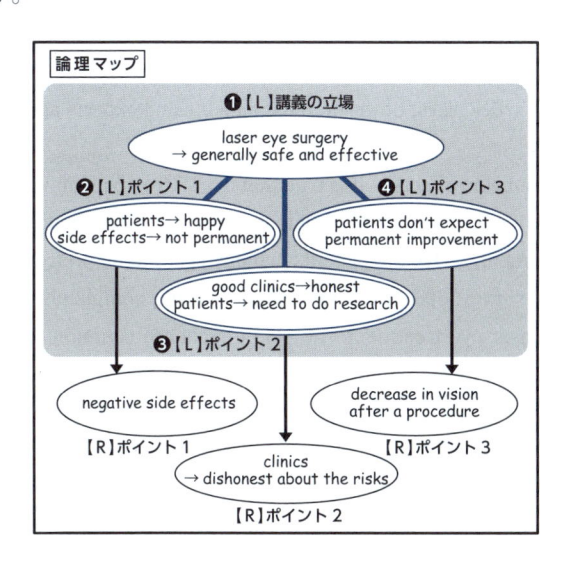

```
┌─ 論理マップ ──────────────────────────┐
│                ❶【L】講義の立場                │
│              laser eye surgery                │
│           → generally safe and effective       │
│  ❷【L】ポイント1              ❹【L】ポイント3   │
│   patients→ happy         patients don't expect│
│   side effects→ not permanent  permanent improvement│
│            good clinics→honest                │
│            patients→ need to do research       │
│           ❸【L】ポイント2                      │
│   negative side effects    decrease in vision  │
│                            after a procedure   │
│   【R】ポイント1              【R】ポイント3      │
│              clinics                          │
│           → dishonest about the risks          │
│              【R】ポイント2                     │
└──────────────────────────────┘
```

【課題文訳】

　レーシック手術のひどい副作用が起きているレーザー眼科手術の患者の症例が，何千件も存在しています。このため，レーザー眼科手術の処置は，今後の調査で大多数の患者に好ましい結果が保証されるまで禁止されるべきです。

　レーザー眼科手術の最大の問題は，患者にはほぼ確実に悪い副作用が起きているということです。最も一般的な副作用は，ドライアイです。実は，最大で30パーセントの患者が，レーシック治療後にドライアイを患うと報告されています。ある患者は，「毎日，1日に何度も目薬をささなければならないので，もうアイメイクができません」と言ったと伝えられています。このような目薬の頻繁な使用は，依存症につながる可能性があり，重度のドライアイは失明につながることさえあります。

　最も悪い点は，レーザー眼科手術で起こり得る副作用について，眼科医が患者に対して誠実でないということです。レーシック手術を受けた3分の2近くの患者が，手術をしても眼鏡をかける必要があるということを知って，落胆しています。最近の独自の研究では，眼科治療クリニックの3分の1以上が，無料相談中にレーザー眼科手術のリスクについて説明していませんでした。

　レーザー眼科手術を受けた患者の大多数が処置後の数週間で視力が向上していますが，長期間に及ぶ副作用は大きな問題です。レーザー眼科手術を受けた患者の最大75パーセントは，10年経つ頃には視力が低下してくるでしょう。このことはつまり，患者のほとんどは後年になってから，特に夜間の運転のような活動では，なお眼鏡が必要となるということです。中には，何年か経ってから著しく視力が低下し，角膜移植といった大がかりな外科手術を受けなければならない患者さえいます。

【リスニングスクリプト】

Now listen to part of a lecture on the topic you just read about.

　It is true that laser eye surgery still has some problems that need to be addressed. Contrary to what this article says, however, most patients and experts agree that it is a safe, effective procedure.

　First, let's talk about side effects... It is true that over 50% of patients experience negative side effects initially, but only around 20% of patients continue to experience these side effects six months after treatment... Overall, patients actually seem to be pretty happy with LASIK surgery. In a recent survey, 80% of patients claimed to be "completely satisfied" or "very satisfied" with their laser eye treatment. So side effects are common, but they're usually short-term, and most patients seem to be pretty pleased with the results.

　It is also true that some clinics do not provide enough information about the risks of eye surgery. This is partially the patients' fault, too, though. Virtually every well-respected medical website warns patients that they should be very careful when choosing an eye clinic, and patients need to make sure that they are being treated by experienced professionals.

Many patients simply choose an eye clinic based on price, and they get poor treatment as a result. In contrast to this, hospital-based eye clinics tend to have very high ratings, and they are good about explaining the risks and possible side effects of laser eye treatment.

As for long-term side effects... Yes, vision may get worse many years after LASIK surgery, but good clinics will explain this to patients. Also, many patients understand that they are paying to have good vision for many years —— but not forever... Indeed, long term side effects should be taken into consideration. These treatments have not been around for a long time, so medical experts still do not know a lot about the long-term effects.

【リスニングスクリプト訳】
今読んだトピックに関する講義の一部を聞きなさい。

　　レーザー手術には，対処すべき問題がまだ存在していることは間違いありません。しかし，この記事に書かれていることとは反対に，ほとんどの患者と専門家は，レーザー眼科手術は安全で効果的な処置であるという意見で一致しています。
　　まず，副作用についてお話ししましょう…。50パーセント以上の患者に手術直後は副作用がありますが，これらの副作用が治療の6カ月後も続く患者は20パーセント前後しかいません…。概して，患者はレーシック手術にかなり満足しているようです。最近の調査では，患者の80パーセントがレーザー眼科手術に「完全に満足している」または「とても満足している」と述べました。ですから，副作用はよく起こりますが，それらは短期間のことが多く，ほとんどの患者は結果にとても喜んでいるようです。
　　眼科手術のリスクについて，十分な情報を提供しないクリニックがあることも確かです。しかし，これには患者の落ち度も一部あります。実際にはすべての評判の高い医療情報サイトが，患者は眼科クリニックを選ぶ際に慎重を期すべきだと警告しており，患者は必ず経験豊富な専門家による治療を受ける必要があると警告しています。多くの患者は，眼科クリニックを価格だけで選んでいて，その結果，下手な治療を受けています。これとは対照的に，病院を基盤とする眼科クリニックは，とても評価が高い傾向にあり，レーザーによる眼治療のリスクと，起こり得る副作用の説明に長けています。
　　長期的な副作用については…。確かに，レーシック手術の後長い年月が経つと視力が落ちるかもしれませんが，よいクリニックはこのことを患者に説明します。それに，多くの患者は，お金を払っているのは，永久にというのではなく，何年間かよい視力を得るためだと理解しています。確かに，長期的な副作用は考慮されるべきです。こうした治療は行われるようになってからまだ長くないため，医療の専門家たちは長期的な副作用についてはまだ多くを知らないのです。

✅ 重要表現チェック

課題文
- ☐ surgery「手術」
- ☐ procedure「処置,手順」
- ☐ guarantee「〜を保証する」
- ☐ quote「〜を引用する」
- ☐ multiple「複数の」
- ☐ vision「視力,視界」
- ☐ undergo「(治療)を受ける,〜を経験する」
- ☐ side effect「副作用」
- ☐ ban「〜を禁止する」
- ☐ treatment「治療」
- ☐ eye drop「目薬」
- ☐ dependency「依存」

リスニングスクリプト
- ☐ initially「初めに,当初は」
- ☐ partially「部分的に」
- ☐ make sure that ...「必ず…するようにする,…を確かめる」
- ☐ take 〜 into consideration「〜を考慮に入れる」
- ☐ be around「存在している,活動している」
- ☐ be pleased with 〜「〜に喜ぶ」
- ☐ fault「落ち度,誤り」

[2] 解答時間：30分

今度は，本番の1.5倍の解答時間で問題に取り組んでみましょう。時間配分を意識して，次のページのスペースに自分で論理マップを作成し，解答の組み立てを行いましょう。

Reading Time: 3 minutes

A tariff is a tax on imported goods and services. One of the primary reasons that countries use tariffs is to protect domestic industries from foreign competition. To explain this, let's look at the United States tariff on auto parts.

Imagine that in order to import auto parts from a foreign country, US companies have to pay a 25% import tax. So if a US company is selling a muffler for $100, then it costs $100 for US customers to buy it. But if a foreign company is selling a muffler for $100, then it costs $125 for US customers to purchase. This type of tax helps to protect US companies from foreign competition, which results in more successful American companies overall. Over time, this also leads to strong, efficient industries that can handle global competition.

Tariffs raise employment rates as well. Many foreign countries have much cheaper labor forces than the United States. A factory worker in the United States typically makes around $12 an hour. A factory worker in a foreign country, however, might work for only $2 an hour. This means that foreign factories can produce auto parts more cheaply. Without a tariff, these cheaper labor forces from other countries would have an unfair advantage, and factory workers in the United States would lose their jobs. By simply charging a small tax on products and services from other countries, the government can save thousands of jobs, decreasing unemployment nationwide.

By protecting domestic companies and saving the jobs of thousands of US workers, the government also strengthens the economy. For example, if an import tax saves 20,000 factory worker jobs, then it would generate over $400 million in salaries per year. These workers can then spend that income on various products and services, fueling the economy.

Now listen to part of a lecture on the topic you just read about.　● CD 03

Summarize the points made in the lecture you just heard, being sure to explain how they challenge specific arguments made in the reading passage.

【設問訳】
今聞いた講義の論点を要約しなさい。その際,課題文で挙げられているどの論点にどのように反論しているかを必ず説明しなさい。

課題文訳,スクリプト ➡ p.42

【解答例】
  The professor talks about how tariffs do not help economies or unemployment rates.
  First, using tariffs to protect domestic companies is not a good thing. Import taxes

40

decrease competition, and this makes businesses less efficient. As a result, industries become weaker in general. This points out flaws in the reading passage's argument, which states that protecting companies with tariffs leads to stronger, more efficient industries.

Second, tariffs decrease employment rates. The professor points out that tariffs cause more people to lose jobs overall. As an example, she cites a tariff on imported goods that saved 10,000 jobs. However, eight jobs were lost per every job that was saved. This is because as people have to pay more to buy goods protected by tariffs, they have less to spend on other goods, which damages other companies. Again, this contradicts the reading passage, which states that import taxes decrease unemployment rates.

Third, tariffs do not help to boost economies. The professor explains that the cost of saving jobs with tariffs is too high, and this hurts the economy overall. She cites a study which estimated that the economy lost over $30 billion due to tariffs in 1994. With this point, the professor takes issue with the reading's claim that import taxes strengthen economies.

In short, the professor disagrees with the reading's claims that tariffs are a good way to decrease unemployment and strengthen economies. (232 words)

（教授は，関税が経済や失業率の支えにはならないということについて話しています。

第1に，国内企業を保護するために関税を使うことはよいことではありません。輸入税は競争を低下させ，このために事業の効率性が下がります。結果として，産業は全体的に弱体化します。このことは，関税で企業を保護することが，より磐石で効率的な産業を育てることにつながると述べている課題文の主張の欠陥を指摘しています。

第2に，関税は雇用率を下げます。教授は，関税のせいで全体的には職を失う人が増えると指摘しています。一例として，教授は，1万件の雇用を守った輸入製品への関税について話しています。しかし，雇用が1件守られるごとに8件の雇用が失われました。これは，関税で守られた製品を買うのに，人々がより多くのお金を支払わなければならないため，その他の製品に費やせる分が少なくなり，他の企業が被害を受けるからです。ここでも，輸入税が失業率を減らすと述べている課題文と相違しています。

第3に，関税は経済を上向かせる助けにはなりません。教授は，関税で雇用を守るコストが高すぎて，このことが経済全体に害を与えていると説明しています。教授は，関税のせいで，1994年に経済が300億ドル以上の損失を出したと推定した研究について述べています。この点で，教授は，輸入税が経済を強化するという課題文の主張に反対しています。

つまり，教授は，関税が失業を減らし，経済を強化する優れた方法だという課題文の主張に異議を唱えています。）

【解説】
反論型の問題ですので，課題文のポイント（関税の3つの利点）に対し，教授が反論する理由を示しながら，講義のポイントを整理しましょう。

教授は冒頭部分で、関税が経済と失業率両面で害を及ぼすと述べ、続いて関税の3つの利点、すなわち、国内企業の保護と磐石で効率的な産業の実現（ポイント1）、雇用率の上昇（ポイント2）、経済の強化（ポイント3）に対し、順に反論を述べています。解答では、まず Introduction で教授の主張を示し、続いて Body の各段落でそれぞれのポイントについてまとめていきましょう。

　ポイント1については、「関税は産業の強化につながらない」という教授の意見に加えて、「事業効率の低下と産業の弱体化」という理由を盛り込みましょう。P.26〜27で［役に立つ表現］として挙げた表現も参考に、論理関係をわかりやすく示すことを意識しましょう。ポイント2に対しては、「逆に雇用率が下がる」という反論を、具体例や数字を含めて説明しましょう。ポイント3でも、「経済の強化につながらない」ことを、「雇用を関税で守る場合のコストの高さ」を主な論点として、具体的な研究事例を加えるという展開にすることができます。こうした情報を盛り込むには、リスニングの際に、講義のどの部分が主張や理由・根拠、例・詳細情報にあたるのかを意識して聞くことが大切です。なお、解答例は最後に In short（要するに）で始まる結論の一文を置いています。

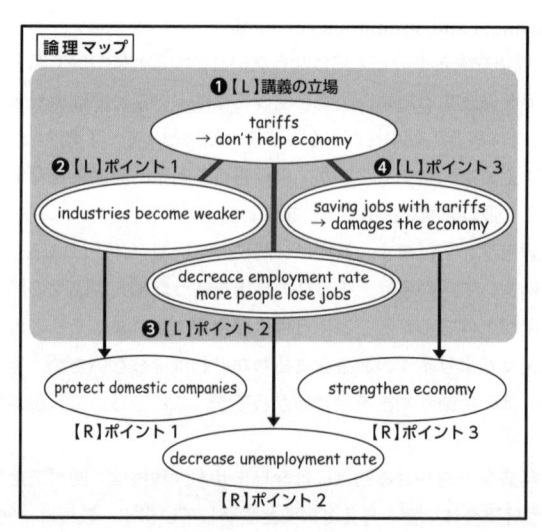

```
論理マップ

                    ❶【L】講義の立場
                         tariffs
                   → don't help economy

    ❷【L】ポイント 1              ❹【L】ポイント 3
                              saving jobs with tariffs
  industries become weaker    → damages the economy

              decrease employment rate
              more people lose jobs
                    ❸【L】ポイント 2

  protect domestic companies       strengthen economy
       【R】ポイント 1                  【R】ポイント 3
              decrease unemployment rate
                    【R】ポイント 2
```

【課題文訳】

　関税とは、輸入された製品やサービスにかけられる税金のことです。国々が関税を使う主な理由の1つは、国内の産業を外国との競争から保護することです。このことを説明するために、自動車部品にかけられているアメリカの関税について考えてみましょう。

　外国から自動車部品を輸入するために、アメリカの企業は25パーセントの輸入税を支払わなければならないという状況を想像してみましょう。あるアメリカの企業が車のマフラー（消音器）を100ドルで売っていたら、アメリカの消費者がそれを買うのにかかる費用は100ドルですが、

もし外国の企業がマフラーを100ドルで販売していたら，アメリカの消費者はそれを購入するのに125ドルかかることになります。この種の税金が，アメリカの企業を外国との競争から保護するのに役立っており，その結果，全体としてより多くのアメリカ企業の成功につながっています。これにより，グローバル競争に対処できる磐石で効率的な産業を徐々に作ることにもつながります。

関税は雇用率も上昇させます。外国の多くは，アメリカよりもずっと安い労働力を有しています。アメリカの工場労働者は，通常時給が12ドル前後です。しかし，ある外国の工場労働者は時給がたったの2ドルであることもあるでしょう。このことはつまり，外国の工場のほうが自動車の部品を安く作ることができるということです。関税がなければ，こうした他国の安い労働力が不公平な優位性を持つことになり，アメリカの工場労働者は仕事を失うでしょう。他国の製品やサービスにわずかな税金を課すだけで，政府は何千もの雇用を守ることができ，国内の失業率を減少させることができます。

国内の企業を保護し，アメリカの何千人もの労働者の職を守ることで，政府は経済を強化することもできます。例えば，輸入税で2万人分の工場労働者の職を守れば，年間4億ドル以上の給与を生むことになります。そして，こうした労働者がさまざまな製品やサービスにその収入を使い，経済を活気づけるのです。

【リスニングスクリプト】
Now listen to part of a lecture on the topic you just read about.

It's really common to hear that tariffs save jobs... The fact is, though, that this is simply not true. When looking from a broader perspective, tariffs almost always hurt both economies and unemployment rates.

The idea of protecting domestic companies from foreign competition sounds nice, but realistically it's not a very good solution for strengthening industries. Numerous studies have shown that import taxes actually harm industries, because they decrease competition. Any time competition is lower, businesses become less efficient, and the economy as a whole suffers... So tariffs actually weaken industries by decreasing competition.

Next, let's take a moment to explore how tariffs actually decrease the number of jobs available. In the year 2000, the US government raised tariffs on imported steel goods. Studies estimate that this saved around 10,000 jobs... Which is a good thing, right? Well, not really... Because it is estimated that eight jobs were lost for every one job that was saved with tariffs. Import taxes raise the prices of goods and services. If consumers are spending more money on steel goods, then they have less money to spend on other goods, and this causes other domestic companies to suffer, and more jobs are lost overall.

Aside from this decrease in employment, the overly high cost of saving jobs with tariffs damages the economy. In the example I just mentioned, 10,000 jobs were saved... That same study concluded that each of these jobs was costing $400,000 to save, which is a lot higher than the salaries of the people keeping their jobs. To give another example, in 1994 a professional study found that tariffs cost the US economy $32.3 billion. In other words, the country lost $170,000 for every job that was "saved." This shows that tariffs cost economies billions of dollars, making them weaker overall.

【リスニングスクリプト訳】
今読んだトピックに関する講義の一部を聞きなさい。

　関税が雇用を守るというのは本当によく聞く話です…。しかし，実際にはこれはまったく事実ではありません。より大きな視点から見てみると，関税はほとんど常に，経済にも失業率にも悪影響を及ぼしています。
　外国との競争から国内企業を保護するという考え方はよいことのように聞こえますが，現実的には，産業を強化する上であまりよい解決策というわけではありません。無数の研究が，輸入税は競争を低下させるため，実際には産業に害であると示しています。競争が低下すると，事業効率が下がり，経済は全体として苦しくなります…。ですから，関税は実際には競争を低下させることによって産業を弱体化させるのです。
　次に，関税が実際に得られる仕事の数をどれだけ減らしているかを，少し見てみましょう。2000年にアメリカ政府は輸入されるスチール製品への関税を引き上げました。研究では，これにより約1万件の雇用が守られたと推定されています…。これはいいことですよね。ところが，そうでもないのです…。というのも，関税によって守られた雇用1件につき，8件の雇用が失われたと推定されているからです。輸入税が製品やサービスの値段を上げます。消費者がスチール製品にかける金額が増えると，他の製品に使うお金が少なくなり，このことがその他の国内企業を苦しめ，全体ではもっと多くの仕事が失われることになるのです。
　この雇用の減少だけでなく，関税によって雇用を守るコストはあまりにも高く，経済にダメージを与えています。先ほど挙げた例では，1万件の雇用が守られましたね…。それと同じ研究が，これらの雇用を守るために1件あたり40万ドルかかっていると結論づけており，この額は職を維持した人の給与額よりもはるかに高いのです。他の例を挙げると，1994年の専門的な研究では，関税がアメリカ経済に負わせるコストは323億ドルだということがわかっています。言い換えると，雇用が1件「守られる」たびに，国は17万ドルを失っていたということです。このことは，関税が経済に何十億ドルものコストを負わせ，そのために経済全体が弱体化するということを示しています。

✓ 重要表現チェック

課題文
- □ tariff「関税」
- □ competition「競争」
- □ over time「時間と共に，徐々に」
- □ import「～を輸入する」
- □ auto parts「自動車部品」

Question 1 | 解答のエッセンス

解答例 リスニングスクリプト	☐ employment rate「雇用率」 ☐ charge a tax on ~「~に課税する」 ☐ unemployment「失業」 ☐ boost「(経済)を回復させる，上向かせる」 ☐ perspective「視点」 ☐ explore「~を検討する」 ☐ aside from ~「~に加えて，~は別として」	☐ labor force「労働力」 ☐ fuel「~を活気づける」 ☐ numerous「数多くの」

Integrated Task Question 1

集中トレーニング

ここからは，実戦形式の問題を解きながら，例題や演習問題で学んだ考え方を確実に定着させていきましょう。解答の作成は，本番と同じく**1問20分間**で行いましょう。不十分な解答例は，情報量の不足や，語彙・文法・構成上のミスがあります。適切な解答例と見比べて，解答のブラッシュアップに役立ててください。

問題1
課題文訳・リスニングスクリプト ➡ 別冊 p.2

Reading Time: 3 minutes

The US government gives space exploration and research over three times as much funding as ocean exploration and research. From a practical viewpoint, however, funding ocean exploration and research makes a lot more sense, because it can lead to discoveries related to national concerns such as climate change and energy and food production.

Climate change is currently a major issue. The international scientific community continues to warn that global warming is a reality, and that governments need to start taking action to preserve the earth's climate. Further exploration and research of oceans could help to produce solutions to this problem. For example, excessive CO_2 emissions are said to be a major cause of climate change, and the earth's oceans absorb a large amount of these gases. With further research, it is possible that oceans could be used to reduce atmospheric CO_2 even further.

Ocean research may also produce solutions to energy production problems. A growing number of people are opposing the production and use of nuclear energy, yet environmentally friendly energy sources are not capable of fully powering cities around the globe. Some scientists claim that there are renewable energy sources in oceans that have yet to be utilized. One example of this is wave energy. The wave energy conversion generates electrical energy from the movement of waves.

Further research funding is also necessary in order to improve and maintain seafood production worldwide. While human populations keep increasing, fish stocks keep decreasing. In fact, many species of fish are facing extinction due to overfishing. In response to this, aquaculture — also called aqua farming — is becoming more popular. However, there is insufficient research regarding its sustainability and ecological impact.

Question 1 | 集中トレーニング

Now listen to part of a lecture on the topic you just read about. ● CD 04

Summarize the points made in the lecture you just heard, being sure to explain how they cast doubt on specific points made in the reading passage.

Response Time: 20 minutes

【設問訳】
今聞いた講義の論点を要約しなさい。その際，課題文で挙げられているどの論点にどのように疑問を投げかけているかを必ず説明しなさい。

解答例

不十分な解答例

★1 The passage say (→says) funding ocean exploration and research is more important than funding space exploration and research. The professor agrees that ocean research could lead to some discoveries about reducing CO_2.

★2 The professor agrees that ★3 the climate change is currently a major issue and further exploration and research of oceans could help to produce solutions to this problem. However, the professor says that we can measure climate change ★4 by using devices developed by NASA.

★2 Ocean research may also produce solution (→solutions) to energy production. One example is wave energy conversion. However, environmentally friendly energy sources cannot fully power cities around world (→the world). The professor says there are ★5 a lot of problems. ★6

★2 The passage say (→says) further research funding is necessary to improve and maintain seafood production; and aquaculture is becoming more popular. However, the professor says that it is not going to increase seafood supply, but companies developing bigger aqua farms do (→will do) that. ★7

●構成と内容の改善ポイント
★1 教授は，海洋研究は二酸化炭素を減らす解決策を生み出すという課題文の主張を認めてはいますが，海洋研究への資金提供の重要性については課題文に反対の立場をとっています。
➡ Introduction ではまず，講義が課題文に反論していることをはっきりと伝えます。本書の解答例などを参考に，さまざまな表現を身につけていきましょう。

★2 ディスコース・マーカーがないため，全体の構成がわかりにくくなっています。
➡ Body の各段落を First / Second / Third から始め，第1文に，各段落で扱う講義の内容を端的に示すキーセンテンスを配置しましょう。

★3 課題文の内容をそのまま書き写してしまっています。
➡ 情報を整理して，要点を自分の言葉で言い換えましょう。多様な表現力は評価のポイントになります。リスニングの際も，一語一句書き留めようとするのではなく，大意を捉えながらメモをとりましょう。

★4 「NASA が開発した装置を使っている」という事例を述べるにとどまっており，教授がそのことをどう捉えているのかが示されていません。
➡ 教授は，「海洋研究による気候変動の理解には，宇宙研究が寄与している」と主張するためにこの事例を挙げています。リスニングの際は，詳細情報を聞き取るだけでなく，どのような主張を裏づけるためにその情報が持ち出されているのかを意識しましょう。

★5 講義で述べられている，波エネルギー変換プログラムの具体的な問題点に触れられていません。
➡ 講義について，できるだけ具体的な内容を述べることも重要です。リスニングでは，大意をつかむと同時に，詳細情報も聞き逃さないようにしましょう。

★6 この段落で扱われている講義の論点が，課題文とどのような関係にあるのかが示されていません。
➡ 設問の指示にあるように，各段落で取り上げる論点における講義と課題文の関係（反論あるいはサポート）を必ず明示しましょう。

★7 語数に余裕のある場合は，エッセイのまとめとして，最終段落で教授の立場を再提示するのが理想です。

《構成の改善例》

❶【L】講義の立場 海洋の研究探査への資金提供の有効性について疑問がある。
- **❷【L】ポイント1** 海洋研究による気候変動の理解には，宇宙研究が寄与している。
  （【R】ポイント1：海洋研究が二酸化炭素の削減など気候の保全に役立つ。）
- **❸【L】ポイント2** 波エネルギー変換のようなプログラムには多くの問題がある。
  （【R】ポイント2：海はエネルギー問題の解決策となり得る。）
- **❹【L】ポイント3** 魚類資源を増やすには，企業が養殖場を開発するほうが有効である。
  （【R】ポイント3：海洋研究が魚類資源を増やす。）

適切な解答例

[★1] The professor explains that funding ocean research and exploration will not produce the expected results.

[★2] First, the professor states that space research contributes more to understanding climate change than ocean research. [★4] As an example, he refers to monitoring devices developed by NASA, which are used to measure gases in the atmosphere. Although the professor acknowledges the reading passage's claim that [★3] ocean research is important for reducing CO_2, he thinks that space research plays a more critical role.

[★2] Second, the professor explains that there are many problems with programs like wave energy conversion. [★5] The ocean is not a good environment for technological devices, and this can cause problems. Also, the scientific community has not yet agreed on the best types of devices for wave energy conversion. [★6] Again, this weakens the reading passage's argument that the ocean is a good resource for energy.

[★2] Third, it is unlikely that ocean research will increase fish populations. The professor explains that companies trying to develop bigger and more efficient fish farms are more likely to improve aquaculture. With this point, the professor opposes the reading's claim that more ocean research funding is needed to increase fish stocks.

[★7] In short, although the professor agrees with some points made in the reading, overall he seems to be skeptical about the claim that ocean research is more important than space research. (223 words)

（教授は，海洋の研究と探査への資金提供が，期待される結果を生み出さないということについて説明しています。

第1に，教授は宇宙研究のほうが海洋研究よりも気候変動の理解に寄与していると述べています。例として，彼は，大気中の気体の計測に用いられている，NASAが開発した観測装置に言及しています。教授は，海洋研究は二酸化炭素を減らす上で重要だという課題文の主張を認めながらも，宇宙研究のほうがより重要な役割を果たしていると考えているのです。

第2に，教授は，波エネルギー変換のようなプログラムには多くの問題があることを説明しています。海はハイテク機器にとって望ましい環境ではなく，このことが問題を起こす可能性があります。また，波エネルギー変換に最適の装置の種類について，科学界はまだ合意に達していません。ここでも，海はよいエネルギー源であるという課題文の主張を弱めています。

第3に，海洋研究が魚の量を増やすことにはならないだろうということです。教授は，より広大で効率的な養殖場の開発に取り組む企業のほうが，養殖技術を向上させる可能性が高いと説明しています。この点で，教授は海洋研究費の増額が魚類資源を増やすために必要であるという課

題文の主張に反対しています。

つまり，教授は課題文で挙げられているいくつかの点には同意していますが，全体としては，宇宙研究よりも海洋研究のほうが重要だという主張には懐疑的であるように思われます。)

✓ 重要表現チェック

課題文
- ☐ exploration「探査」
- ☐ scientific community「科学界」
- ☐ excessive「過度の」
- ☐ atmospheric「大気の」
- ☐ environmentally friendly「環境に優しい」
- ☐ utilize「~を活用する」
- ☐ generate「~を作り出す」
- ☐ aquaculture「水産養殖」
- ☐ ecological「生態上の」
- ☐ fund「~に資金を提供する」
- ☐ preserve「~を保全する」
- ☐ absorb「~を吸収する」
- ☐ conversion「変換」
- ☐ extinction「絶滅」
- ☐ sustainability「持続可能性」
- ☐ impact「影響」

適切な解答例
- ☐ acknowledge「~を認める」
- ☐ overall「全般的に言えば」
- ☐ weaken「~を弱める」
- ☐ skeptical「懐疑的な」

問題 2

課題文訳・リスニングスクリプト ➡ 別冊 p.5

Reading Time: 3 minutes

The introduction of the assembly line revolutionized manufacturing and led to great cost cuttings. The idea was to assign people individual tasks, which they could repeat quickly instead of using workers who did a whole series of tasks one after another. If the tasks themselves were unchanged, why was it more efficient to use the assembly line?

First, time was not lost as individual workers brought pieces from many different locations to the place where the object was being assembled. Instead, workers used all their time attaching pieces. Items for assembly would be carried on a conveyor belt to the workers, who would stay in one place as the items came to them.

Also, each worker could achieve a high level of expertise performing the assigned task. Repeating the same action hundreds or even thousands of times a day eliminated confusion about the task and its performance. Equally important for peak efficiency was determining the rate for each task and the speed at which the assembly line should move. Time and motion studies have continually made adjustments to create maximum speed with minimum effort.

Finally, automatic measurement of products freed the workers from testing the item slowly by hand. By automatically separating well-made from poorly-made goods, the manufacturing process could turn out products at the lowest possible cost. This maximized profits and allowed prices to be kept low enough to permit mass sales.

Now listen to part of a lecture on the topic you just read about. 🔘 CD 05

Summarize the points made in the lecture you just heard, being sure to explain how they challenge specific arguments made in the reading passage.

Response Time: 20 minutes

【設問訳】
今聞いた講義の論点を要約しなさい。その際，課題文で挙げられているどの論点にどのように反論しているかを必ず説明しなさい。

解答例

不十分な解答例

　The reading passage is about ★1 good things of the assembly line, but the professor disagrees with the passage. ★2 The good thing is efficiency, and the professor talks about its problems.

　★3 First, by using the assembly line, time is not lost because workers stay in one place. They don't have to move around because items come to them.

　Second, each worker become (→**becomes**) bored or stressed by doing the same ★1 thing again and again. However, repeating the same ★1 thing hundreds or thousands of times wears people out. ★4 I think I will get bored and stressed too if I have to repeat something every day.

　Third, though the automatic measurement reduces the cost, workers don't feel involve (→**involved**) because they see only pieces, not a whole. Therefore, they might make a mistake and not even notice it. ★5

●構成と内容の改善ポイント

★1 thing は色々な場面に使える便利な単語ですが，その分意味が曖昧になりがちです。
➡ benefit / task などのように，状況に応じて適切な単語を選択しましょう。

★2 前の文から，1文に課題文と講義両方の情報が盛り込まれた構造の文が続いています。単調な表現は，段落全体にまとまりのない印象を与えます。
➡ ここでは情報を1文に詰め込まず，複数の文に分けて整理するとよいでしょう。ディスコース・マーカーを効果的に用いて，講義の立場と課題文との関係をわかりやすく示すように心がけましょう。

★3 課題文の内容だけが述べられており，講義の内容が述べられていません。
➡ Question 1 は，講義の論点を要約する問題です。設問の指示に従い，講義で述べられている問題点を中心に書きましょう。リスニングの際は，それぞれのポイントについて教授が述べている内容をきちんと聞き取るようにしましょう。

★4 自分の意見が述べられています。
➡ Question 1 では，自分の意見は不要です。課題文や講義の内容を的確に答えることを意識しましょう。

★5 全体として，情報量が少なく，語数が不足しています。
➡ 適切な解答例を参考に，盛り込むべき情報を確認しましょう。

《構成の改善例》

- **❶【L】講義の立場** 組み立てラインにはいくつか問題がある。
  - **❷【L】ポイント1** 何か問題が起こるとライン全体を止めることになり，非効率である。
    - (【R】ポイント1：部品がベルトコンベヤーで運ばれて来るので，時間の損失がない。)
  - **❸【L】ポイント2** 作業員が飽きたりストレスを感じたりする恐れがある。
    - (【R】ポイント2：同一作業の反復により，各々の作業員が高い専門性を獲得した。)
  - **❹【L】ポイント3** 作業員は最終製品を見ないので，責任を感じにくくなる。
    - (【R】ポイント3：完成品の自動測定のおかげで，時間短縮と低コストが実現した。)

適切な解答例

The reading passage focused on the ★1 benefits the assembly line brought to manufacturing. ★2 It described how the assembly line made production faster and cheaper. Then, the product could be sold at a lower price. In contrast, the lecture mentioned numerous problems that came with the change to assembly line production.

★3 First, time is lost when the assembly line stops. Although the reading passage said it can save time to bring pieces, the efficiency of the system depends on all of the parts moving in a smooth flow. If there is a problem, the whole line stops and products cannot be made.

Second, each worker becomes bored or stressed by doing the same ★1 task again and again. As the reading passage mentioned, this reduces the amount of labor a finished product needs. However, repeating the same ★1 task hundreds or thousands of times wears people out. ★4 Workers may have trouble concentrating and may not do the task correctly due to the repetitive and boring nature of their work.

Third, though the automatic measurement system reduces the cost, it makes it harder for workers to feel responsible because they never see the finished product. Some workers may let the quality of their work fall. They might make a mistake that they don't notice, but that affects the finished product. For an assembly line to be as efficient as it is supposed to be, workers need to have a better sense of what they are making.　　　　　　　　(242 words)

　（課題文は組み立てラインが製造業にもたらした恩恵に焦点を当てていました。そこには組み立てラインがどれほど製品をより速くより安く作るようになったかが述べられていました。そして製品はより安い値段で販売されることが可能になったのです。一方，講義では，組み立てライン製造への転換とともに起こった諸問題について述べていました。
　まず組み立てラインが止まると時間が無駄になります。課題文は，部品を運ぶ時間を節約できると述べていますが，このシステムの効率性は，全部品が円滑に流れているかどうかにかかっています。もし何か問題が起これば，全ラインが止まり，製品を作ることができません。
　第2に，各々の作業員が同じ作業を何度も何度も行うことで，飽きたりストレスを感じたりするようになります。課題文で述べられていたように，これにより製品が完成するために必要な労働量は減ります。しかし，同じ作業を何百回，何千回と繰り返すことによって，人々は疲れ果ててしまうのです。反復的で退屈なこの作業の性質のため，作業員が集中できないということや，作業を正しく行えないということがあるかもしれません。
　第3に，自動測定装置はコストを削減しますが，作業員が最終製品を見ることがないため，責任を感じることが難しくなります。仕事の質を落としてしまう作業員もいるかもしれません。自分では気づかない間違いをしてしまうことがあるかもしれませんが，そのことが最終製品に影響を及ぼすのです。組み立てラインが，本来そうあるべき効率性の高さを保つためには，作業員が自分たちが作っているものをより深く理解する必要があります。）

✓ 重要表現チェック

課題文	☐ assembly line「組み立てライン」	
	☐ revolutionize「～に革命をもたらす」	
	☐ one after another「次から次へと」	☐ expertise「専門技術，専門知識」
	☐ eliminate「～を取り除く」	☐ turn out「～を生産する」
不十分な解答例	☐ wear ～ out「～を疲れさせる」	
適切な解答例	☐ repetitive「反復的な」	☐ nature「性質，本質」
	☐ be supposed to *do*「本来…するはずである」	

問題 3

Reading Time: 3 minutes

The writings and beliefs of Thomas Jefferson, the third President of the United States, have been the subject of debate for many years. As the author of the Declaration of Independence, he will forever be a towering figure among the founding fathers of the United States.

Regarding foreign affairs, in his Inaugural Address on March 4, 1801, he endorsed, "Peace, commerce and honest friendship with all nations, entangling alliances with none." His view was that the United States' relations with other countries should remain commercial in nature. This was a continuation of George Washington's view that the U.S. should "steer clear of permanent alliance with any portion of the foreign world." In fact, from 1789 until the end of World War II, the United States entered no treaties of alliance with any foreign countries.

On the subject of amending the laws of the land, he wrote in a letter to Samuel Kercheval: "I am certainly not an advocate for frequent and untried changes in laws and constitutions." He also said that the Constitution should not be "a mere thing of wax in the hands of the judiciary, which they may twist, and shape into any form they please." Instead of changing the laws, he argued, we should interpret them based on the explanations of those who wrote them.

And on religion, Jefferson called himself a Christian and expressed faith in the existence of God and God's role in human affairs. He attended church regularly, sometimes even going by himself when his family could not attend. His moral sense was clearly guided by his religious faith.

Now listen to part of a lecture on the topic you just read about. CD 06

Summarize the points made in the lecture you just heard, being sure to explain how they challenge specific arguments made in the reading passage.

Response Time: 20 minutes

【設問訳】
今聞いた講義の論点を要約しなさい。その際，課題文で挙げられているどの論点にどのように反論しているかを必ず説明しなさい。

> 解答例

不十分な解答例

★1 The professor is clearly at odds with the reading passage. He says writings and beliefs of Thomas Jefferson seem to be mistakenly understood.

★2 As the reading passage says, the United States did not enter into alliances with foreign countries while he was president. However, the professor says Jefferson stayed in France for several years and he loved the country and the people there.

★2 The reading passage says that he wrote in his letter that ★3 he did not want to change the law. However, the professor points out that in the very same letter, he also wrote that the laws should progress along with human development. Therefore, the professor think (→**thinks**) that Jefferson clearly approved of changing the law.

★2 Finally, according to the reading passage, Jefferson was a believer in God and a follower of Christianity. This may be true, but the professor says that ★4 he coined the phrase, "wall of separation between church and state" and he saw Jesus as a good man but not a God's son. ★1

●構成と内容の改善ポイント

★1 Introduction で講義の立場が明確に述べられているのはよいですが，第2段落以降で展開される具体的な論点については述べられていません。また，結論にあたる部分もないため，★2 で指摘する点も合わせて，全体の構成が捉えにくくなっています。

➡ Introduction で課題文の3つの論点を簡潔に提示し，その1つ1つについて議論を展開していくということが読み手に伝わるように工夫します。また，時間や語数に余裕がある場合には，再度教授の立場を提示して締めくくります。Introduction・Body・Conclusion がそれぞれの役割をきちんと果たすように書いていくことが，伝わりやすいエッセイを書くポイントです。

★2 しばらく読み進めなければ，段落の要点が掴めません。

➡ 第1文を読むだけで，その段落の要点がすぐに分かるように工夫しましょう。ここでは，on foreign affairs / on changing the law / on religion と，各段落の初めにそれぞれの論点を端的に示すとよいでしょう。

★3 課題文よりも断言的なニュアンスに変わってしまっています。課題文ではジェファーソンの書いた手紙を引用していますが，「法改正をしたくなかった」と直接的には述べていません。

➡ 婉曲的に表現したい場合には，seem to do や is likely / unlikely to do などを用いましょう。パラフレーズの際は，伝わるニュアンスが変わらないように慎重に

★4 教授が引用したフレーズがそのまま書かれています。
　➡引用などの詳細情報は，主張を裏づけるために持ち出されます。ここでは，「ジェファーソンは政治と宗教は分離されるべきであると考えていた」という事実を裏づけるために引用がなされています。その情報を持ち出すことで教授が何を主張したいのかを捉え，自分の言葉で言い換えるようにしましょう。

《構成の改善例》

❶【L】講義の立場　　課題文では，トーマス・ジェファーソンについて正しく理解されていない。

　❷【L】ポイント1　数年間フランスに住み，フランスを大変気に入っていた。
　（【R】ポイント1：いかなる国とも，煩わしい同盟関係を結ばないという見解だった。）
　❸【L】ポイント2　法律と制度は人間の進歩に伴って改正されるべきだと考えていた。
　（【R】ポイント2：法律は，改正するよりも，解釈すべきものであると考えていた。）
　❹【L】ポイント3　イエスを善人だとは思っていたが，神の子だとは思っていなかった。
　（【R】ポイント3：信心深いキリスト教徒であり，神の存在を信じていた。）

適切な解答例

　★1 In the reading passage, Thomas Jefferson is portrayed as reluctant to engage in foreign affairs, opposed to the changing of laws, and strongly religious. However, the professor gives evidence from his writings that none of these claims are fully accurate.

　★2 On foreign affairs, as the reading passage says, though officially the United States did not enter into alliances with other nations while he was president, Jefferson did spend time in France. Not only did he spend time there, but he loved it. He wrote about the generosity and kindness of the French people long after he had visited the country.

　★2 On changing the law, the reading passage quotes a letter that ★3 seems to suggest he was against amendments. However, the professor points out that in the very same letter, he also wrote that laws and institutions should progress along with human development. Therefore, the professor thinks Jefferson was clearly an advocate for amendments to the laws.

　Finally, ★2 on religion, the reading passage portrays Jefferson as a believer in God and a follower of Christianity. This may be true, but the professor says that ★4 his views on religion were markedly different from others of the time. He said that government and religion should be separated and saw Jesus as a good man but not a God's son. These views almost caused him to lose the election.

🔸In conclusion, the professor is clearly at odds with the writer of the reading passage. (240 words)

（課題文では，トーマス・ジェファーソンは外交問題には関わりたくないと思っていて，法改正には反対の立場をとり，非常に信心深いと表現されています。しかしながら，教授は，これらの主張はどれも完全に正確だとは言えないことを，彼の著書を引用して証言しています。

外交問題については，課題文で述べられている通り，ジェファーソンが大統領を務めていた期間に，合衆国は公式には他の国と同盟関係を結びませんでしたが，彼はフランスで時を過ごしたのです。そこで時を過ごしただけではなく，それが大変気に入っていました。その国を訪れて随分経った後で，彼はフランス人の寛容さや優しさについて書いています。

法改正については，課題文は，彼が改正に反対だったと示唆するような手紙を引用していますが，教授は，まさに同じ手紙の中で，彼が法律と制度は人間の進歩と共に前進すべきだとも書いていると指摘しています。ゆえに教授は，ジェファーソンは明らかに法改正を支持していたと考えています。

最後に，宗教についてですが，課題文はジェファーソンのことを，神の存在を信じていて，そしてキリスト教徒であると表現しています。これは正しいのでしょうが，教授は，彼の宗教に関する見解は当時の他の人とは著しく異なっていたと述べています。彼は，政府と宗教は分離されるべきであると述べ，イエスを神の子としてではなく善人として見ていました。これらの見解のために，彼は危うく選挙に負けるところだったのです。

結論としては，教授は明らかに課題文の著者と意見が食い違っています。）

✓ 重要表現チェック

課題文
- ☐ the Declaration of Independence「アメリカ独立宣言」
- ☐ towering「非常に優れた」　☐ founding father「建国の父」
- ☐ foreign affairs「外交問題」　☐ Inaugural Address「就任演説」
- ☐ endorse「(主張など)を公式に承認する」
- ☐ commerce「貿易」　☐ entangle「込み入らせる」
- ☐ alliance「同盟」　☐ steer clear of ~「~を避ける」
- ☐ treaty「条約」　☐ amend「~を改正する」
- ☐ advocate「擁護者，支持者」　☐ untried「未審理の」
- ☐ constitution「憲法」　☐ wax「意のままになるもの」
- ☐ judiciary「司法(制度)，裁判官」
- ☐ twist「(意味など)を曲解する，誤解する」
- ☐ moral sense「道徳感」

不十分な解答例　□ at odds with ～「～と反目しあって，争って」
適切な解答例　□ portray「～を描写する」　　□ be reluctant to *do*「しぶしぶ…する」
　　　　　　　　□ generosity「寛容さ」　　　　□ markedly「著しく」

問題 4

課題文訳・リスニングスクリプト ➡ 別冊 p.10

Reading Time: 3 minutes

Microcredit refers to very small loans, also called microloans, for poor people that are unable to borrow money from traditional lending institutions like major banks, and it is one of the most effective and sustainable methods for fighting poverty in developing countries.

Many professional studies have shown that microfinance programs, in particular microcredit loans, are beneficial to the poor. Disadvantaged citizens of developing countries cannot qualify for loans from major banks, but microcredit loans give them the opportunity to receive small loans with generous payment terms. These loans then aid them in improving their financial situation. For example, a microfinance company reported that the weekly income of their clients increased by 145%.

Perhaps the greatest benefit of microcredit programs is their high sustainability. Many contributors to microcredit loans find that it is a preferable alternative to charitable donations in the traditional sense. With charity, money is given so that disadvantaged people can spend it. With microloans, however, money is used to help people develop higher, more stable incomes. With money from this loan, borrowers can set up businesses that will support themselves economically. After the money is paid back in full, the lender then has the option of loaning it to someone else.

Aside from the way it supports entrepreneurial efforts among the poor, microcredit programs have also been praised for empowering less fortunate social groups, such as women in male-dominated societies. The most famous example of this is a bank in Bangladesh. The bank has helped millions of women in Bangladesh to achieve economic independence. As a result, it won the Nobel Peace Prize.

Now listen to part of a lecture on the topic you just read about. CD 07

Summarize the points made in the lecture you just heard, being sure to explain how they challenge specific arguments made in the reading passage.

Response Time: 20 minutes

【設問訳】
今聞いた講義の論点を要約しなさい。その際，課題文で挙げられているどの論点にどのように反論しているかを必ず説明しなさい。

|解答例|

不十分な解答例

★1 The professor explains what she doesn't like about the reading passage's arguments. First, she talks about how microloans can harm poor people. ★2 Microloans, she explains, tend to have high-interest rates. Also, it takes too much administrative time to set up the loan. These directly refute the reading passage, which states that microcredit loans have generous payment terms and improve the financial situations of borrowers.

Second, she argues that creating jobs are (→is) a more sustainable way to fix poverty. As an example, she talks about lending $100 to 1,000 different women, so that they can buy sewing machines. ★3 If they buy their sewing machines, however, they will end up closing their businesses. Again, this is contradicting (→contradicts) the reading passage, which states that microloans are (→不要) enable people to generate a more stable income.

Third, she claims that microcredit programs cannot fix discrimination against woman (→women). Although she agrees to (→that) giving woman (→women) more opportunities is a good thing, she says that only changing a culture's values will solve gender inequalities. With this point, the professor opposes to (→不要) the reading's claim that microcredit programs empower woman (→women).

★4 In conclusion, she thinks only changing a culture's values gradually can fix both poverty and gender inequalities.

●構成と内容の改善ポイント

★1 単に「課題文の主張の気に入らない点を説明している」と述べるだけでは，教授の立場を適切に伝えていません。
→教授はマイクロローンの背景にある考えには好意的な一方，貧困を解決するという効果については，はっきりと反論しています。教授の課題文に対する立場を正確に述べましょう。

★2 教授が述べた情報の論理関係を正確に捉えられていません。教授は，「管理コストが高いこと」について詳しく説明していますが，これは「マイクロローンの金利が高いこと」を論証するためであり，論理的に並列の関係ではありません。
→適切な解答例では，「管理コストが高いことによって高金利になる傾向があり，それが借り手の財政状況を悪化させる」と講義の論点をまとめています。適切な

ディスコース・マーカーを用いて論理関係を示しましょう。

★3 なぜ彼女たちがそれぞれミシンを買うと事業が失敗するのか，この場合どのような方法が有効だと考えられるのかが不明であり，「雇用を創出するほうがより持続的な方法だ」という主張の根拠についての説明が不足しています。
→ 講義では，個人に融資するよりも，1つの優良な会社に融資した方が持続可能な雇用が創出されることが説明されています。具体例がどのような論理で主張をサポートしているのかをしっかりと聞き取り，記述しましょう。

★4 「文化的価値観を変えることでしか男女間の不平等は解決できない」という3つ目の論点の結論を，全体の結論として述べてしまっています。
→ 「マイクロローンは貧困を解決しない」というのが講義全体の主張です。結論では講義全体の主張を再度まとめて締めくくりましょう。

《構成の改善例》

- **❶【L】講義の立場** マイクロクレジット・プログラムは貧困を解決しない。
  - **❷【L】ポイント1** 高金利が財政状況を悪化させるなど，貧しい人々の害になり得る。
  （【R】ポイント1：マイクロローンは貧しい人々の財政状況を改善する。）
  - **❸【L】ポイント2** 安定した雇用を創出するほうが持続性が高い。
  （【R】ポイント2：マイクロローンは安定した収入を生み出すため，持続可能性が高い。）
  - **❹【L】ポイント3** 文化的価値観を変えることでしか，女性の地位を向上させることはできない。
  （【R】ポイント3：マイクロローンは女性の地位を向上させる。）

適切な解答例

★1 The professor talks about how microcredit programs do not cure poverty, pointing out some flaws in the reading passage's arguments.

First, she talks about how microloans can harm poor people. **★2** Microloans, she explains, tend to have high-interest rates due to the high administrative costs. This means that some borrowers' financial situation is worse after getting a loan. This directly refutes the reading passage, which states that microcredit loans have generous payment terms and improve the financial situations of borrowers.

Second, she argues that creating jobs is a more sustainable way to fix poverty. As an example, she talks about lending $100 to 1,000 different women, so that they can buy sewing machines. **★3** Buying a sewing machine does not guarantee that these women will succeed, but lending all of that money to build a clothing factory would create more stable jobs.** Again, this contradicts the reading passage, which states that microloans enable people to generate a more stable income.

Third, she claims that microcredit programs cannot fix discrimination against women. Although she agrees that giving women more opportunities is a good thing, she says that only changing a culture's values will solve gender inequalities. With this point, the professor opposes the reading's claim that microcredit programs empower women.

★4 **In short, the professor clearly does not believe that microcredit is one of the most effective cures for poverty.** (226 words)

（教授は，マイクロクレジット・プログラムが貧困を解決しないということについて話しており，課題文の主張に見られるいくつかの欠点を指摘しています。

第1に，教授は，マイクロローンが貧しい人々の害になり得ることについて話しています。教授の説明では，高い管理コストにより，マイクロローンは高金利になる傾向があります。これはつまり，融資を受けた後に，財政状況がさらに悪化する借り手もいるということです。このことは，マイクロクレジット・ローンは寛大な支払い条件を設けており，借り手の財政状況を改善すると述べている課題文に，直接的に反論しています。

第2に，教授は，雇用を創出するほうが貧困を解消するより持続的な方法だと主張しています。例として，ミシンを買うことができるように，1,000人の女性に100ドルの融資をすることについて話しています。ミシンを買うことは女性の成功を保証するものではなく，全額を縫製工場の建設のために融資するほうが，より安定した雇用を生むでしょう。ここでも，マイクロローンは人々により安定した収入を生み出せるようにすると述べている課題文と相違しています。

第3に，教授は，マイクロクレジット・プログラムは女性に対する差別を解消することはできないと主張しています。教授は，女性により多くの機会を与えることはよいことだということには賛同していますが，文化的価値観を変えることでしか，男女間の不平等は解決できないだろうと述べています。この点で，教授は，マイクロクレジット・プログラムが女性の地位を向上させるという課題文の主張に反対しています。

つまり，教授は明らかに，マイクロクレジットが貧困をなくす最も効果的な解決法の1つだとは思っていません。）

✓ 重要表現チェック

課題文
- ☐ microcredit「マイクロクレジット，少額融資」
- ☐ institution「銀行，会社」　☐ major「大きい（ほうの）」
- ☐ sustainable「持続できる」　☐ disadvantaged「不利な，恵まれない」
- ☐ qualify「資格を得る」　☐ generous「寛大な」
- ☐ terms「（支払い・値段などの）条件」
- ☐ contributor「寄付する人，貢献する人」
- ☐ alternative「代わるもの」　☐ in full「全部，全額」
- ☐ loan「～を貸す」　☐ entrepreneurial「起業家の」

不十分な解答例　☐ discrimination「差別」

適切な解答例　☐ cure「～を解決する」

問題 5

課題文訳・リスニングスクリプト ➡ 別冊 p.13

Reading Time: 3 minutes

Genetic engineering is the process of adding DNA from one organism to another that did not already have it. It's already being used in some fascinating and beneficial ways.

In Canada, there is a pig that has been genetically engineered to digest phosphorous, a chemical that causes large amounts of algae to form in waters. When too much algae forms, it takes away oxygen and kills marine life. The genetically-altered pigs process the phosphorus so that their waste contains less of it. This reduces the pigs' impact on the environment.

In another development, agricultural scientists at a university in China have added scorpion venom to cabbages. This is intended to kill caterpillars that damage cabbage crops. They have modified the venom so that it kills caterpillars, but does no harm to humans. Growing this cabbage will result in a reduction in pesticide use, saving farmers money and also reducing the amount of chemicals used on the crops.

Finally, a company in the United States has modified the genes of salmon to make them grow faster. It has spent about $77 million to develop the salmon, which combines a gene from a different species to produce more growth hormone. The Food and Drug Administration has said that it appears to be safe to eat and unlikely to harm the environment, although they have not yet approved it. If it can be sold in supermarkets, it will help to satisfy the increasing global demand for fish.

Now listen to part of a lecture on the topic you just read about. ● CD 08

Summarize the points made in the lecture you just heard, being sure to explain how they cast doubt on specific points made in the reading passage.

Response Time: 20 minutes

【設問訳】
今聞いた講義の論点を要約しなさい。その際,課題文で挙げられているどの論点にどのように疑問を投げかけているかを必ず説明しなさい。

> 解答例

不十分な解答例

★1 The reading passage says about genetic engineering and shows three examples. The professor is doubtful about **★2** those good points.

　First, in Canada there is a pig that has been genetic (→**genetically**) engineered so that its waste contains less phosphorus, which produces algae. However, the professor says the experiments only lasted about two years and the pig had to be kept away from other animal (→**animals**). The professor also says it would take some time before the approval of using the pig for food even if the research started again.

★3 Second, the professor talks about the cabbage with scorpion venom which is intended to kill caterpillars which damage cabbage crops without harm (→**harming**) humans and the professor makes a point that no one would like to buy it in a rush even if told it is safe. The professor also believes that the toxin may not work because of the way it is (→**was**) tested. So pesticides will be used anyway.

　Third, the professor talks about the modified salmon to grow faster. **★4** The FDA says the salmon seems to be safe but they have not approved it. Some supermarket chains have said they will not sell it and many people is (→**are**) against eating it. **★1**

> ●構成と内容の改善ポイント

★1 Introduction でトピックが明確に述べられているのはよいですが，第2段落以降で展開される具体的な論点については述べられていません。
➡ 適切な解答例のように，Introduction の中で課題文で挙げられた事例についてより具体的に言及し，教授がその利点に反論しているという構成を示すと，より読み手が構成をつかみやすくなります。また，結論で教授の立場を再度提示し，エッセイのまとめができるとよりよいでしょう。

★2 教授は課題文で述べられている遺伝子工学の利点に対して疑いを持っています。good points という語彙の選択は，誰の立場から見て good なのかが伝わりづらく，誤解を招く可能性があるため，あまり適切ではありません。
➡ ここでは supposed benefit とし，遺伝子工学の取り組みを有益と考えているのは課題文であることを明確に示します。課題文の立場からの記述なのか，教授の立場からの記述なのかが読み手に伝わるように書くことを意識しましょう。

★3 一文が長すぎて読みにくくなっています。
➡ 英文ライティングでは，1つ1つの内容をわかりやすく端的に述べるのが鉄則です。日本語では一文で書くことだとしても，読みやすいように2〜3文に分けましょう。

★4 課題文と講義がそれぞれどのような主張をしているかが明確に示されていません。
→ 講義が課題文に反論するパターンの問題では，「課題文では〜と述べられているが，教授は…と述べている」などの流れで，課題文と講義の関係を明確に示しましょう。

《構成の改善例》

❶【L】講義の立場　遺伝子工学の恩恵とされていることに対し疑問を投げかけている。

❷【L】ポイント1　遺伝子操作された豚の研究は止まっている。食用としての承認も容易ではない。
（【R】ポイント1：遺伝子操作された豚は，環境に対する影響を減少させる。）

❸【L】ポイント2　サソリ毒の入ったキャベツは誰も食べたいとは思わない。検証方法にも疑問がある。
（【R】ポイント2：サソリ毒入りキャベツは，殺虫剤の使用の減少などをもたらす。）

❹【L】ポイント3　遺伝子操作されたサケはまだ承認されておらず，販売拒否の動きもある。
（【R】ポイント3：速く成長するサケは安全だと言われており，販売されれば，魚の需要を満たすのに役立つ。）

適切な解答例

★1 The reading passage gives three examples of how genetic engineering is being used on plants and animals to improve the environment and benefit humankind. The professor casts doubt on those ★2 supposed benefits.

First, there is a pig that has been modified so that its waste contains less phosphorus, which produces algae. The professor says the experiments only lasted about two years, and the modified pig could not be kept with other animals. The professor also says that it's unlikely the pigs would be readily approved for use as food by humans.

★3 The second example was a cabbage with scorpion venom that kills the insects that eat the cabbage. The professor makes a point that people would not want to eat such a thing, even if told it's safe. There was also an issue regarding how the venom was tested, leading the professor to believe the toxin may not work. If pesticides have to be used anyway, there is no point in this modification.

Third, the professor talks about the salmon that was genetically modified to grow faster. ★4 The reading passage says the FDA has said the salmon seems to be safe, but the professor says they haven't approved it yet, which is a big difference. The professor also says some supermarket chains refuse to sell it, so even if approved, it won't achieve its goal.

★1 **Therefore, these may be good ideas to help people, but they probably won't be effective in their goals.**　　　　　　　　　　　　　　　　(243 words)

（課題文は，環境を向上させたり人間の利益となるように，遺伝子工学がどのように植物や動物に利用されているかを示す３つの例を挙げています。教授は，恩恵とされているそれらのことに疑問を投げかけています。

第1に，排泄物に含まれる，藻を作り出すリンが，通常より少なくなるように遺伝子操作された豚がいます。教授は，その実験はたった２年間続いただけで，その遺伝子組み換え豚は他の動物と一緒にしておくことはできなかったと言っています。また教授は，そのような豚が人の食用としての使用を容易に承認されることはなさそうだ，とも言っています。

第２の例は，キャベツを食べる虫を殺すサソリ毒の入ったキャベツでした。教授は，たとえ安全だと言われても，人々はそのようなものを食べたいとは思わないだろうと指摘しています。毒の試され方に関する問題もありました。そのことにより，教授は，毒は作用しないかもしれないと考えています。もしいずれにしても殺虫剤が使用されなければならないのなら，この組み換えには意味がありません。

第３に，教授はより速く成長するように遺伝子操作されたサケについて話しています。課題文にはFDAがそのサケを安全だと思われると述べていると書かれていますが，教授は彼らはまだサケを承認しておらず，それは大きな違いだと述べています。また，それを販売することを拒んでいるスーパーマーケットチェーンもあり，たとえ承認されたとしても目的を達成することはないだろうとも述べています。

したがって，これらは人々の役に立とうとするよい考えかもしれませんが，その目的を達成するという点においてはおそらく効果はないでしょう。）

✓ 重要表現チェック

課題文
- ☐ genetic engineering「遺伝子工学，遺伝子組み換え技術」
- ☐ engineer「(遺伝子)を操作する」
- ☐ phosphorous「リン」　　☐ algae「藻」
- ☐ waste「排泄物」　　☐ scorpion venom「サソリ毒」
- ☐ caterpillar「イモムシ」　　☐ modify「～を変更する，～を修正する」
- ☐ Food and Drug Administration「食品医薬品局」

適切な解答例
- ☐ readily「すぐに，容易に」

問題6

Reading Time: 3 minutes

3D printing is a process of making solid, 3D objects from a digital file. 3D printers are special, because they can produce different kinds of objects, in different materials, all from the same machine. The 3D printing industry is expected to grow consistently over the next few decades, making for a number of promising investment opportunities.

3D printing is going to completely change the way the world manufactures products. 3D printing could potentially give consumers the ability to manufacture virtually anything from the comfort of their own homes. For example, if a designer has an idea for a new piece of jewelry, he or she could go from concept all the way to final product within only hours by using a 3D printer.

There are already a number of companies that are capitalizing on this new industry, many of which have promising futures. Some companies produce and sell personal 3D printers. Others focus on building and implementing designs. With experts predicting that the 3D printing industry will continue to grow steadily for the next few years, we can expect to see more and more successful companies taking advantage of this new and exciting technology.

Many financial experts recommend investing in a variety of the major companies in this emerging industry. It is likely that these companies will continue to grow as the 3D printing industry continues to develop. In addition, spreading investment out across multiple companies lowers any risks involved.

Now listen to part of a lecture on the topic you just read about. CD 09

Summarize the points made in the lecture you just heard, being sure to explain how they challenge specific arguments made in the reading passage.

Response Time: 20 minutes

【設問訳】
今聞いた講義の論点を要約しなさい。その際，課題文で挙げられているどの論点にどのように反論しているかを必ず説明しなさい。

> 解答例

不十分な解答例

 ★1 The 3D printing industry is expected to grow over the next few decades. Investing in this industry is being recommended.

 First, the future of 3D printing is not clear. As an example, the professor points out that most 3D printer (→**printers**) can only make very simple products, but the cost of making simple products with 3D printer (→**printers**) is not low. ★2 This is true even if some believe that 3D printing will enable us to manufacture virtually anything.

 Second, many companies are likely to fail in an emerging industry like 3D printing. The professor mentions how some experts say that consumer models of 3D printers will never become popular. ★3 It means we can't expect to see more and more successful companies in this industry.

 Third, the professor points out that no one know (→**knows**) which 3D printing companies will succeed. ★4 In other words, it is very difficult to judge which companies are safe to invest in. With this point, the professor opposes to (→不要) the reading's claim that investing in many 3D printing companies lows (→**lowers**) risks.

 In short, ★5 the professor doesn't agree with the 3D printing industry.

●構成と内容の改善ポイント

★1 課題文の内容のみが述べられており、教授の立場が述べられていません。
→ Introduction ではまず、教授の立場を明確に述べましょう。これから展開するのは課題文の要約ではなく、講義の要約です。課題文の立場については、余裕があれば言及する程度で構いません。

★2 「たとえ…と考える人がいたとしても」と書かれているだけで、課題文との関係性が明示されていません。
→ 課題文に対する反論であることがわかるように記述しましょう。

★3 ★2 と同様に、講義と課題文との関係に言及していません。また、課題文の表現をそのまま用いています。
→ 適切な解答例では、教授が、「3D プリンティング産業に参入する多くの会社が成功するだろう」という課題文の主張に反論していることを説明しています。表現については、なるべく自分の言葉で言い換えるようにしましょう。

★4 前の文で述べた内容に似たことを繰り返しているだけで、教授がそのように主張する理由が述べられていません。
→ 教授は 3D プリンティング産業への投資が危険である理由として、日の浅い産業に投資する危険性を指摘しています。主張とその理由を合わせて把握し、記述し

★5 講義全体の主張を正確に伝えられていません。
➡教授は3Dプリンティング産業自体を批判しているのではなく,「3Dプリンティング企業への投資はよい考えではない」と主張しています。言葉足らずにならないように気をつけ,教授の立場を正確に表現しましょう。

《構成の改善例》

❶【L】講義の立場　3Dプリンティング産業への投資はよくない考えである。

　❷【L】ポイント1　3Dプリンティングの未来ははっきりしない。
　（【R】ポイント1：3Dプリンティングが製造業界を完全に変えるだろう。）

　❸【L】ポイント2　新興の産業では多くの会社が失敗する傾向にある。
　（【R】ポイント2：多くの企業が3Dプリンティングにより成功する。）

　❹【L】ポイント3　新技術に投資をすることはリスクが高い。
　（【R】ポイント3：多くの3Dプリンティング企業への投資はリスクが低い。）

適切な解答例

★1 The professor talks about how investing in 3D printing companies might be a bad idea.

First of all, the future of 3D printing is not clear. As an example, the professor points out that most 3D printers can only make very simple products, but the cost of making simple products with 3D printers is not low. ★2 This is different from the reading passage, which states that 3D printing is going to completely change the manufacturing industry.

On the second point, many companies are likely to fail in an emerging industry like 3D printing. The professor mentions how some experts say that consumer models of 3D printers will never become popular. ★3 Again, this contradicts the reading passage, which states that many new, successful companies are expected to profit from 3D printing.

Third, ★4 investing in new technology is risky. In young industries, it is difficult to know how the market will change. The professor points out that no one knows which 3D printing companies will succeed. With this point, the professor opposes the reading's claim that investing in many 3D printing companies is low-risk.

In short, ★5 the professor seems to believe that investing in 3D printing companies is not advisable, because there is too much risk. This is completely at odds with the reading passage, which suggests that the 3D printing industry will continue to advance. (218 words)

(教授は，3D プリンティングの企業に投資をすることがいかによくない考えであるかについて話しています。

第1に，3D プリンティングの未来ははっきりしません。例として，教授は，ほとんどの3D プリンターはとても単純なものしか作れませんが，3D プリンターで単純なものを作るコストが低いわけではないと指摘しています。このことは，3D プリンターが製造業界を完全に変えようとしていると述べている課題文と異なります。

第2の点については，3D プリンティングのような新興の産業では，多くの企業が失敗する傾向にあります。教授は，3D プリンターの消費者向けモデルがありふれたものになることはないだろうと言う専門家もいると述べています。ここでも，多くの新しく躍進する企業が3D プリンティングから利益を得ると期待されると述べられている課題文に反論しています。

第3に，新技術に投資をすることはリスクが高いです。日の浅い産業では，市場がどのように変化するかを知るのは容易ではありません。教授は，3D プリンティングのどの企業が成功するかはだれにもわからないと指摘しています。この点で，教授は，多くの3D プリンター企業への投資はリスクが低いと主張する課題文に反対しています。

つまり，教授は，3D プリンティングの企業に投資をすることは，あまりにもリスクが高いので，賢明ではないと考えているようです。これは，3D プリンティング産業が進歩し続けるだろうと述べる課題文と，完全に意見が食い違っています。)

✓ 重要表現チェック

課題文
- ☐ 3D「3次元（の），立体（の）」
- ☐ solid「固体の」
- ☐ object「物体」
- ☐ material「物質，材料，素材」
- ☐ consistently「絶えず，一貫して」
- ☐ promising「有望な」
- ☐ investment「投資」
- ☐ manufacture「〜を製造する」
- ☐ virtually「実質的には，事実上」
- ☐ from the comfort of 〜「〜にいながらにして」
- ☐ jewelry「宝石類，宝飾品」
- ☐ capitalize on 〜「〜を利用する，つけこむ」
- ☐ emerging「新興の」
- ☐ multiple「複合的な，多様の」
- ☐ lower「〜を低くする」

適切な解答例
- ☐ advisable「賢明な，得策である」

問題7

課題文訳・リスニングスクリプト ➡ 別冊 p.18

Reading Time: 3 minutes

Scientists have confirmed that a mass extinction event is currently taking place. What this means is that numerous species of plants and animals are disappearing at an unnaturally high rate. In fact, this is the fastest that animal species have been disappearing since the age of the dinosaurs. In addition, scientists claim that humans are the cause of this mass extinction event.

Perhaps the largest factor contributing to this event is climate change. Thanks to a number of technological advances over the last thousand years or so, human populations have skyrocketed. One negative result of this is global warming, which is causing harmful changes to climate patterns. Human vehicles and factories are changing the climate, and thousands of species are dying off as a result.

Another major cause of this is oceanic devastation. In other words, ocean ecosystems are being destroyed, and many fish species are dying as a result. This is almost entirely due to overfishing by humans. With increased population, overfishing has become a major global problem. Humans are simply eating more fish than the oceans can produce.

On land, the most significant contributor to species loss is deforestation. This refers to the removal of forests for non-forest use. For example, expanding populations often destroy forested areas in order to build homes. Forests are also destroyed in order to provide the lumber to make these homes. Put simply, growing human populations are putting the earth's plants and animals at risk in a number of ways. If something does not change soon, there could be dangerous consequences.

Now listen to part of a lecture on the topic you just read about. ● CD 10

Summarize the points made in the lecture you just heard, being sure to explain how they cast doubt on specific points made in the reading passage.

Response Time: 20 minutes

【設問訳】
今聞いた講義の論点を要約しなさい。その際，課題文で挙げられているどの論点にどのように疑問を投げかけているかを必ず説明しなさい。

解答例

不十分な解答例

★1 The reading passage says that a mass extinction event is currently taken (→**taking**) place. The professor also says this is true.

　First, though climate change is a major cause of the disappearance of species, the professor clarifies that climate change is not only about global warming. ★2 Many people agree that humans cause climate change. She explains that harming natural environments in general also causes damage **to** animals and plants. For example, pollution damages the environment. With this point, her opinion is (→不要) differs from the reading passage, which states that global warming is the primary cause of the problem.

　Second, the professor talks about oceanic devastation. She says that it refers to more than overfishing. As one example, she talks about ★3 major accidents. They kill a lot of animals and plants. She disagrees with the passage that says ocean devastation is mainly caused by overfishing.

　Third, ★4 the professor talks about the cause of species loss on land. The professor says the problem is not only destroying forests. She says humans should be blamed for the cause of this problem. Humans destroy large areas for their homes or farms. The main cause of species loss is not destroying forests. Humans should be blamed. She again disagrees with the passage, which claims that the deforestation is the primary contributor to species' disappearing on land.

　In short, the professor argues that the mass extinction event is a major problem with many complicated causes.

●構成と内容の改善ポイント

★1 教授が課題文に賛成しているような印象を与えます。
　➡教授は，大量絶滅が起きていること自体には同意していますが，課題文の与える情報は誤解を招くとし，その問題点を指摘しています。課題文の内容を補足しているのか，反論しているのかを正しく理解し，Introduction で明確にしましょう。

★2 「多くの人が，人間が気候変動を引き起こしているということに同意する」という内容の文ですが，前後の文との論理的なつながりが不明です。
　➡前の文で「気候変動とは地球温暖化のことだけではない」と述べ，後の文で「自

然環境を破壊すること全般が原因である」と述べており，これらが論理的につながっているため，該当の文は削除します。文と文の自然な論理の流れを作りましょう。

★3 major accidents の内容が具体的に述べられていません。
→ 講義では，石油流出による海洋汚染が例として挙げられています。なるべく詳しい情報まで聞き取り，具体性の高い要約にしましょう。

★4 同じ内容が繰り返し述べられ，says / cause / should be blamed などの同じ表現が繰り返し用いられているため，冗長で単調な印象です。
→ 適切な解答例のように，課題文や講義の内容を，多様な表現を用いて簡潔に説明することを心がけましょう。解答例の中で使える表現を見つけてメモしておくなど，工夫するとよいでしょう。

《構成の改善例》

- **❶【L】講義の立場** 課題文の動植物の大量絶滅の原因の説明には，問題がある。
  - **❷【L】ポイント1** 気候変動の原因は，単なる地球温暖化ではなく，自然環境の破壊全般である。
    （【R】ポイント1：地球温暖化が気候変動の主な原因である。）
  - **❸【L】ポイント2** 気候変動や，石油流出などによる海洋汚染も原因となっている。
    （【R】ポイント2：海洋破壊の原因のほとんどは，人間による魚の乱獲である。）
  - **❹【L】ポイント3** 森林だけではなく，土地一般を破壊していることが原因である。
    （【R】ポイント3：陸上で生物種の消滅を招いている主な原因は，森林破壊である。）

適切な解答例

★1 **The professor talks about the causes of the current mass extinction event and points out some flaws in the reading passage's arguments.**

First, though climate change is a major cause of the disappearance of species, the professor clarifies that climate change is not only about global warming. She then explains that harming natural environments in general causes damage to animals and plants. One example of this is pollution. This directly refutes the reading passage, which states that global warming is the primary cause of the problem.

Second, "ocean devastation" refers to more than just overfishing. As an example, she points out that **★3** marine pollution such as oil spills sometimes kills large amounts of animals and plants. This is one way that humans cause damage to ocean ecosystems. Again, this contradicts the reading passage, which states that ocean devastation is almost entirely caused by overfishing.

　　Third, ★4 **a major cause of species loss on land is humans changing and destroying land. The professor mentions that the problem is not only destroying forests. Instead, the problem is destroying land in general. For example, when humans convert open fields into farms, they can damage the environment.** With this point, the professor opposes the reading's claim that destroying forests is the primary contributor to species' disappearing on land.

　　In short, the professor argues that the mass extinction event is a major problem with many complicated causes.　　　　　　　　　　　　　　　　　　　(231 words)

（教授は，現在の大量絶滅の原因について話しており，課題文の主張に見られるいくつかの問題点を指摘しています。

　第1に，気候変動は生物種の消滅の大きな原因ではありますが，教授は，気候変動とは地球温暖化のことだけではないということを明確にしています。そして，教授は，自然環境を破壊すること全般が動植物に損害を与えると説明しています。この一例が汚染です。このことは，地球温暖化がこの問題の主たる原因だと述べている課題文に直接的に反論しています。

　第2に，「海洋破壊」とは魚の乱獲のことだけを指すのではありません。一例として，教授は，石油流出のような海洋汚染がたくさんの動植物を死に至らせることがあると指摘しています。このような形でも，人類は海洋の生態系にダメージを与えています。このことも，海洋破壊の原因はほとんどが乱獲であると述べている課題文に異議を唱えています。

　第3に，陸上での生物種の損失の主な原因は，人間が土地に変化を与え，破壊していることです。教授は，森林を破壊していることだけが問題ではないと述べています。そうではなく，土地一般を破壊していることが問題なのです。例えば，人間が開けた野原を農場に変える時，環境にダメージを与えることがあります。この点で，教授は，森林を破壊することが，陸上での生物種の消滅を引き起こしている主たる原因であるという，課題文の主張に反対しています。

　つまり，教授は，大量絶滅はたくさんの複雑な原因が絡む大きな問題であると主張しています。）

✓重要表現チェック

課題文　　　□ skyrocket「急増する」　　□ devastation「破壊」
　　　　　　□ deforestation「森林破壊」

問題 8

Reading Time: 3 minutes

In the last few decades, the Internet has become flooded with articles on diet and nutrition, many of which have contradictory claims. With so many differing opinions, it can be difficult to know what is sound nutritional advice. As such, I would like to introduce some dietary advice that is backed by solid scientific research.

For our first tip, we will look at recommended daily protein intake. Many bodybuilders and weight-loss experts recommend a high-protein diet that includes protein supplements such as shakes or protein powder. The general consensus of such proponents seems to be "the more protein, the better." However, a research study produced by the Board of the Institute of Medicine concluded that the recommended daily protein intake for those 18 years of age and older was .36 grams per pound of body weight.

Point three six (.36) grams per pound of body weight is not that much protein. For a 160-pound person, this means only 57.6 grams of protein per day. The best way to meet these requirements is by eating high-quality, protein-rich foods such as seafood, lean chicken, and low-fat dairy products. For example, a 4 ounce skinless chicken breast has around 30 grams of protein, over half of that recommended daily requirement.

For those trying to lose weight, eating multiple small meals throughout the day may be a better option than eating two or three large meals. Some diet experts claim that eating multiple small meals per day can increase the speed of one's metabolism, which leads to more calories burned per day. Also, it is a good diet practice, because frequent small meals can keep one from getting too hungry and, as a result, overeating during meals.

Now listen to part of a lecture on the topic you just read about.   CD 11

Summarize the points made in the lecture you just heard, being sure to explain how they challenge specific arguments made in the reading passage.

Response Time: 20 minutes

【設問訳】
今聞いた講義の論点を要約しなさい。その際，課題文で挙げられているどの論点にどのように反論しているかを必ず説明しなさい。

> 解答例

不十分な解答例

　The professor talks about how science-backed dieting advice also have (→**has**) problems.
　★1 First, for example, some working people who are 18 years of age or older need .36 grams of protein per pound of body weight, but some athletes might need .8 grams per pound per day. That means we need different amount of protein.
　Second, ★2 the reading passage says that we should eat a high-quality, protein-rich foods to intake .36 grams per pound of body weight because it is not much when calculated. For a 160-pound person, he or she needs only 57.6 grams of protein per day. However, the professor says the body does not necessarily need protein-rich foods. That is because (→**why**) some great athletes are vegetarians. Our body can create protein from nutrient-rich foods.
　★3 Third, it may be good advice to eat multiple small meals for some people because it can keep them from getting too hungry, so they can avoid overeating. However, some people may eat too many calories by this method.
　In short, the professor would like to say that giving ★4 good advice which is useful for everyone's diet is difficult.

> ●構成と内容の改善ポイント

★1 具体例から述べられており，この段落の主旨が把握しづらくなっています。また，課題文と講義の関係が述べられていません。
　➡各段落の第1文には，キーセンテンスとなる文を配置しましょう。抽象→具体の順に書くと，読みやすくなります。また，1つ1つの主張が課題文と講義のどちらのものなのか，課題文と講義の論点がどのように対応しているのかを明確にしましょう。
★2 要約としては不要な具体的情報が長々と述べられており，講義の論点との対応関係がわかりにくくなっています。
　➡教授は，「必要な摂取量を満たすには，たんぱく質の豊富な食品を食べるのが一番だ」という課題文の主張に反論しています。課題文の主旨を読み取り，必要な情報に絞って記述しましょう。適切な解答例では，講義の主張を示した上で，それに対応する課題文の主張を簡潔にまとめています。
★3 ★1 と同様に，課題文と講義の関係が述べられていません。

➡解答を見直す時間を必ず設け，課題文と講義がそれぞれどのような主張をしているのか，解答を読むだけで伝わるかどうかを確かめましょう。

★4 説明的で冗長な表現になっています。
➡適切な単語を用いて，端的に状況を説明することができると，より読みやすく，スマートなエッセイになります。

《構成の改善例》

- ❶【L】講義の立場　科学的根拠に基づくダイエットにも問題がある。
    - ❷【L】ポイント1　人によって必要な量は異なるため，決まったやり方として提示することはできない。
    - (【R】ポイント1：成人のたんぱく質の推奨摂取量は，1日あたり，体重1ポンドにつき0.36グラムである。)
    - ❸【L】ポイント2　必ずしもたんぱく質に富む食品を食べる必要はなく，たんぱく質を作ることのできる食品を食べればよい。
    - (【R】ポイント2：推奨摂取量を満たすためには，良質でたんぱく質に富む食品を食べるのが一番だ。)
    - ❹【L】ポイント3　1日に複数回少量の食事をとることは，一部の人にはよいアドバイスだが，カロリーを摂りすぎる人もいる。
    - (【R】ポイント3：体重を減らすには，1日に少量ずつ複数回の食事をとるとよい。)

適切な解答例

The professor talks about how science-backed diet tips have problems, as well.

First, ★1 different people need different types of diets. She points out that diet formulas cannot be trusted. As an example, she mentions that athletes need more protein than average people. This refutes the reading passage, which states that adults need .36 grams per pound of body weight per day.

Second, the body does not necessarily need protein-rich foods. The body can create protein from nutrient-rich foods. To illustrate this, she refers to how some of the world's greatest athletes are vegetarians. ★2 Again, this contradicts the reading passage, which states that eating high-quality, protein-rich foods like seafood and lean chicken is the best way to meet daily protein requirements.

★3 Third, eating many small meals per day can cause people to gain weight. Although the professor acknowledges that eating multiple small meals is good advice for some people, she clarifies that other people have gained weight on these types of diets. With this point, the professor somewhat opposes the reading's claim that eating multiple small meals per day could be preferable to eating two or three large meals.

In short, the professor seems to believe that giving ★4 general dieting advice is difficult, because different types of diets are necessary for different types of people.

(214 words)

（教授は，科学的根拠に基づいたダイエットのアドバイスにも問題があるということについて話しています。

第1に，人によって必要な食事のタイプは異なります。教授は，ダイエットの決まったやり方は信用できないと指摘しています。例として，スポーツ選手は平均的な人々よりも多くのたんぱく質を必要とすると述べています。このことは，成人は1日あたり体重1ポンドにつき0.36グラムのたんぱく質が必要だと述べている課題文に反論しています。

第2に，身体は必ずしもたんぱく質に富んだ食品を必要としません。身体は，栄養が豊富な食品からたんぱく質を作ることができます。これを説明するために，教授は，世界最高のスポーツ選手の中には菜食主義者もいるということに触れています。これもまた，海産物や脂肪分の少ない鶏肉のような良質でたんぱく質に富んだ食品を食べることが，1日に必要なたんぱく質摂取量を満たす一番の方法だと述べている課題文に相反しています。

第3に，1日に複数回少量の食事をとると，体重が増えるかもしれません。教授は，複数回少量の食事をとることが一部の人々にとってはよいアドバイスになるとは認めているものの，このようなダイエットをすると体重が増えてしまう人もいることを明らかにしています。この点で，教授は，2，3回たくさんの食事をとるよりも複数回少量の食事をとるほうが望ましいだろうとする課題文の主張に，ある程度反対しています。

つまり，教授は，人によって必要な食事のタイプが異なるため，一般的なダイエットのアドバイスをすることは難しいと考えているように思われます。）

✓ 重要表現チェック

課題文		
	☐ contradictory「相反する」	☐ sound「理にかなった」
	☐ solid「信頼のおける，確実な」	☐ protein「たんぱく質」
	☐ lean「低脂肪の」	
	☐ dairy products「乳製品」	☐ multiple「多数の」
	☐ metabolism「新陳代謝」	
適切な解答例	☐ formula「決まったやり方，公式」	☐ acknowledge「〜を認める」

問題 9

Reading Time: 3 minutes

Compared to other areas of society, higher education has changed very little over the last few hundred years. Due to the ongoing technological advances of the 21st century, however, university education is facing more and more problems, and some analysts estimate that a significant number of universities will go bankrupt within the next two decades.

The main problem —— in the United States, at least —— is that universities are in a funding crisis. The costs of running a world-class university keep rising, but government funding continues to drop. For example, in the five years leading up to 2012, public universities increased their fees by 27%. Almost all universities have been passing this cost onto their students. As a result, American student debt has added up to over $1 trillion.

Future students are starting to look for alternatives to expensive university education. One of these alternatives is online learning. A popular example of this is massive open online courses, commonly referred to as MOOCs. Students take these courses via the web, meaning that large numbers of students can take the same courses. This makes their cost dramatically lower than universities. Some of them are even beginning to offer official degrees, making them viable alternatives to universities.

Universities, however, are not changing much at all. Defenders of traditional university education point out that there are still advantages to studying at a university, such as opportunities to network with students and teachers. However, online schools are quickly adapting to these disadvantages. Some online education companies are beginning to offer online seminars, in which students have a high degree of interaction with a small group of classmates and highly skilled university professors. This is one example of how online schools are improving rapidly.

Now listen to part of a lecture on the topic you just read about. 🔘 CD 12

Summarize the points made in the lecture you just heard, being sure to explain how they challenge specific arguments made in the reading passage.

Response Time: 20 minutes

【設問訳】
今聞いた講義の論点を要約しなさい。その際，課題文で挙げられているどの論点にどのように反論しているかを必ず説明しなさい。

解答例

不十分な解答例

　　The professor talks about how universities are changing and improving in response to modern trends.
　　First, ★1 universities are experimenting with new ways of teaching. The professor mentions how some universities are beginning to include online courses in their study programs. This enables students to save money while also getting a high-quality education. This directly refutes to (→不要) the reading passage, which says that almost all universities have been charging students for (→不要) more money.
　　Next, online education is not a threat to universities. ★2 If you are taking online courses, you have to study alone at home. On the other hand, in university, students can learn with their classmates and rely on tutors, teaching assistants, and professors. It is highly beneficial to students. ★3 Some universities offers (→offer) facilities to help students start businesses. This contradicts to (→不要) the reading passage, which states that online learning is a viable alternative.
　　Third, universities are changing and innovating. Aside from experiments with online learning, many universities are also testing other ways to improve education. ★4 In short, the professor seems to disagree with the idea that universities cannot keep up with the way that education is rapidly changing. Indeed online schools are improving rapidly, but they will not be alternatives to universities.

●構成と内容の改善ポイント

★1 「大学が新しい教育の方法を試している」という内容は講義全体に共通するものであり，この段落で扱う論点を的確に伝えられていません。

➡️講義は，課題文の「財政難の大学のほとんどが，学生に費用を負担させている」という1つ目の主張に対し，「大学は新しい財政モデルの開発に取り組んでいる」と反論しています。つまり，この段落の論点は「財政難に対する大学の対応」と言えます。これを第1文で簡潔に示します。各段落の論点が明確に伝わるように，内容・表現を吟味しましょう。

★2 オンライン教育が大学にとって脅威でないことの根拠について，講義の主旨を正確に伝えていません。

➡️教授は，オンライン教育が大学にとって脅威でないと述べた直後に，「始めるのは簡単だが，修了することは難しい」と述べ，モチベーションの維持が課題であることを，具体的な数値を挙げて指摘しています。主張と根拠を合わせて聞き取り，記述しましょう。

★3 大学の利点を挙げた流れで，学生の事業の立ち上げを支援する大学の例に言及していますが，これは「オンライン教育は大学にとって脅威ではない」という主張を裏づけるために挙げられたものではありません。

➡️この大学の例は，「大学が変革を試みている」という3つ目の論点をサポートするために挙げられています。この具体例は次の段落で言及しましょう。

★4 学生の事業の立ち上げを支援する大学について，前の段落で述べてしまったため，3つ目の論点の内容が薄くなっています。また，3つ目の論点について述べる段落で，全体の結論まで述べています。

➡️教授は複数の論点に言及するので，それぞれの主張とそれを支える根拠の結びつきに注意を払って聞き取ることが大切です。「1段落に1つの論点」を原則とし，この段落では3つ目の論点に絞って，課題文との関係を記述します。全体の結論は段落を変えて述べましょう。

《構成の改善例》

❶【L】講義の立場 大学は現代の潮流に応じて変化し，改善されている。

　❷【L】ポイント1 大学は学費を減らす選択肢を模索している。
　（【R】ポイント1：ほとんどすべての大学が学生に課す費用を増やしている。）

　❸【L】ポイント2 大学にとって，オンライン教育は脅威ではない。
　（【R】ポイント2：オンライン教育は大学に代わる実効性を持つ。）

　❹【L】ポイント3 大学は変革しようと新たな方法を試している。
　（【R】ポイント3：大学は変革しようとしていない。）

適切な解答例

The professor talks about how universities are changing and improving in response to modern trends.

First, ★1 universities are exploring options for reducing student fees. As an example, the professor mentions how some universities are beginning to include online courses in their study programs. This enables students to save money while also getting a high-quality education. This directly refutes the reading passage, which says that almost all universities have been charging students more money.

Second, online education is not a threat to universities. ★2 There is the problem that it is difficult to maintain motivation until the student completes the course. Data shows only 10% of students complete online courses after enrolling. On the other hand, in university, students can learn with their classmates and rely on tutors, teaching assistants, and professors. It is highly beneficial to students. This contradicts the reading passage, which states that online learning is a viable alternative.

Third, universities are changing and innovating. Aside from experiments with online learning, many universities are also testing other ways to improve education. ★3 For example, a university in the U.S. developed a new building to help students start businesses. ★4 With this point, the professor opposes the reading's claim that universities are not changing.

★4 In short, the professor seems to disagree with the idea that universities cannot keep up with the way that education is rapidly changing.　　　(225 words)

（教授は，大学がどのように現代の潮流に応じて変化し，改善されているかについて話しています。

第1に，大学は学費を減らす選択肢を模索しています。例として，教授は，履修課程にオンライン講座を取り入れはじめている大学もあることに言及しています。これにより，学生たちは質の高い教育を受けながら費用を節約することができます。このことは，ほとんどすべての大学が学生に課す費用を増やしていると述べている課題文に直接的に反論しています。

第2に，大学にとって，オンライン教育は脅威ではありません。オンライン講座には，修了するまでモチベーションを保つことが難しいという課題があります。登録後の修了率はたったの10パーセントというデータもあります。一方，大学では，仲間と共に学んだり，無料の個人教師，教育協力者，教授に頼ったりすることができます。これは生徒にとって非常に有益です。オンライン学習は大学に代わる実効性を持つものであると述べる課題文と相違しています。

第3に，大学は変化し，変革しています。オンライン学習を試しているだけでなく，多くの大学は教育をよくする他の方法も試しています。例えば，アメリカのとある大学は学生たちが事業を立ち上げるのに役立つ新しい建物を開発しました。この点で，教授は，大学が変わっていない

という課題文の主張に反対しています。
　つまり，教授は，大学が，教育の急速な変化の仕方に対応できていないという考えに反対していると思われます。)

✓ 重要表現チェック

課題文
- □ estimate「～と見積もる」
- □ bankrupt「破産した」
- □ funding「資金（提供），財源」
- □ crisis「危機」
- □ add up to ～「合計～になる」
- □ trillion「1兆」
- □ dramatically「劇的に」
- □ viable「実行可能な」
- □ network「ネットワークを持つ，人脈を築く」
- □ interaction「相互作用，ふれあい」

問題 10

課題文訳・リスニングスクリプト ➡ 別冊 p.27

Reading Time: 3 minutes

The US government has a larger military budget than any other country in the world, which leads to a large number of critics demanding a decrease in spending. Many supporters of increased military spending, however, argue that it advances technological discoveries, creates jobs for US citizens, and strengthens national security.

In the 21st century, nothing will drive economies more than technological innovation, and military spending leads to greater advances in technology. Most US citizens would have a hard time imagining a world without the Internet, satellite communication, and high-speed jet engines, because these are all essential to the modern economy. All of these technologies got started in the military. From a logical viewpoint, continued military spending will lead to further technological discoveries.

Another major benefit of military spending is that it creates so many jobs for US citizens. Experts estimate that $1 billion of military spending creates around 11,000 jobs. Cutting the defense budget would result in many Americans losing their jobs. At the time of this writing, it is estimated that roughly 10 million US citizens have jobs that depend on US military spending. That is a lot of jobs that will be at risk with budget cuts.

Finally, there is nothing more important than national security. The world does not fight traditional wars anymore. Rather, citizens face different types of threats in the 21st century —— threats like cyberattacks, terrorism, weapons of mass destruction, and climate change. Having a large defense budget gives the government the ability to protect its citizens from these threats.

Now listen to part of a lecture on the topic you just read about. CD 13

Summarize the points made in the lecture you just heard, being sure to explain how they challenge specific arguments made in the reading passage.

Response Time: 20 minutes

Question 1 | 集中トレーニング

Question 1

【設問訳】
今聞いた講義の論点を要約しなさい。その際、課題文で挙げられているどの論点にどのように反論しているかを必ず説明しなさい。

解答例

不十分な解答例

　The professor talks about some flaw (→flaws) in the passage about high military spending.
　First of all, the professor says military spending is not the most effective way to improve technology. As an example, he tells about companies which made technological discoveries. He lists many discoveries that **are** being made using ★1 a tiny friction (→fraction) of the US military's budget. ★2 This means that military spending is not the best way. So he ★3 opposes the reading passage, which says that high military spending is necessary for technological discoveries.
　Second, other government sectors create more jobs than the military. According to the passage, 11,000 jobs can be created with $1 billion of military spending. The professor says that education and healthcare would create more jobs than the military if given the same money (→same amount of money) . He ★3 opposes the reading passage, which says that the military spending creates a lot of jobs.
　Third, cutting military spending would increase national security. National security is not only by military spending. By having a strong economy, good healthcare and high-quality education, the country's national security gets better. The professor ★3 opposes the reading passage, which says that nothing is more important than national security.
　In short, the professor ★3 disagrees with ★4 the passage, which says military spending strengthens national security.

●構成と内容の改善ポイント

★1 聞き取った表現をそのまま書こうとしていますが、語彙のミスが多くなっています。a tiny fraction of ～ で「ほんのわずかな～」という意味になります。friction は「摩擦」という意味です。
➡ 多様な表現で言い換えることが高得点につながります。また、多少のスペルや文法のミスは、意味を把握する上で支障にならないレベルであれば問題になりませんが、スペルに自信がない場合は正しく使える別の表現を使いましょう。

★2 講義で述べられていた具体例に言及していません。
➡ 教授は、「自動運転する車、より安全な航空機、糖尿病患者の助けとなるコ

ンタクトレンズ，再生可能なエネルギー源」を例に挙げています。できるだけ具体的に記述しましょう。

★3 同じ表現を繰り返し使っています。
　➡同じ内容を表す場合にも，できるだけ多様な表現を用いることを意識しましょう。よく使う単語については，適切な解答例や本書P.25の［役に立つ表現］を参考にいくつか同義語を覚えておくとよいでしょう。

★4 全体のまとめとなる結論部分で，国家の安全保障という講義の3つ目の論点についてのみまとめています。
　➡結論を書く場合は，講義全体の主張や立場を簡潔にまとめましょう。

《構成の改善例》

❶【L】講義の立場　多額の軍事支出を支持する主張には，いくつか問題がある。

　　❷【L】ポイント1　軍事支出は，技術を高める最善の方法ではない。
　　（【R】ポイント1：多額の軍事支出は技術的発見にとって重要である。）
　　❸【L】ポイント2　軍事以外の部門のほうが，より多くの雇用を創出する。
　　（【R】ポイント2：軍事支出が多くの雇用を生む。）
　　❹【L】ポイント3　軍事支出を減らすことが国家の安全保障を向上させる。
　　（【R】ポイント3：多額の防衛予算が，国家の安全保障にとって必要である。）

適切な解答例

　The professor talks about how there are some flaws in the reading passage's arguments for high military spending.

　First of all, military spending is not the most effective way to improve technology. As an example, the professor looks at companies making technological discoveries. He lists a variety of discoveries that are being made using ★1 much less money than the US military, ★2 such as cars that drive themselves and high-performance airplanes. This means that military spending is probably not the best way to improve technology. This directly ★3 refutes the reading passage, which states that high military spending is important for technological discoveries.

　On the second point, other sectors of the government can create more jobs than the military. The reading passage says that 11,000 jobs can be created with $1 billion of military spending. The professor points out that education and healthcare can both create more jobs than the military with the same amount of money. Again, this ★3contradicts the reading passage, which states that military spending creates a lot of jobs for US citizens.

Third, decreased military spending could improve national security. National security is not only about military spending. By improving areas like education, healthcare and the economy, the country's national security improves. With this point, the professor ★3challenges the reading passage's claim that having a large defense budget is necessary for national security.

In short, the professor ★3disagrees with ★4the points made in the reading passage.

(238 words)

（教授は，多額の軍事支出を支持する課題文の主張にはどのような問題点があるのかについて話しています。

第1に，軍事支出は技術を高める最も効果的な方法ではありません。例として，教授は，技術的な発見をしている企業について考察しています。彼は，アメリカ軍よりもずっと少額の資金でなされた，自動運転する自動車や高性能の航空機などのさまざまな発見をリストアップしています。このことが意味するのは，軍事支出はおそらく，技術を高める最善の方法ではないということです。このことは，多額の軍事支出は技術的発見にとって重要であると述べている課題文に直接的に反論しています。

第2に，政府の他の部門は，軍事よりも多くの雇用を創出することができます。課題文では，10億ドルの軍事支出で11,000件の雇用が創出されると書かれています。教授は，教育や医療はどちらも，軍事よりももっと多くの雇用を同じ額で創出できると指摘しています。ここでも，軍事支出がアメリカ国民に多くの雇用を生むと述べている課題文を否定しています。

第3に，軍事支出を減らすことは国家の安全保障を向上させることになる可能性があります。国家の安全保障とは，軍事支出だけではありません。教育や医療，経済のような分野を改善することによって，その国の安全保障は改善されます。この点で，教授は，多額の防衛予算を組むことが国家の安全保障にとって必要であるという課題文の主張に反対しています。

つまり，教授は課題文で挙げられている論点に対して異なる意見を持っています。）

✓重要表現チェック

課題文
- □ military budget「軍事予算」　□ military spending「軍事支出」
- □ national security「国家安全保障」
- □ satellite communication「衛星通信」
- □ defense budget「防衛予算」　□ weapon「兵器」
- □ mass destruction「大量破壊」

問題 11

Reading Time: 3 minutes

Koalas are fuzzy, bear-like creatures that are symbols of their native Australia. They spend most of their time in trees, eat eucalyptus leaves, and are the only living representatives of their biological family. However, these unique creatures are facing extinction due to various factors, including the overdevelopment of agricultural and residential land, excessive hunting, disease, and forest destruction caused by global warming. Their habitats have been significantly reduced, and the remaining koalas have become overcrowded in what habitats remain.

Koalas live in the wild in four states: Queensland, New South Wales, Victoria, and South Australia. Each of these states has implemented legislation to protect the environment. These laws strengthen the national protection of koalas and require the assessment of any development project that is likely to have a significant impact on koala populations.

Several environmental organizations are also engaged in tree-planting projects to improve habitats and protect the koalas. One of these has set up an informative website with information on how to plant trees and donate to reforestation projects. Private companies are also doing their part. A Japanese automaker has started a tree-planting project in Australia, in which 1763 hectares of eucalyptus trees have been planted near Perth and Melbourne.

Finally, zoos throughout the world can assist in preservation efforts by taking in koalas from Australia. Zoos in Japan, Singapore, the U.S., and other regions now care for koalas. They are cute and popular with visitors, which benefits the zoos as well. As long as these efforts continue, the koala should be safe from extinction.

Now listen to part of a lecture on the topic you just read about. CD 14

Summarize the points made in the lecture you just heard, being sure to explain how they challenge specific arguments made in the reading passage.

Response Time: 20 minutes

Question 1

【設問訳】
今聞いた講義の論点を要約しなさい。その際，課題文で挙げられているどの論点にどのように反論しているかを必ず説明しなさい。

> 解答例

不十分な解答例

★1 The reading passage points out that Koalas are in danger due to various factors, such as the overdevelopment of land, hunting, disease and forest destruction. Also, their habitats have been significantly reduced. On the other hand, the professor acknowledges that there are efforts to protect koalas, but says it is (→**they are**) insufficient. ★2 She states that the national government's approach has been to declare the species "Vulnerable," but they should have been classified as "Endangered."

First, the reading passage states that laws have been passed by individual state governments, but the professor says these laws are not enough strong (→**strong enough**). ★3 The states governments should put forth more enforceable legislations. Otherwise developers can still take actions that threatens (→**threaten**) koalas.

Second, the reading passage mentions about (→不要) the tree-planting projects of environmental groups and companies, but the lecture points out the difficulties they face. The trees that koalas eat are specific kinds of eucalyptus and ★4 they don't grow fast. Even if humans plant more eucalyptus trees, it will soon disappear because koalas usually eat a large amount of the leaves.

Third, the reading passage says that koalas can be sent to zoos overseas, but the lecture makes it clear that ★5 sending koalas outside of Australia causes greater problems. Plus, the number taken in by zoos is too little (→**small**) to have any real effect.

In conclusion, ★6 although both the reading passage and the professor are saying that koalas are endangered, the professor states that the government of Australia needs to do (→**take**) a much more decisive approach to the problem.

> ●構成と内容の改善ポイント

★1 コアラが絶滅の危機にある状況や原因についての記述が冗長になっています。
　➡これらは，課題文のトピックの導入として説明されている情報です。設問の指示は講義のポイントの要約ですので，該当部分は削除し，講義の立場を簡潔に伝えましょう。

★2 Introduction で，講義のポイントのうちの1つについて話を展開してしまっています。また，教授は，コアラを"Vulnerable"に分類するだけでは不十分だとは

述べていますが，より強力な国の法律が必要だと主張しており，"Endangered" に分類すべきであるという主張はしていません。

→ まずは，講義の主張を正確に捉えましょう。また，Introduction で示したポイントと Body で展開されるポイントが一致していないと，要約としてまとまりのない印象を与えます。Introduction では，各ポイントを簡潔に挙げて全体の構成を示すか，あるいは適切な解答例のように講義の立場だけを確実に示し，Body を充実させることに焦点をおきましょう。ここでは該当部分は削除します。

★3 教授が，「オーストラリア政府」がすべきだと述べたことを，「各州の政府」と誤解して述べています。

→ 教授は，法的な対策が州以下レベルでの取り組みにすぎないことを指摘し，国が法律を強化する必要があると主張しています。ここでは州ではなく国の取り組みの必要性について述べましょう。

★4 「木が速く成長しない」「コアラが大量の葉を食べる」といった，推測による情報を加えてしまっており，ユーカリの植林の難しさについて，間違った理由を述べています。

→ 「コアラの好きな種類の木が限られていて，いくつかは消失しつつある」という植林の問題点を説明します。無理に推測した情報は書かないようにしましょう。適切な解答例では，人間がコアラの好みの木を知る努力が必要だという情報を加えています。

★5 コアラを海外の動物園に送ることにより生じる問題について，具体的に説明できていません。

→ 講義では，動物園が受け入れるコアラの数が少ないことを述べる前に，ユーカリのコストの問題や，コアラが自然の生息地を好むことを述べています。漏れなくすべて挙げることが難しくとも，可能な限り詳しく説明しましょう。

★6 「コアラが絶滅の危機に瀕している」という内容を課題文と講義の共通点として挙げていますが，これは両者の前提となっている事実であり，両者の関係を示すために持ち出すことは効果的ではありません。

→ 課題文は，結論としてコアラは絶滅の危機から救われるはずだと述べているのに対し，講義ではその取り組みの問題点を指摘して反論しています。適切な解答例では，課題文と講義の論調の違いを強調することで，両者の関係を明確に示して締めくくっています。

《構成の改善例》

- **❶【L】講義の立場**　現在なされているコアラ保護の取り組みは不十分である。
  - **❷【L】ポイント1**　各州の政府による法律に十分な効力はなく，より強力な国の法律が必要である。
    - (【R】ポイント1：各州の政府により保護のための法律が制定されている。)
  - **❸【L】ポイント2**　コアラにはユーカリの好みがあり，植林を効果的なものにするにはそれを把握する必要がある。
    - (【R】ポイント2：さまざまな団体が植林事業に従事している。)
  - **❹【L】ポイント3**　コアラの移送には問題点がある。
    - (【R】ポイント3：コアラを海外の動物園に送ることができる。)

適切な解答例

　The professor acknowledges that there are efforts to protect koalas, but says the ones mentioned in the reading passage are insufficient.

　First, the reading passage states that laws have been passed by individual state governments, but the professor says these laws are not strong enough ★3 **and stronger national laws are necessary. The national government's approach has been to declare the species "vulnerable,"** but developers can still take actions that threaten koalas.

　Second, the reading passage mentions the tree-planting projects of environmental groups and companies, but the lecture points out the difficulties they face. The trees that koalas eat are specific kinds of eucalyptus. ★4 **The ones they like are disappearing, and humans need to know which kinds of trees are preferred by koalas in the area to make these reforestation efforts effective.**

　Third, the reading passage says that koalas can be sent to zoos overseas, but the lecture makes it clear that ★5 **koalas need their natural habitats.** Plus, the number taken in by zoos is too small to have any real effect.

　In conclusion, the professor states that the government of Australia needs to take a much more decisive approach to the problem. ★6 **This is a much more urgent tone than that of the reading passage, which states that current efforts are sufficient.**

(213 words)

(教授はコアラを保護する取り組みがなされていることは認めていますが，課題文で述べられているものは不十分だと言っています。

　第1に，課題文は各州の政府により法律が制定されていると述べていますが，教授はこれらの

法律には十分な効力がなく，より強力な国の法律が必要であると述べています。中央政府は取り組みとしてコアラを "Vulnerable"（絶滅危惧Ⅱ類）と言明していますが，土地開発業者は依然としてコアラを脅かす行動をとることができてしまいます。

　第2に，課題文は環境保護団体や企業の植林事業に言及していますが，講義はそれらが直面する困難を指摘しています。コアラが食べる木は特定の種類のユーカリです。彼らが好む種は消失しつつあり，こうした森林再生の取り組みを効果的なものにするには，人間が，その地域のコアラがどの種類の木を好むのかを把握する必要があります。

　第3に，課題文はコアラを海外の動物園に移送することができると言っていますが，講義では，コアラが繁栄するためには，自然な生息地が必要であるとはっきり述べられています。加えて，動物園に受け入れてもらえる数はあまりに少ないので，実際の効果をもたらすことができません。

　結論として，教授は，オーストラリア政府は，問題に対しもっと決定的な取り組みをする必要があると述べています。これは，現在の取り組みが十分だと述べている課題文よりずっと緊迫した論調です。)

✓ 重要表現チェック

課題文
- ☐ fuzzy「毛羽立った，短い毛で覆われた」
- ☐ creature「生物」　　　　　☐ eucalyptus「ユーカリ」
- ☐ family「（生物分類学上の）科」　☐ extinction「絶滅」
- ☐ overdevelopment「過度の開発」　☐ residential「住宅の」
- ☐ remaining「残りの」　　　　☐ overcrowded「過密状態の」
- ☐ implement「〜を実行する，〜を施行する」
- ☐ legislation「法律，法律制定」　☐ assessment「評価，判定」
- ☐ population「個体数，個体群」
- ☐ informative「情報を提供する，有益な」
- ☐ reforestation「植林」　　　☐ preservation「保護，保存」

問題 12

課題文訳・リスニングスクリプト ➡ 別冊 p.32

Reading Time: 3 minutes

The majority of large businesses have a hierarchical management structure. This means that the company's management is organized like a pyramid. Employees report to general managers; general managers report to area managers, and so on. Finally, at the top of the organization you have executive managers like CEOs and CFOs. Most believe that this is the best way to organize a large business.

For one thing, having a hierarchical management structure improves communication. Managers can make sure that all of their subordinates are communicating properly and working together. Also, there is a clear communication line from executive management all the way down to entry-level employees. This means that important, executive-level decisions and policies can easily be distributed to all of the members of a company.

A clearly defined management structure can also be motivating for lower-level employees, as it gives them an easily understandable idea of their possible future with a company. The possibility of advancing in a company is a great motivator, and employees will work harder if they can see that their efforts will lead to promotions.

Most importantly, managers are responsible for ensuring that their teams achieve company goals. One side of this is assigning work and communicating expectations. In addition, it is also a manager's job to offer guidance in difficult situations and to help lower-level employees to develop skills. While mangers are technically bosses, directing tasks and assignments, they also serve as mentors, giving both moral and professional support.

Overall, hierarchical management structures are highly effective for running companies with hundreds —— and sometimes thousands —— of employees.

Now listen to part of a lecture on the topic you just read about.　● CD 15

> Summarize the points made in the lecture you just heard, being sure to explain how they cast doubt on specific points made in the reading passage.
>
> Response Time: 20 minutes

【設問訳】
今聞いた講義の論点を要約しなさい。その際，課題文で挙げられているどの論点にどのように疑問を投げかけているかを必ず説明しなさい。

|解答例|

不十分な解答例

★1 The professor talks about a company which has about 400 employees and sells a lot with no bosses, or no promotions. Surprising (→ **Surprisingly**), it is working very well for them.

First, the company's system improves communication. Employees of this company do not have to ask their bosses before deciding something. This increases productivity and decreases time for unnecessary meetings. ★2

Second, the company does not have any promotion system. Employees make more money when they have more responsibilities. ★3 95% of **the** employees said that they like this method. ★4 Because they feel they are being rewarded for producing high-quality work. This contradicts the reading passage, which says that the employees get motivation from hierarchical company structures.

Third, all members of the team are responsibly (→**responsible**) for achieving the goals. ★5 Newer employees seek help and experienced employees help newer employees to improve. The professor opposes the reading passage that says managers are needed to guide employees and help them develop their skills to achieve the goals.

In short, the professor talks about a large company that is success (→**successful**) without a traditional system.

|●構成と内容の改善ポイント|

★1 この企業について話すことで，教授が何を主張しようとしているのかがわかりにくくなっています。
➡教授はこの企業を例にとることで，「企業は従来の階層的な経営構造がなくとも

うまく機能しうる」ということを説明しています。この点について、課題文との違いに触れながら簡潔に述べると、講義の主旨が読み取りやすくなります。

★2 課題文との関係について言及されていません。
➡ この論点が、課題文とどのように相違しているのかがわかるように記述しましょう。

★3 アカデミック・ライティングでは、読みづらさを考慮し、文頭に数字を用いることは避けられます。
➡ 文頭に数字がこないように文を修正するか、アルファベットで表記（スペルアウト）しましょう。

★4 従位接続詞 Because による節が、単独で用いられています。
➡ Because / If / When / Before などの従位接続詞は、2つの節を結びつけるために用いられます。ここでは前の文と結びつけて書きましょう。

★5 新入社員と先輩社員の行動について事実が述べられているだけで、それぞれがなぜそのように行動するのかの理由が書かれていません。
➡ 講義では、責任をキーワードに、それぞれの理由に基づく行動により、チームワークが強化される様子が描かれています。それらを具体的に述べましょう。ある事実に対して理由・根拠が述べられている場合は、合わせて書くようにしましょう。

《構成の改善例》

❶【L】講義の立場 従来の階層的な経営構造を持たずに、うまく機能している会社がある。

　❷【L】ポイント1 管理職からの承認が不要なので、意思伝達が容易である。
　（【R】ポイント1：階層的な構造は意思伝達を向上させる。）

　❸【L】ポイント2 より多くの責任を負うことで給与が増える制度が、社員のやる気につながる。
　（【R】ポイント2：階層的な構造と昇進の可能性が社員のやる気につながる。）

　❹【L】ポイント3 全社員が目標達成に責任を負っており、新入社員はスキル向上のため努力し、先輩社員は自然と後輩を助けている。
　（【R】ポイント3：目標達成とスキルの向上には管理職が必要である。）

適切な解答例

★1 **The professor talks about a company that has a unique management structure with no bosses. This is different from the hierarchical structure mentioned in the reading,** and it is working very well for the company.

First, it improves communication. Employees of this company have the ability to make decisions without approval from management. This increases productivity and decreases time wasted in meetings. ★2 **This directly refutes the reading passage, which states that hierarchical management structures improve communication.**

Second, the company does not have any promotion system. Employees make more money when they have more responsibilities. ★3 ★4 **Ninety-five percent (95 %) of the company's employees reported that they prefer this method of determining salaries, because they feel that they are being rewarded for producing high-quality work.** Again, this contradicts the reading passage, which states that employees get motivation from hierarchical company structures and the opportunity for advancement.

Third, all members of the team are responsible for achieving the goals. ★5 **Newer employees seek help, because they want to improve skills and get more responsibilities. Senior employees help their less experienced coworkers, because they want the team to perform well.** With this point, the professor opposes the reading's claim that managers are needed to guide employees and help them develop their skills to achieve the goals.

In short, the professor gives an example of a large company that is successful without a traditional, hierarchical management structure. (231words)

（教授は，上司がいないというユニークな経営構造の会社について話しています。これは，課題文で述べられていた階層構造とは異なり，しかも，この会社ではとてもうまく機能しています。

第1に，この構造は意思伝達を向上させます。この会社の社員は，管理職からの承認なしに決定をすることができます。これにより生産性が高まり，会議で無駄にされる時間が減ります。このことは，階層的な経営構造が意思伝達を向上させると述べている課題文に直接的に反論しています。

第2に，この会社には昇進のシステムがまったくありません。社員は，より多くの責任を負うことによって得られるお金が増えます。同社の社員の95％が，この給与決定方法のほうが，質の高い仕事に対して報酬を受けられると感じるのでよいと報告しています。ここでも，社員は階層的な会社構造と昇進の機会によって動機づけを得ると述べている課題文に異議を唱えています。

第3に，チームの全員が目標達成に責任を負っています。新入社員は，スキルを向上して，もっと多くの責任を負うことを望んでいるため，周囲へサポートを求めます。先輩社員は，チームの仕事ぶりを上げたいので，経験の少ない同僚を助けます。この点で，教授は，目標達成に向け

て社員を導き，彼らのスキルの向上を手助けするために管理職が必要とされるという課題文の主張に反対しています。

　つまり，教授は，従来の階層的な経営構造がなくても成功している大企業の例を提示しています。）

✓ 重要表現チェック

課題文
- □ hierarchical「階層制の」
- □ general manager「部長，ゼネラルマネジャー」
- □ executive manager「経営幹部，エグゼクティブマネジャー」
- □ CEO「最高経営責任者」　□ CFO「最高財務責任者」
- □ subordinate「部下」　□ entry-level「新入社員の，初心者の」
- □ define「～を定義する」　□ ensure「～を確実にする」

問題 13

課題文訳・リスニングスクリプト ➡ 別冊 p.35

Reading Time: 3 minutes

Impressionism began when painters started using natural methods of lighting their work and painting with bright, broad strokes. The name came from the Claude Monet painting Impression: Sunrise of 1873. And in the following year, the first independent Impressionist exhibition was held in Paris at the studio of the photographer Nadar.

One characteristic of Impressionists' painting is that they worked for very short periods of time during the day. They would go to the site of their scene or landscape and paint quickly. Then, when the light changed, they would stop working. They came back to the scene when the light was similar to when they had started painting. Nevertheless, their paintings took considerably less time than more traditional styles.

The use of color and thick brush strokes are another characteristic of their painting. Their focus was on tone and color, not so much on detail. They used brighter, more saturated colors and even painted color in their shadows, adding to the overall brightness of their paintings. They produced grays and dark colors by mixing complementary colors, and tried to avoid the use of black.

Finally, their subjects were common scenes and common people. They painted modernity and scenes of leisure, such as cafes, hotels, and beaches. Painters had been painting mundane scenes for over a century, but the Impressionists did not focus on any particular component, letting the entire scene take over the painting like a stolen snapshot. Though their work was questioned by traditionalists at the time, it soon took hold among the public and has remained hugely popular to this day. Hundreds of thousands of people visited recent exhibitions in Chicago and Boston.

Now listen to part of a lecture on the topic you just read about.　● CD 16

Summarize the points made in the lecture you just heard, being sure to specifically explain how they support the explanations in the reading passage.

Response Time: 20 minutes

Question 1 | 集中トレーニング

【設問訳】
今聞いた講義の論点を要約しなさい。その際，課題文で挙げられているどの説明をどのようにサポートしているかを必ず説明しなさい。

| 解答例 |

不十分な解答例

　The reading passage gives **an** overview of the Impressionists. In the lecture, the professor talks about how other artists and critics reacted to the Impressionists' works in the very beginning.

　First, ★1 traditionalists criticized the speed **with** which Impressionists painted in those days. As the reading passage describes, the Impressionists completed their paintings in a short time.

　Second, the color and painting style was criticized. According to the reading passage, Impressionists made thick brush strokes and used lots of color, even in their shadows. In contrast, traditionalists valued composition and their paintings were more shaded and subdued in color. ★2 Some people asked them to make their paintings darker so that they did not stand out too much.

　Lastly, the subjects of the Impressionists' paintings are (→were) also criticized. The reading passage says that they were common and people did not understand them at the time. ★3 The paintings were thought to be common and vulgar.

　★4 In, summary, the professor criticizes the Impressionism by refering (→ **referring**) to criticisms of the time.

●構成と内容の改善ポイント

★1 「伝統主義者は印象派の画家たちが絵画を描くスピードを批判していた」という事実のみが述べられています。
　➡なぜ批判していたのか，理由も合わせて述べましょう。講義では，「伝統主義者は，絵画とはゆっくりと注意深く制作されるものだと考えていた」と述べられています。事実や主張には，必ず理由や根拠となる情報がセットで述べられているため，聞き逃さないように注意しましょう。

★2 前の文とのつながりを，より伝わりやすく表現することができます。
　➡ここでは ask の前に even を加え，「～する人さえいた」とすることで，前文の内容を強調していることが伝わりやすくなります。場面に応じて色々な表現を使いこなしましょう。

101

★3 具体的な詳細情報が述べられていません。
➡ 講義では，ルイ・ルロワという評論家の発言について詳しく述べられています。細かい情報が聞き取れない場合でも，大意をつかみ，できるだけ具体的な情報を記述するようにしましょう。

★4 教授は印象派を批判しているのではなく，当時の批判を紹介することで，課題文の内容を発展させています。
➡ 講義の立場を正確に把握して記述しましょう。リスニングの際は，1つ1つの情報だけに気をとられず，全体として何を述べようとしているのかを聞き取るように意識しましょう。

《構成の改善例》

- ❶【L】講義の立場　印象派の作品に対し，当初どのような反応があったのかについて話している。
  - ❷【L】ポイント1　伝統主義者は，絵画はゆっくりと注意深く制作されるべきだと考えていた。
    （【R】ポイント1：印象派の画家は，短い時間で絵を完成させた。）
  - ❸【L】ポイント2　伝統主義者によって色彩や画風が批判された。
    （【R】ポイント2：太い筆使いで，多くの色を使って描いた。）
  - ❹【L】ポイント3　ある評論家は，印象派の題材をありきたりで下品だと酷評した。
    （【R】ポイント3：平凡な題材を描いたことが，当時は理解されなかった。）

適切な解答例

　The reading passage gives a general overview of the Impressionists' style. In the lecture, the professor talks about how other artists and critics reacted to the Impressionists' works in the very beginning.

　First, ★1 in terms of the speed with which Impressionists painted, the traditionalists thought that paintings should be made slowly and carefully. As the reading passage describes, the Impressionists completed their paintings in a short time. This fact seemed to imply that they were not taking enough care with their work.

　Second, the color and painting style was criticized. According to the reading passage, Impressionists made thick brush strokes and used lots of color, even in their shadows. In contrast, traditionalists valued composition and their paintings were more shaded and subdued in color. ★2 Some people who collect Impressionists' works even asked them to make their paintings darker so they didn't stand out too much.

Lastly, the subjects of the Impressionists' paintings were criticized. The reading passage says that they were common and people did not understand them at the time. ★3 The professor mentions one critic writing in a French magazine who attended the first Impressionist exhibition in Paris. He said that the paintings were commonplace and vulgar, and that the wallpaper had probably required more work.

★4 In summary, the professor refers to criticisms of the time against the Impressionism, and provides details expanding on the ideas of the reading passage.

(230 words)

（課題文は印象派の表現方法について総括しています。講義では，教授が，当初その他の芸術家や評論家がどのように印象派の作品に反応したのかについて話しています。

第1に，印象派の画家が描く際の速さに関しては，伝統主義者は，絵画はゆっくりと注意深く制作されるべきだと考えていたのです。課題文にあるように，印象派の画家は，短い時間で絵を完成させました。この事実は，彼らが作品に十分に気を配っていなかったということを暗示しているように思えたのです。

第2に，色彩や画風が批判されました。課題文によれば，印象派の画家は，太い筆使いで多くの色を使い，影さえもそのように描きました。それとは対照的に，伝統主義者たちは構図を大切にしていましたし，彼らの絵画は印象派のものよりも陰影が多く，地味な色使いでした。印象派の作品を収集していた人の中には，目立ちすぎないように絵をもっと暗くしてほしいと頼んだ人さえいました。

最後に，印象派の絵画の題材が批判されました。課題文では，その題材が平凡なものであり，その当時の人々はそれらを理解していなかったと述べられています。教授は，フランスの雑誌に記事を書き，パリで行われた第1回展示会を訪れた1人の評論家について述べています。彼は，その絵画はありきたりで下品なものであり，壁紙の方が多くの労力を必要としただろうと表現しました。

要するに，教授は，印象派に対する当時の批判を紹介し，課題文の見解をさらに詳しく述べています。）

✓重要表現チェック

課題文	☐ impressionism「印象主義」	☐ saturated color「飽和色」
	☐ dark color「暗色，黒ずんだ色」	☐ complementary color「補色」
	☐ mundane「現世の，ありふれた」	
	☐ take over ～「～を引き受ける，～を引き継ぐ」	
	☐ take hold「根づく」	
不十分な解答例	☐ subdue「（光，色）を和らげる」	
適切な解答例	☐ expand on ～「～についてさらに詳しく述べる」	

問題 14

課題文訳・リスニングスクリプト ➡ 別冊 p.38

Reading Time: 3 minutes

Although it is one of the Earth's seven continents, Antarctica remains mostly uninhabited. That is because it is extremely difficult to build a permanent community there in which humans can live. There are research stations that have over 100 people living in them during the winter, and this number rises to a few thousand in the summer. However, these stations exist for research purposes only, and they are not communities with children and elderly people.

One reason for this is that Antarctica is much too cold for humans to settle. The warmest area of the Antarctic Peninsula has a mean winter temperature of −40 degrees Celsius and the coldest areas far inland have mean winter temperatures of −70 degrees Celsius. Spending any time outside in these conditions would be intolerable.

Another reason is that conditions on the continent make it very difficult to grow plants. The Antarctic Peninsula has what little life can be found on the continent. Everywhere else, the huge ice mass prevents plant life from thriving.

Finally, the lack of plants makes it impossible for an ecosystem to survive. This means there are almost no animals, especially inland away from the oceans. Hunting and fishing to collect food are essential activities for humans. Without the vegetation to build an ecosystem, humans cannot build societies. For these reasons, the Antarctic is virtually lifeless.

Now listen to part of a lecture on the topic you just read about.   ● CD 17

Summarize the points made in the lecture you just heard, being sure to specifically explain how they strengthen specific points made in the reading passage.

Response Time: 20 minutes

Question 1 | 集中トレーニング

【設問訳】
今聞いた講義の論点を要約しなさい。その際，課題文で挙げられているどの論点をどのように強めているかを必ず説明しなさい。

解答例

不十分な解答例

★1 The reading passage states that it is colder in the Antarctic than in the Arctic. The lecture points out how so (→**much**) harsher conditions are in the Antarctic than in the Arctic.

First, the reading passage describes the extremely cold temperatures on the Antarctic continent. ★2 This is partly because of the thickness of the ice.

Second, there is the lack of plant life. As stated in the reading passage, plants can only be found on the Antarctic Peninsula. ★3 Because the warmest area of the Antarctic Peninsula has a mean winter temperature of -40 degrees Celsius, it has what little life can be found on the continent. The interior of the continent is solid ice and much too cold.

Third, there is the lack of **an** ecosystem, including animals for human (→**humans**) to hunt for food. The professor tells (→**talks**) about the many animals that live in the Arctic. ★4 The professor also mentions on (→不要) the whales and seals found both in the Arctic and Antarctic, and says that no big animals like the polar bear live in Antarctica.

In short, the professor provides details to support to (→不要) the reading passage, which states that Antarctica is barely suitable for human life.

●構成と内容の改善ポイント

★1 ただ「南極は北極より寒い」と述べているだけで，「南極には人が住んでいない，生命がほとんどない」という課題文と講義の主旨に言及していません。
  ➡ 課題文，講義ともに，主旨や要点は冒頭で述べられていることが多いので，確実に押さえましょう。

★2 北極のほうが温暖であることの説明として，「氷が厚いこと」については述べられていますが，海と気温の関係についての説明がありません。
  ➡ 教授は「北極はほとんどを海が占めている」ことを説明しています。教授が述べている説明を正確に聞き取りましょう。

★3 課題文からの引用が長く，教授による説明について述べられていません。
  ➡ 教授は，南極では植物が育ちにくいのに対して，北極では植物が豊富であることを説明しています。前の文で課題文の内容に触れていますので，ここでは課題文の情報にさらに詳しく言及するより，教授による「北極では比較的温暖な海があり，植物が豊富である」という説明を漏らさずに伝える必要があります。

★4 「北極と南極ではともにクジラやアザラシが見られる」,「南極にはホッキョクグマのような大きな動物は生育していない」と言うだけでは,北極と南極の動物の違いを比較した教授の説明を十分に伝えていません。
➡教授は北極と南極の動物について,特に陸上の動物について比較することで,南極の環境の過酷さを論証しています。何を主張するために持ち出された情報であるかを意識し,具体例から導びかれる主旨を端的に記述しましょう。

《構成の改善例》

❶【L】講義の立場　南極は北極よりはるかに過酷な環境である。
　　　❷【L】ポイント1　南極が寒いのは氷が厚く海から離れているためであり,北極は大部分が海であるため比較的暖かい。
　　（【R】ポイント1：南極大陸の気温は極めて寒い。）
　　　❸【L】ポイント2　北極では豊富な植物が見られる。
　　（【R】ポイント2：南極では,植物は南極半島でしか育たない。）
　　　❹【L】ポイント3　北極にはホッキョクグマが生育しているが,南極には陸上で生活する動物はほとんどいない。
　　（【R】ポイント3：南極には人間が生きるために必要な生態系がない。）

適切な解答例

★1 The reading passage gives reasons that humans cannot live on Antarctica, and the lecture points out how much harsher conditions are in the Antarctic than in the Arctic.

First, the reading passage describes the extremely cold temperatures on the Antarctic continent. ★2 The professor explains that this is a result of the greater thickness of the ice and the distance of inland Antarctica from the ocean. In contrast, the thinner ice and the fact that the ocean covers much of the Arctic keeps the area warm enough for people to live there.

Second, there is the lack of plant life. As stated in the reading passage, plants can only be found on the Antarctic Peninsula. The interior of the continent is solid ice and much too cold. ★3 In contrast, the professor explains that the Arctic, with its relatively warmer oceans, has an abundance of plant life.

Third, according to the reading passage, there is the lack of an ecosystem, including animals for humans to hunt for food. The professor talks about the many animals that live in the Arctic. ★4 There are some similarities in marine life, but the temperature differences mean that land animals are completely different. No animals which live entirely on land evolved. **The Arctic has the huge polar bear, while the largest land animal in Antarctica is a mosquito.**

　　In short, the professor provides details to support the reading passage, which states that Antarctica is barely suitable for human life.　　　　　　　　　　　　　　(242 words)

　（課題文は，人間が南極に住むことができない理由を述べ，講義は，南極が北極よりどれほど過酷な環境かを指摘しています。

　第1に，課題文は南極大陸の極めて低い気温について説明しています。教授は，これは氷がより厚く，南極の奥地が海から離れていることの結果であると説明しています。それに対して，氷がより薄いことと，海が北極の大部分を占めていることが，その地域を人が暮らすのに十分な程暖かくしています。

　第2に，植物がないことが挙げられます。課題文に述べられているように，植物は南極半島でしか見ることができません。大陸の内陸地は固い氷になっていてあまりにも寒すぎます。対照的に，教授は，北極では比較的暖かい海があるので植物が豊富だということを説明しています。

　第3に，課題文によれば，人間が食べるために狩ることのできる動物を含めた生態系がありません。教授は，北極に住む多くの動物について述べています。海洋生物にはいくつかの類似点がありますが，気温が異なるということは，陸の動物が完全に異なるということです。南極には，もっぱら陸地で生活するように進化した動物はいません。北極には大きなホッキョクグマがいますが，南極の最も大きな陸の生物は蚊なのです。

　つまり教授は，南極は人間の生活にほとんど適さないと述べている課題文をサポートする詳細情報を提供しています。）

☑ 重要表現チェック

課題文		
	□ Antarctica「南極大陸」	
	□ uninhabited「人の住んでいない，住むのに不適な」	
	□ settle「定住する」	□ the Antarctic Peninsula「南極半島」
	□ mean「平均の」	□ Celsius「摂氏」
	□ inland「内陸の，奥地の」	□ intolerable「耐えられない」
	□ what little ～「なけなしの～，あるだけの～」	
	□ mass「かたまり」	□ thrive「（植物などが）成長する」
	□ ecosystem「生態系」	□ vegetation「植物」
	□ the Antarctic「南極（地方）」	□ lifeless「生物のいない」

問題 15

課題文訳・リスニングスクリプト ➡ 別冊 p.40

Reading Time: 3 minutes

The brain has always been a mystery even to the scientists who devote their lives to studying it. Recent research has unlocked a number of mysteries about the brain, especially in relation to the mechanisms of memory.

First is the mechanism of forgetting. It was long assumed that a person could not forget certain memories, especially those that elicit a strong negative reaction. Recent studies have shown that those memories could actually be erased. Researchers found that mice without a certain gene feared a cage in which they had been given an electric shock, but mice with that gene formed new memories and no longer feared the cage.

The second is the role of sleep. In another study, researchers learned more about the mechanism through which sleep improves memory and learning. Scientists have long understood that sleep plays an important role in memory, but they did not know for sure why. This study in the U.S. and China showed that sleeping mice formed more connections between neurons in their brains after learning a new skill.

Finally, a recent study has helped scientists understand how memories are formed. Scientists previously had limited understanding of what makes a memory. They knew that protein synthesis and changes in neuron structures were involved, but other mechanisms were a mystery. Now researchers have learned that one part of a group of molecules in a part of the brain involved in emotional memory may promote protein synthesis. They saw that levels of this molecule decreased when learning was taking place.

Now listen to part of a lecture on the topic you just read about.　　CD 18

Summarize the points made in the lecture you just heard, being sure to specifically explain how they support the explanations in the reading passage.

Response Time: 20 minutes

Question 1 集中トレーニング

【設問訳】
今聞いた講義の論点を要約しなさい。その際，課題文で挙げられているどの説明をどのようにサポートしているかを必ず説明しなさい。

解答例

不十分な解答例

　　The reading passage says that recent studies have given scientists clues to the inner workings of the brain. ★1 The proffesser (→**professor**) says that thanks to the advancements in the technology, we can gain the knowledge about the brain.
　　★2 First, there is a study that suggests people can forget bad memories. It was shown that mice forget a bad experience. The proffesser (→**professor**) explains that new memories ★3 might be formed to replace old memories and that this study could be used to develop a drug that help (→**helps**) people get over various kinds of fear.
　　Second is a study on the role of sleep. In the study, researchers found that mice formed more neuron connections during deep sleep. The proffesser (→**professor**) talks about the importance of sleep. He talks about the microscopes used to determine this.
　　Finally, there is a study about memory formation. The levels of a molecule decreased when learning was taking place. ★4 The proffesser (→**professor**) says that it was interesting to see how the molecule was supresed (→**suppresssed**).

●構成と内容の改善ポイント

★1 教授はこのことに触れてはいますが，あくまでトピックの導入として述べており，講義の主旨ではありません。
　➡ Introduction では，講義の立場や全体の主旨を短くまとめましょう。ここでは，教授は課題文を補足しているので，expand on（〜について詳しく述べる）などを用いて講義の立場を伝えます。

★2 この段落のキーワードでもある遺伝子の条件に関する記述が抜けています。この記述からは，すべてのマウスについて同様の結果が得られたと受け取られてしまいます。
　➡ ある遺伝子を持ったマウスについての結果であることを明確にしましょう。短い字数制限の中で解答をまとめる必要がありますが，省略してもよい部分と，できない部分があることを意識するようにしましょう。

★3 教授の説明を正しく伝えられていません。
　➡ 教授は「古い記憶を消すためには新しい記憶を形成する必要がある」と述べているので，might（…するかもしれない，…する可能性がある）では講義の内容が

正しく伝わりません。各段落のトピックを意識しながら、教授の詳細な説明を正確に聞き取るようにしましょう。

★4 この研究に関して、教授が最も言いたいことではありません。
→教授は、課題文にも書かれている研究結果だけではなく、今後開発されうる薬の可能性について話を展開しています。講義が課題文をサポートしている問題の場合でも、教授がどのように課題文を補足しているのかについて、必ず触れるようにしましょう。

《構成の改善例》

❶【L】講義の立場 課題文で説明されている研究を補足し、開発可能な薬についても言及している。

❷【L】ポイント1 あらゆる種類の恐怖を克服するのに役立つ薬が開発される可能性がある。
(【R】ポイント1:悪い記憶を忘れるのに役立つ遺伝子の研究が行われている。)

❸【L】ポイント2 睡眠中脳内で何が起こっているのか、最先端の顕微鏡を使って見ることができた。
(【R】ポイント2:記憶における睡眠の役割が、研究によって明らかになった。)

❹【L】ポイント3 miR-182という分子の量を調整することで、記憶機能の修復が可能かもしれない。
(【R】ポイント3:学習が行われている時、ある分子の量が減少することが研究によってわかった。)

適切な解答例

　The reading passage cites three studies that have given scientists clues to the inner workings of the brain. **★1** <u>The professor expands on that information and, in two of the cases, describes the possibilities for drugs that could be developed.</u>

　★2 <u>First, the reading passage refers to a study on a gene that can help people forget bad memories. It was shown that mice forget a bad experience if they have this gene.</u> The professor explains that new memories **★3** <u>have to be formed</u> to replace old memories, and that this study could be used to develop a drug that helps people get over various kinds of fear, including war veterans.

　The second is a study on the role of sleep. In the study shown in the reading passage, mice were found to form more neuron connections during deep sleep. The professor goes on to talk about how necessary sleep is, because the mice could not achieve the same level of learning if they did not have enough sleep. The professor also mentions the microscopes used to determine this.

Finally, there is a study about memory formation. The reading passage mentions that a certain molecule decreases in amount in the brain when learning is happening. **★4**<u>According to the professor, this molecule, miR-182, could be controlled, again by drugs, in the brains of people suffering from dementia. It is another potential benefit for humankind from brain research.</u> (228 words)

（課題文は，科学者に脳内の働きの手がかりを与えた3つの研究について述べています。教授はその情報について詳しく述べ，そのうち2つにおいては，開発され得る薬の可能性について説明しています。

第1に，課題文は，人々が悪い記憶を忘れるのに役立ち得る遺伝子についての研究に言及しています。この遺伝子を持っていれば，マウスが嫌な経験を忘れるということが明らかになりました。教授は，古い記憶を置き換えるために新しい記憶が形成される必要があると説明しています。そして，退役軍人などの人々が，あらゆる種類の恐怖を克服するのに役立つ薬を開発する上でこの研究が使われる可能性についても，教授は説明しています。

2つ目は，睡眠の役割に関する研究です。課題文で示された研究では，マウスが深く眠っている間に神経細胞間でより多くのやりとりが行われたことがわかりました。教授は引き続き睡眠がどんなに必要であるかについて話を続けます。というのは，十分な睡眠が得られなかった場合，マウスは同程度の学習を達成することができなかったからです。教授はまた，このことを確認するために使われた顕微鏡についても言及しています。

最後に，記憶の形成について研究が行われています。課題文は，学習が行われている時に，脳内のある分子の量が減少すると述べています。教授によれば，この miR-182 という分子も，認知症に苦しむ人々の脳内において薬によって調整することが可能です。そのことも，脳の研究が人類にとって役立つもう1つの可能性なのです。）

✓ 重要表現チェック

課題文		
	☐ devote「〜にささげる」	☐ unlock「〜を解明する」
	☐ assume「〜と仮定する」	☐ elicit「〜を引き起こす」
	☐ gene「遺伝子」	☐ neuron「神経細胞」
	☐ previously「以前は」	☐ protein synthesis「たんぱく質合成」
	☐ molecule「分子」	☐ promote「〜を促進する」
適切な解答例	☐ cite「〜に言及する」	☐ clue「手がかり」
	☐ war veteran「退役軍人」	☐ dementia「認知症」

Independent Task

Question 2 の概要とポイント

■ Independent Task の特徴

ライティングセクションの Question 2 は，提示されたトピックに対して，自分の意見や考えを解答する「独立型問題（Independent Task）」です。与えられたトピックに対して，自分の意見や考えをいかに論理的に組み立てて解答できるかという「論述」の力が問われます。

■ 設問形式

Question 2 で出題されるトピックは，主として以下の2つのパターンに分けられます。
　　agree / disagree 型：ある事柄や意見に対して，「賛成」か「反対」かを問うもの。
　　prefer 型：挙げられている2つの事柄や意見のうち，どちらを好むかを問うもの。
　また，設問指示文のほとんどには，自分の意見の根拠となる具体的な理由や事例を挙げなさいという条件がついています。

　解答時間は **30 分**，適切とされる解答の語数は **300 語以上**です。トピックと残り時間，使用語数はコンピューター画面に表示され続けます。
　Question 1 と同様，アイディアを書き留めるために，鉛筆とメモ用紙を使用することができます。

■ Independent Task の評価基準

　解答は，最低2名の採点者が，以下の3つの観点から，0～5点まで段階的に採点します。
① **課題の指示に対して的確に答えているか。**
② **構成・展開に一貫性・まとまりがあるか。**
③ **文法・語彙に誤りがなく，表現は多様であるか。**

　すなわち高得点をとるためには，①「賛成」か「反対」か，あるいはどちらを選ぶかという**自分の立場をはっきり示し，その根拠となる情報を盛り込む**こと，②自分の立場を一貫して通し，**途中でぶれない**こと，③綴りや文法の間違いを極力減らし，できるだけ**バラエティに富んだ語彙と構文**で書くことが必要ということになります。
　他にも，会話で用いる「話し言葉」ではなく，アカデミックなライティングにふさわしい，フォーマルな文体で書くということも留意すべき点です。
　また，語数は 300 語を超えるようにしましょう。語数が少ないと，減点の対象となる可能性があります。
　以下が，ETS の採点者が解答を評価する際に用いる基準の概略です。

評価	評価の基準
5	このレベルのエッセイは，以下の点をほぼ満たしている。 ・与えられたトピックに対して的確に解答している。 ・明らかに適切な説明，例，詳細情報が用いられており，構成・内容展開が優れている。まとまり，流れ，一貫性がある。 ・小さな語彙的・文法的誤りは見受けられるものの，一貫して多様な構文，適切な語彙・慣用表現が使用されている。
4	このレベルのエッセイは，以下の点をほぼ満たしている。 ・やや不足も見られるが，与えられたトピックに対して十分に解答している。 ・十分な説明，例，詳細情報が用いられており，構成・内容展開が概ねよくできている。時折，冗長な表現や話の脱線，つながりの不明瞭な箇所が見られるものの，まとまり，流れ，一貫性がある。 ・文構造や語彙・表現面に，意味の伝達を阻害しない程度の誤りが時折見られるものの，多様な構文，語彙が使用されている。
3	このレベルのエッセイは，以下の点のうち1つかそれ以上に当てはまる。 ・ある程度よく展開された説明や，例，詳細情報を用いて，解答している。 ・考えのつながりが不明瞭な箇所があるものの，まとまり，流れ，一貫性がある。 ・意味の不明瞭さのもととなるような，文構造や語彙選択に関する能力のむらが見られる。正確だが，構文や語彙選択の幅が限られている。
2	このレベルのエッセイは，以下の弱点のうちの1つかそれ以上が認められる。 ・与えられたトピックに対する内容展開が限られている。 ・内容構成や考えのつながりが不適切で，盛り込まれた例や説明，詳細情報が不適切，あるいは不十分である。 ・語彙選択が明らかに不適切で，文構造に誤りが多く見られる。
1	このレベルのエッセイは，以下の弱点のうちの1つかそれ以上によって，著しく損なわれている。 ・内容構成あるいは内容展開に著しい欠点がある。 ・詳細情報がほとんど，あるいはまったく書かれていない。具体例が的外れで，課題に対する答えとして不適切である。 ・文構造の誤りが顕著で，かつ頻繁に見られる。
0	トピックの単語を写しているだけ，またはトピックに無関係である。英語以外の言語で書かれている。ただキーを押しただけ，あるいは白紙のままである。

Independent Task　Question 2

解答のエッセンス

> **出題内容**
> 《設問形式》提示されたトピックに対し，理由やその根拠となる具体例や詳細情報を挙げながら，自分の意見を答える。
> 《設問タイプ》
> 　　agree / disagree 型：トピックに対する賛否を問うもの。
> 　　prefer 型：2つの立場のうち，どちらを好むかを問うもの。
> 《解答時間》30分（準備時間を含む）

　Question 2 では，「**トピックに対する自分の意見を明確に答えているか**」，「**全体の構成がまとまっていて，論理的に文章が展開されているか**」という点が特に重要です。与えられたトピックから話がそれたり意見がぶれたりすることなく，**具体例や詳細説明を加えながら**いかに論理的な文章を展開できるかがポイントになります。

　出題傾向としては，agree / disagree 型が多くなっています。そのため，例題・演習問題では agree / disagree 型を扱いますが，解答に必要な考え方は prefer 型においても共通です。集中トレーニングには prefer 型の問題も含まれていますので，ここで学ぶ考え方を応用して取り組んでください。

　ここでは，解答を論理的に展開するためのポイントを学びましょう。基本的な解答構成は次の通りです。

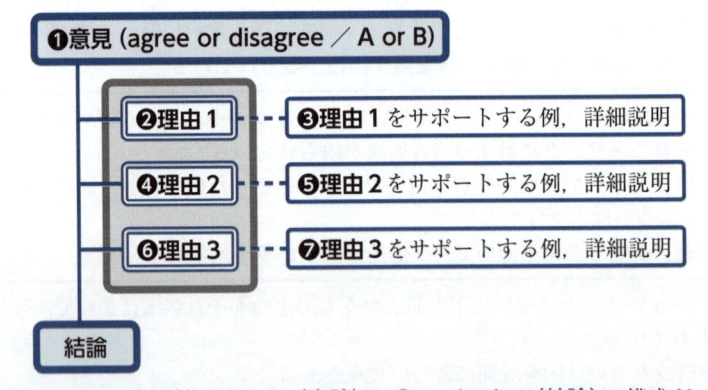

```
❶意見 (agree or disagree ／ A or B)
    ├─ ❷理由1 ─── ❸理由1をサポートする例，詳細説明
    ├─ ❹理由2 ─── ❺理由2をサポートする例，詳細説明
    └─ ❻理由3 ─── ❼理由3をサポートする例，詳細説明

結論
```

　Introduction（序論）→ Body（本論）→ Conclusion（結論）の構成が，英文ライティングの基本スタイルです。Introduction では，与えられたトピックに対する自分の**意見**（❶）を簡潔かつ明確に示します。また，これからこのエッセイがどのように展開していくのか，読み手が予測しながら読み進められるよう，全体の構成を示しましょう。Body では，1段落に1つずつ，意見をサポートする**理由**（❷❹❻）を展開します。それぞれの理由を簡潔にまとめた**キーセンテンス**を述べた上で，それらをサポートする**例や詳細説明**（❸❺❼）をできるかぎり具体的に記述していきます。理由は必ずしも3つ挙げる必要は

ありませんが，上の図のように，Introduction（1）・Body（3）・Conclusion（1）の**5段落構成**を目安とすると，バランスのとれた説得力のあるエッセイを展開しやすくなります。Conclusion では，**結論**として自分の意見を再提示して締めくくります。なお，結論は，述べるべきポイントが意見（❶）と共通であるため，以降の論理マップや解答の構成図では省略します。

　解答を作成する際には，まず意見（トピックに対する立場）を決め，解答に必要な要素を書き出します。それらを先ほどの構成に整理した上で，実際にエッセイを作成し，**書き終わったら必ず見直し**を行って英文を修正します。

　まずは，Question 2 の代表的な出題例を用いて，解答のための考え方を学んでいきましょう。

例題

> **Do you agree or disagree with the following statement?**
> **Parents should limit the amount of time their children watch TV and play video games.**
> **Use specific reasons and examples to support your answer.**

【設問訳】
あなたは以下の主張に賛成ですか，反対ですか。
「親は子供がテレビを見たりテレビゲームをしたりする時間を制限するべきである。」
あなたの意見の根拠となる具体的な理由や事例を述べなさい。

I アイディア・情報を論理マップに整理する

例題について、次の手順に沿い、論理マップを使ったアイディア整理・構成の仕方を見ていきましょう。

(1) 図の中央部分にトピックを書き出します。(2)以降に取り組む際も、与えられたトピックからそれないよう、常にここを意識します。

(2) 次にトピックに対する立場・意見(❶)を決めます。例題は agree / disagree 型なので、どちらかを選んで青色の枠の中に書き込みます。

(3) 続いて、意見をサポートする理由(❷❹❻)を灰色の範囲に書き出します。Body の各段落におけるキーセンテンスの元になるので、「その理由を一言で表すと何か」を端的に書き出します。この時点では3つに絞らず、思いつくだけ挙げます。

(4) (3)で挙げた理由の根拠となる具体例や詳細説明(❸❺❼)のキーワードを挙げていきます。(3)で思いついた理由の中から、具体的に説明しやすいもの、英語に置き換えやすいものを選んで展開します。

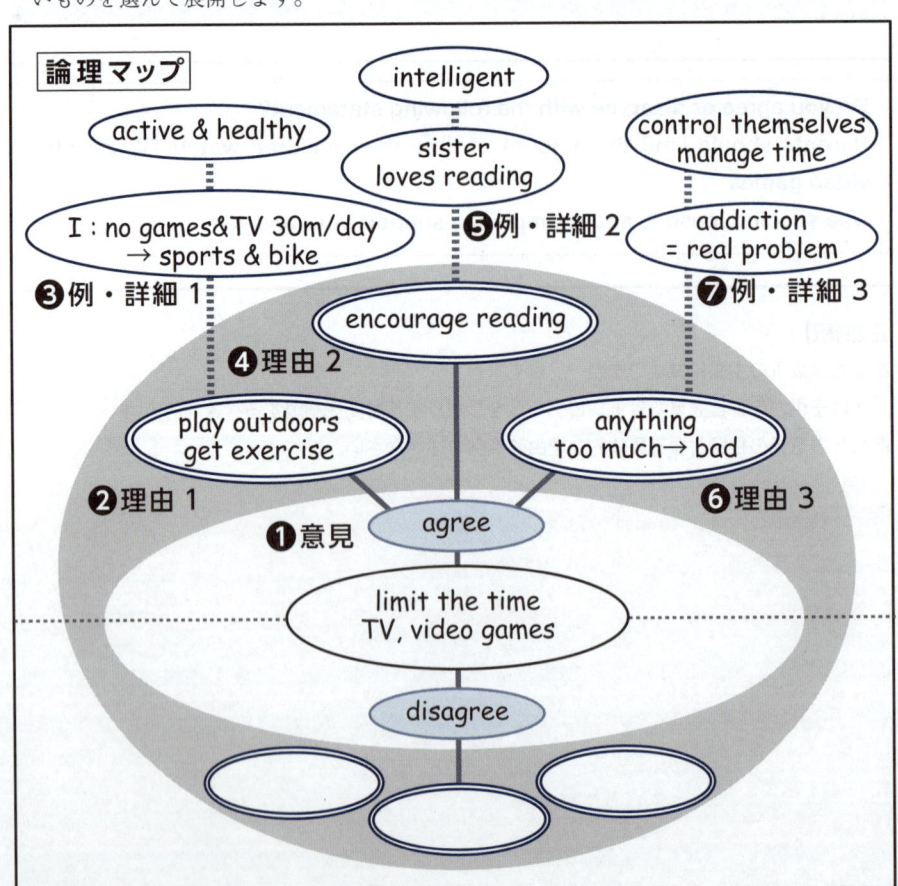

論理マップ

- intelligent
- active & healthy
- sister loves reading
- control themselves manage time
- I : no games&TV 30m/day → sports & bike
- ❺例・詳細2
- addiction = real problem
- ❸例・詳細1
- ❼例・詳細3
- encourage reading
- ❹理由2
- play outdoors get exercise
- anything too much → bad
- ❷理由1
- ❻理由3
- ❶意見　agree
- limit the time TV, video games
- disagree

論理マップのポイント

☆意見はすばやくどちらかに決める
　賛成か反対か、あるいはどちらを好むかは、**どちらかが高く評価されるということはない**ので、時間をかけずに決めましょう。多くの問題に触れ、自分の考え方の傾向を知っておくとよいでしょう。自分の考えに固執しすぎず、理由を展開しやすいものを選ぶことも戦略の1つです。

☆例・詳細を考える際は、自分や周囲の人の経験を思い返す
　実経験を挙げるとより具体的になり、説得力が増します。例題では、子供の頃の経験を含めてわかりやすく展開しています。ただし、主観的なエピソードの羅列にならないよう注意し、**自らの意見をサポートするという目的に沿っているか**を意識しましょう。

☆同一線上にある意見〜理由〜例・詳細の論理的つながりをチェックする
　1つ1つの要素が論理的につながっているか、**飛躍がないか**を確認します。その際、理由〜例・詳細の階層をそろえるようにしましょう。その理由全体をカバーする**抽象的説明から、それを掘り下げる具体的説明に**向かうように、線を外側に伸ばしていきます。

　例題では、「テレビやテレビゲームの時間を制限すべきだ」という❶意見に対し、❷理由1として play outdoors / get exercise「子供は外で遊び、運動すべきだから」という内容を挙げています。❸例・詳細1では、I: no games&TV 30m/day → sports & bike「私の場合、テレビゲームはせず、テレビは1日30分に限り、スポーツや自転車で遊んだ」という経験を例として挙げ、さらにその結果 active & healthy「活発で健康になった」と述べて、理由1をサポートしています。

　ここで例えば、「テレビやテレビゲームの時間を制限すべきだ。それは、活発で健康になるからだ。」とだけ述べ、他に説明がなかったとします。その場合、なぜ書き手が「テレビやゲームを制限すると活発で健康になる」と考えたのかが、読み手に伝わりません。ここでは、「テレビを見たりテレビゲームをしたりする代わりに、体を動かして遊ぶことで、活発で健康になる」という論理の流れを、エッセイの中できちんと示す必要があるのです。

　読み手に論理展開を推測させるのではなく、**書き手が論理のすきまを埋め、順序立てて自分の考えを伝えることに責任を持つ**のが、エッセイライティングの基本です。

Ⅱ 解答を組み立てる

論理マップに整理したアイディアを，解答にまとめていきます。まずは，Ⅰで挙げた意見〜理由〜例・詳細のそれぞれについて，キーワードに必要な言葉を補い，キーセンテンスとなる文を作成します。

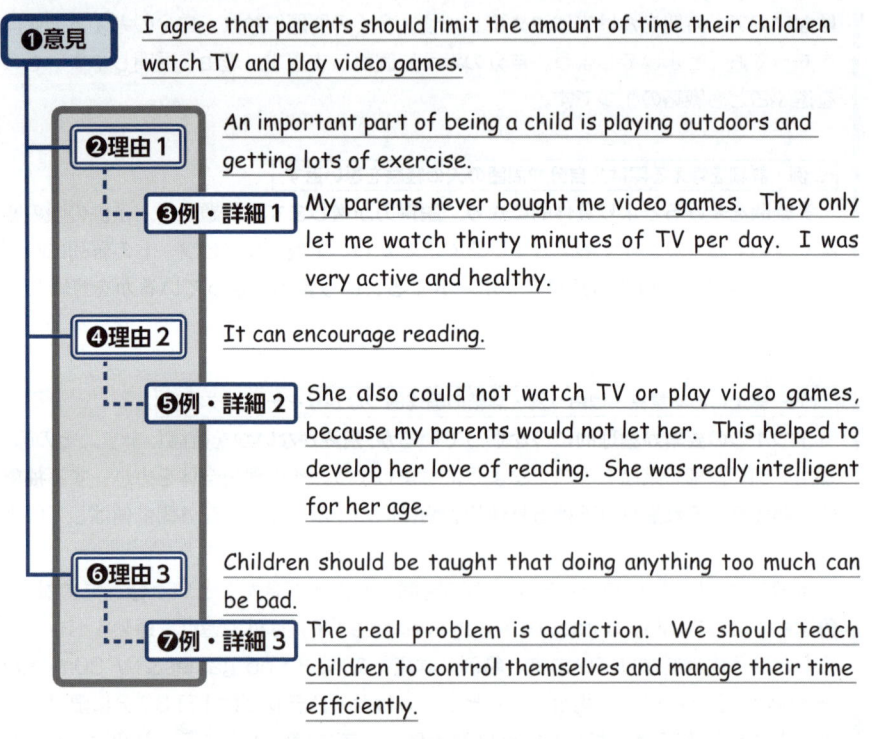

❶意見 I agree that parents should limit the amount of time their children watch TV and play video games.

❷理由1 An important part of being a child is playing outdoors and getting lots of exercise.

❸例・詳細1 My parents never bought me video games. They only let me watch thirty minutes of TV per day. I was very active and healthy.

❹理由2 It can encourage reading.

❺例・詳細2 She also could not watch TV or play video games, because my parents would not let her. This helped to develop her love of reading. She was really intelligent for her age.

❻理由3 Children should be taught that doing anything too much can be bad.

❼例・詳細3 The real problem is addiction. We should teach children to control themselves and manage their time efficiently.

各段落のキーセンテンスができたら，実際にエッセイを書き始めます。以下のポイントに注意しながら解答を作成してみましょう。

● Introduction（序論）では，自分の意見を明確に提示する

　自分の意見を明確に表す一文を，**キーセンテンス**として必ず含めます。また，全体の構成を示すために，解答例のように理由をダイジェスト的に述べる手法もありますが，「〜という人もいますが，私は…」と反対の立場に触れたり，「理由は3つあります」と全体の構成をシンプルに示したりすることもできます。

　あくまで Introduction なので，**長々と書かないこと，時間をかけすぎない**ことに留意します。Body から書き進め，後でその内容をまとめるという手順でもよいでしょう。

[役に立つ表現]

＊賛成・反対を示す
- □ I agree with 〜 . / I am in favor of 〜 .「私は〜に賛成です。」
- □ I disagree with 〜 . / I am against 〜 .「私は〜に反対です。」

＊意見・好みを述べる
- □ in my opinion / from my point of view「私の考えでは」
- □ I prefer 〜 to ....「私は…よりも〜を好みます。」

＊反対の立場に触れる
- □ Some people 〜 . However, ...「〜という人もいます。しかしながら，…」
- □ Although 〜 , ...「〜ですが，…」

● Body（本論）は，論理マップを常に意識し，相手が読みやすいように展開する

　1段落に1つずつ理由を展開させていきますが，ディスコース・マーカーを用いてわかりやすく構成を示すことがポイントです。下記に挙げた表現も参考にしてください。

　また，1つ1つの文が論理的につながっているか，書いているうちにトピックや自分で挙げた理由からそれていないかについてもよく確認しましょう。論理マップで挙げた要素を膨らませていくことになりますが，新たな要素を増やすと話がそれやすくなります。あくまで最初の論理マップの構成に沿って文章を展開しましょう。

　さらに，各段落の語数が同じくらいになるように調整します。あまりに短い場合，説得力のある説明が不足している恐れがあります。長すぎる場合も，同じ内容を繰り返していないか，不必要な情報が書かれていないか，冗長な表現になっていないかなどを確認しましょう。

[役に立つ表現]

＊順序立てて書く
- □ First(ly), 〜 . Second(ly), 〜 . Third(ly), 〜 .「第1に，〜。第2に，〜。第3に，〜。」
- □ First of all / To begin with「まず初めに」
- □ Next / Also / In addition / Moreover / Furthermore「次に，さらに，その上」
- □ Finally / Last(ly) / In the end「最後に」

＊理由を書く
- □ because / since / as「〜なので」
- □ The reason is that ....「その理由は…だからです。」
- □ This is because ....「これは…だからです。」

＊例を挙げる
- □ for example / for instance「例えば」　　□ as an example「一例を挙げると」
- □ such as 〜「〜のような」　　□ in particular「とりわけ，特に」

● Conclusion（結論）は，自分の意見を再提示する

エッセイのまとめとして，最後にもう一度自分の意見を提示します。間違いを避けるためにほぼ同じ語句を用いてもよいですが，少し言い換えて**多様な表現を用いる**ことを目指すとよいでしょう。以下の表現も利用しましょう。

[役に立つ表現]
- ☐ Therefore / Thus「それゆえに」　　☐ In conclusion「結論として」
- ☐ For these reasons「こうした理由で」　☐ After all「結局のところ」
- ☐ In short / In summary / To sum up「つまり」

● 必ず見直し・修正の時間（3〜5分）を設ける

ここまでの解答のポイントや p.19 のような評価基準に照らして見直しを行い，解答を修正します。修正までがエッセイライティングのプロセスです。

ここまでの時間配分は，**論理マップの作成（5〜7分），解答作成（20分），見直し・修正（3〜5分）**ほどが目安となります。時間の感覚を身につけ，見直しまで確実にするようにしましょう。

【解答例】　　：ディスコース・マーカー

　I agree that parents should limit the amount of time their children watch TV and play video games. Children should spend more time outdoors. Also, limiting these activities can encourage reading. Finally, children should be taught that spending too much time doing only one thing is not good.

　An important part of being a child is playing outdoors and getting lots of exercise. My parents never bought me video games when I was growing up, and they only let me watch thirty minutes of TV per day. However, I loved playing sports such as baseball, basketball, and soccer. Also, when I had free time, I often rode bikes with my friends. As a result, I was very active and healthy. I am so glad that I spent my time like this and not playing video games or watching TV.

　Another positive benefit is that it can encourage reading. For example, my younger sister was never very interested in sports, so she did not spend as much time outdoors as I did. However, she also could not watch TV or play video games, because my parents would not let her. This helped to develop her love of reading. She read more books than any child that I knew, and she was really intelligent for her age.

　Perhaps most importantly, children should be taught that doing anything too much can be bad. People often say that television and video games have bad influences, but I think that the real problem is addiction. We should teach children to control themselves and manage their time efficiently. Even a good thing like playing sports can have negative consequences, as it could start to interfere with a student's studies.

　For these reasons, I agree that parents should not let their children play video games or watch television too much. While these are not necessarily bad things, children also need to get lots of exercise, read lots of books, and learn to manage their time effectively.

(329 words)

（私は親が，子供がテレビを見たりテレビゲームをしたりする時間を制限するべきだという意見に賛成です。子供たちはもっと屋外で時間を過ごすべきです。また，こうした行動を制限することは読書を促すことにもなります。最後に，子供たちは，1つのことだけにあまりにも時間を費やすのはよくないということを教えられるべきです。

　子供であることの重要な要素の1つは，外で遊び，たくさん運動することです。私の両親は私が子供の頃，テレビゲームを買ってくれず，テレビも1日に30分しか見せてくれませんでした。しかし，私は野球やバスケットボール，サッカーといったスポーツが大好きでした。また，時間がある時は，私はよく友人たちと自転車に乗りました。その結果，私はとても活発で健康でした。私はテレビゲームをしたりテレビを見たりせずに，このように時間を過ごせてとてもよかったと思います。

　また別の利点は，それが読書を促すことになり得る点です。例えば，私の妹はまったくスポーツに興味がなかったので，私ほどは外で時間を過ごしませんでした。しかし，両親が許さなかったので，やはりテレビを見たりテレビゲームをしたりすることもできませんでした。このおかげで，妹は読書が大好きになりました。彼女は私の知るどんな子供よりもたくさんの本を読み，年の割にとても物知りでした。

　そしておそらく最も重要なことは，子供は何でもやりすぎることはよくないことを学ぶべきだということです。人はよく，テレビやテレビゲームは悪い影響を与えると言いますが，私は，真の問題はそれにのめり込んでしまうことだと思っています。私たちは子供たちに，自らをコントロールし，時間を有効に管理することを教えるべきです。スポーツをするといったよいことでさえ，学生の勉強を妨げ始めているかもしれないように，ネガティブな結果をもたらすことはあるのです。

　こういった理由から，私は親が子供にあまりテレビゲームをしたりテレビを見たりしすぎることを許すべきではないという意見に賛成です。これらのものは必ずしも悪いとは言い切れませんが，子どもたちはたくさん運動をし，たくさんの本を読み，時間を効果的に管理することを学ぶ必要もあるのです。）

✓ 重要表現チェック

- [ ] for *one's* age「年の割には」
- [ ] addiction「中毒」
- [ ] consequence「結果」

仕上げ

- [ ] アイディアを出すトレーニングとして，例題において disagree を主張する場合について，論理マップを書いてみましょう。
- [ ] 解答例をパソコンで入力する練習をしてみましょう。その際，スペルチェック機能をオフにします。メモ帳ソフトを利用してもよいでしょう。

演習問題

【1】 解答時間：制限なし

例題で学んだ考え方を，演習問題を通して実践します。1問目は制限時間を設けず，じっくりと取り組んでみましょう。次の設問について，下のスペースに論理マップを作成し，先ほどの手順で解答を組み立ててください。円や線は自由に書き加えて構いません。

Do you agree or disagree with the following statement?
Improving technology is always a good thing.
Use specific reasons and examples to support your answer.

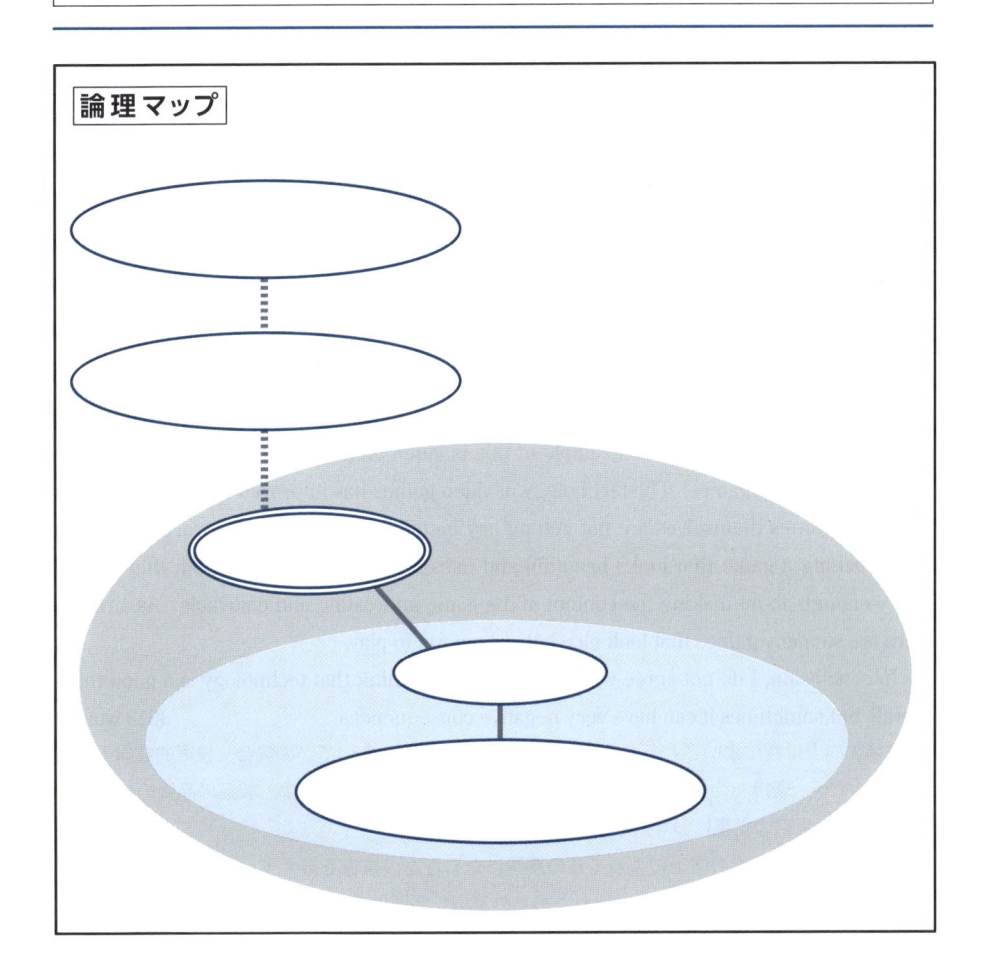

論理マップ

【設問訳】

あなたは，以下の主張に賛成ですか，反対ですか。
「技術の向上は常によいことである。」
あなたの意見の根拠となる具体的な理由や事例を説明しなさい。

【解答例】

　I disagree with the opinion that improving technology is always a good thing. For the most part, technological improvements are good, but sometimes they can lead to negative consequences such as damage to the environment, decreased communication between people, and lower quality products.

　First, humans have caused a lot of damage to the planet because of improving technology. Right now, the world is facing many serious problems like global warming and the destruction of the rainforests. These problems occurred because technology improved so quickly and humans were not careful enough. I am concerned that if we continue to improve technology without being careful, we might cause even bigger problems.

　Second, improving technology is not good for human relationships. Friends, family, and business acquaintances used to always communicate either in person or on the phone. Today, however, due to improved technology, it is more common to send messages and emails, and it causes distance between people. I cannot remember the last time that I spoke to my father on the phone, for example, because we always send messages to each other, and this decreases the quality of our relationship.

　Finally, many technological improvements can seem exciting, but sometimes they result in lower quality products. One example of this is video games. Since I was a child, I have always loved video games. The technology of video games has improved a lot in the last few years, but games themselves are not getting any better. Game developers worry too much about making a game that looks beautiful and uses advanced technology, but they do not worry enough about making the content of the game interesting and enjoyable. As a result, there are so many games that look nice but are not fun to play.

　In conclusion, I do not agree with the statement. I think that technology is a good thing overall, but sometimes it can have very negative consequences.　　　　　　(318 words)

　(技術の向上は常によいことであるという意見に反対です。たいていの場合，技術的な向上はよいことですが，環境への被害や，人と人とのコミュニケーションの減少，製品の品質の低下などといったマイナスの結果につながることもあります。

　第1に，人間は技術の向上によってこの惑星にたくさんの被害を与えています。今まさに，世界は地球温暖化や熱帯雨林の破壊といった多くの深刻な問題に直面しています。これらの問題は，技術がとても急速に向上し，人間が十分に配慮していなかったために起こりました。私は，もし

私たちが慎重さを欠いたままで技術を向上し続ければ，さらに大きな問題を引き起こすかもしれないと心配しています。

　第2に，技術の向上は人間関係によくありません。かつては，友人や家族，仕事上の知人は，直接会うか電話でコミュニケーションをするのが常でした。しかし今日では，向上した技術のために，メッセージやメールを送るほうが一般的になり，人と人との間に距離を生み出しています。例えば，私と父はいつもお互いにメッセージを送信し合っているので，父と最後に電話で話したのがいつだったか覚えていません。このことは私と父の関係の質を低下させています。

　最後に，技術的な向上の多くは，わくわくすることのように思えるかもしれませんが，結果として品質の低下した製品をもたらす時もあります。この一例は，テレビゲームです。私は子供の頃からずっとテレビゲームが大好きです。過去数年間でテレビゲームの技術は向上しましたが，ゲーム自体は全然よくなっていません。ゲームの開発者たちは，見た目がきれいで，先進的な技術を使ったゲームを作ることばかりを気にかけて，ゲームのコンテンツをおもしろく楽しいものにすることには十分に気を配っていません。その結果，見た目はよいが，やっていておもしろくないゲームがあまりにもたくさんあります。

　結論として，私はこの主張に反対です。技術は概してよいものだとは思いますが，とても悪い結果をもたらすこともあると思います。）

【解説】

　「技術の向上は常によいことである」というのが設問のトピックです。これに対する賛否を示し，次に理由と具体例を挙げる構成でエッセイを書きましょう。以下に解答例の構成を示します。

　第1段落の Introduction では，「技術の向上は常によいことである」というトピックに対し，I disagree with the opinion that ... という表現を用いて反対の立場を示しています。opinion の代わりに statement / idea / view などを使うこともできます。さらに，Body で展開する3つの論点を簡潔に示しています。次に Body では，First / Second / Finally で示した各段落で，これらを具体的に説明しています。第2段落では，「技術の向上は環境に被害を与える」というキーセンテンスで理由1を示しています。その後，「温暖化」や「熱帯雨林破壊」といった具体的な事例を挙げ，それらが技術の向上とどのように関連しているかを記述しています（例・詳細1）。第3段落では，「人間関係によくない」というキーセンテンスで理由2を示し，これについて，メッセージやメールといった具体的な技術を挙げ，対面や電話でのコミュニケーションとの比較や，自分の体験を盛り込みながら説明しています（例・詳細2）。第4段落では，「品質の低下した製品をもたらす」というキーセンテンスで理由3を示し，テレビゲームについて，自分の実際の経験から気づいた問題点を示しています（例・詳細3）。最終段落の Conclusion では，トピックに反対である旨を改めて示し，全体の内容をまとめています。

　次に示した解答例の論理マップも参考に，自分の作成した論理マップと解答について，

意見〜理由〜例・詳細の論理展開の仕方に特に注意しながら見直してみましょう。

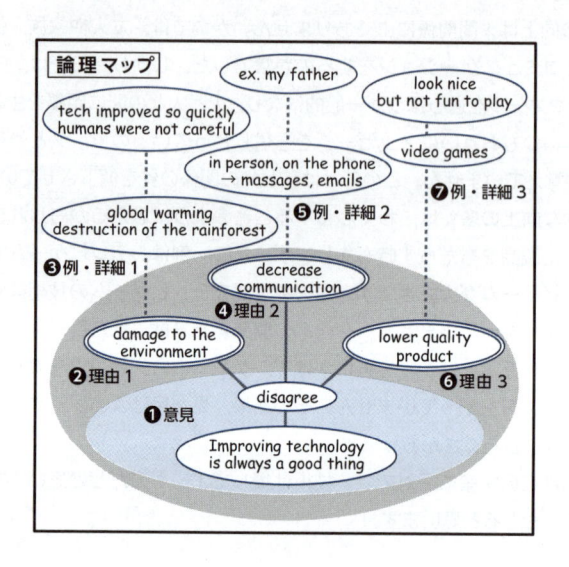

論理マップ

- ❶意見: Improving technology is always a good thing
- disagree
- ❷理由1: damage to the environment
- ❸例・詳細1: global warming / destruction of the rainforest
- ❹理由2: decrease communication
- ❺例・詳細2: in person, on the phone → massages, emails / ex. my father
- ❻理由3: lower quality product
- ❼例・詳細3: video games / look nice but not fun to play
- tech improved so quickly humans were not careful

✓ 重要表現チェック

- □ global warming 「地球温暖化」
- □ destruction of the rainforest 「熱帯雨林の破壊」
- □ acquaintance 「知人」
- □ in person 「直に，直接会って」
- □ distance 「距離」
- □ result in 〜 「〜という結果になる」
- □ developer 「開発者」
- □ advanced 「先進的な」

【2】解答時間：45分

2問目は，本番の1.5倍の解答時間を設けます。ブレインストーミングを行った上で，下記のスペースに自分で論理マップを作成し，解答を組み立てましょう。時間配分を意識しながら，見直し・修正まで行いましょう。

Do you agree or disagree with the following statement?
All children should be required to play team sports like baseball and soccer.
Use specific reasons and examples to support your answer.

【設問訳】

あなたは以下の主張に賛成ですか，反対ですか。
「すべての子供たちに，野球やサッカーのようなチームスポーツをするよう義務づけるべきだ。」
あなたの意見の根拠となる具体的な理由や事例を説明しなさい。

【解答例】

  I completely agree with the opinion that all children should be required to play team sports like baseball and soccer. Playing team sports is good exercise, helps children to build social skills, and teaches them about teamwork.

  First, all children should get lots of exercise, and playing team sports is one of the best ways to do this. When I was younger, I played a variety of sports, and I was always busy with practice and games. As a result, I was very healthy. If I had not played sports, I probably would have stayed at home all the time and played video games, which is not good. In this way, team sports are good for children's health.

  Second, playing team sports is good for building social skills. To give another example from my childhood, I was always very shy. I only had a few friends at school, and I was not good at talking to other students. On my sports teams, though, I had to communicate with my teammates, and this improved my ability to talk with others. Over time, I became much less shy, and now I have many friends. This shows how sports can help children build social skills.

  Finally, team sports can teach children about teamwork. For example, many companies require employees to work in teams in order to complete projects. Employees that have no experience working on a team face a difficult challenge. By playing a team sport, children can prepare for working with others in order to achieve difficult goals. This is a highly valuable skill later in life. In addition, children can learn how good it feels to achieve great results working with others.

  In conclusion, I believe that playing team sports is very important for children, and it prepares them for the future in a number of ways. (305 words)

  (私は，子供たち全員に野球やサッカーのようなチームスポーツをするよう義務づけるべきだという意見に，まったく賛成です。団体競技をすることは，よい運動になり，子供たちが社会的な能力を築くのに役に立ち，彼らにチームワークについて教えます。

  第1に，子供たちは皆，たくさん運動をするべきです。そうするためには，チームスポーツをすることは最もよい方法の1つです。私は子供の頃，さまざまなスポーツをしていて，練習と試合でいつも忙しくしていました。その結果，私はとても健康でした。スポーツをしていなかったら，私はたぶん家にずっといて，テレビゲームをしていただろうと思いますが，それはよくありません。このように，チームスポーツは子供の健康によいのです。

第2に，チームスポーツをすることは社会的な能力を築くのに有効です。子供の頃の例をもう1つ挙げると，私はいつもとても内気でした。学校では少ししか友達がおらず，他の生徒に話しかけるのが得意ではありませんでした。しかし，スポーツチームでは，チームメイトとコミュニケーションをしなければならなかったので，このことが他者と話す能力を改善してくれました。そのうち，私は以前よりもずっと内気ではなくなり，今ではたくさんの友人がいます。このことは，スポーツがいかに子供たちが社会的な能力を築くのに役立ち得るかを示しています。

最後に，チームスポーツは子供たちにチームワークについて教えます。例えば，多くの会社は社員に対し，プロジェクトを遂行するためにチームで働くことを求めます。チームで働いた経験のない社員は困難な課題に直面することになります。チームスポーツをすることによって，子供たちは難しい目標を達成するために他者と協力する準備をすることができるのです。このことは後に人生において極めて貴重なスキルになります。加えて，子供たちは他者と協力して素晴らしい成果を達成した時に，どれほどよい気分を味わうのかを知ることができます。

結論として，チームスポーツをすることは子供たちにとってとても重要で，さまざまな方法で子供たちに将来の備えをさせることになると，私は思います。)

【解説】

今回は，「すべての子供にチームスポーツを義務づけるべきである」というトピックです。以下に解答例の構成を示します。

Introduction は，I completely agree with the opinion that ... という賛成の表現で始まっています。その後，Body で説明していく3つの理由を要約しています。Body では，「よい運動になる」というキーセンテンスで理由1を示し，自分がスポーツの練習や試合を通じて健康になった体験を，If I had not played sports, I probably would have stayed home ... という仮定表現も交えて詳しく述べています（例・詳細1）。続いて，「社会的な能力を養える」という利点をキーセンテンスにして理由2を示しています。ここでも根拠として，自分の経験（チームスポーツがもたらした変化）を例に挙げています（例・詳細2）。最後に理由3として「子供にチームワークについて教える」と述べ，大人になってからの職場でのチームワークの重要性を例に挙げ，その準備として子供にとってチームスポーツがどのように有効であるかを説明しています。Conclusion では，it prepares them for the future in a number of ways という表現で，同じ表現を反復することなく，全体の内容を総括しています。

次に示した解答例の論理マップも参考に，自分の作成した論理マップと解答を見直してみましょう。本番では30分の解答時間の中でこれらを行うということを意識し，時間配分についても振り返りをしましょう。

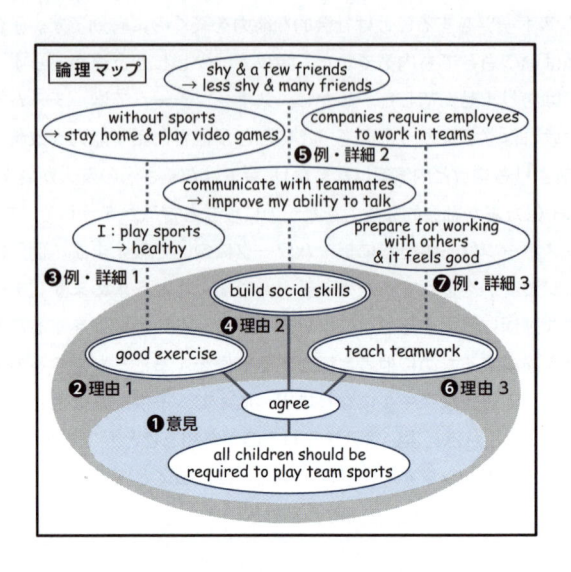

```
論理マップ
                shy & a few friends
              → less shy & many friends
      without sports              companies require employees
    → stay home & play video games    to work in teams
                                    ❺例・詳細2
              communicate with teammates
            → improve my ability to talk
       I : play sports          prepare for working
       → healthy                  with others
                                 & it feels good
     ❸例・詳細1                    ❼例・詳細3
              build social skills
                   ❹理由2
        good exercise      teach teamwork
       ❷理由1                        ❻理由3
                   agree
           ❶意見
           all children should be
         required to play team sports
```

✓ 重要表現チェック

- be required to *do* 「…することを要求される，義務づけられる」
- social skill 「社会的な能力」
- employee 「従業員，社員」
- valuable 「貴重な，価値のある」
- prepare 〜 for ...「〜に…の準備をさせる」
- childhood 「子供時代」
- face a challenge 「課題に直面する」

MEMO

Independent Task　Question 2
集中トレーニング

　ここまで，英文ライティングの基本や，論理マップを使った Question 2 の考え方，解答の組み立て方について学んできました。ここからは，実戦形式の問題を解きながら，例題や演習問題で学んだ考え方を確実に身につけていきます。実際に本番と同じく **1 問 30 分間**で演習を行いましょう。

問題 1

Do you agree or disagree with the following statement?
Loyal employees are more valuable than skilled employees.
Use specific reasons and examples to support your answer.

【設問訳】
あなたは以下の主張に賛成ですか，反対ですか。
「忠実な従業員は，有能な従業員よりも貴重である。」
あなたの意見の根拠となる具体的な理由や事例を述べなさい。

解答例　「忠実な従業員のほうが貴重である」に賛成の場合

不十分な解答例

　　I agree with the idea that loyal employees are more valuable than skilled employees ★1 because employees that are not loyal can be dangerous to a company.
　　First, a company can teach skills to its employees but not loyalty.　★2 When a company hire (→**hires**) a new employee, it may be difficult for its personnel staff to see whether a candidate is loyal or not at the interview.　If their decisions were wrong, it could be dangerous.　So a company's personnel staff cannot be too careful to hire a new employee. On the other hand, when a staff member's skill was not sufficient, then the company can train him or her.
　　Second, ★3 I think skilled employees are (→不要) tend to be more aggressive than loyal employees.　It is true that skilled employees can do the jobs efficiently.　However, if employees are too aggressive, it may be dangerous to the company.　★4 When I was a freshman in high school, I worked at a local coffee shop.　Our boss was rude to us and we didn't want to obey him.　We even gave away free food and drinks to our friends and family members.　★5 It was bad for that coffee shop.
　　★6 Last, an owner of a company would expect his or her staff to be more loyal, especially when the company is small.　This is because loyal employees are less likely to behave badly.　Moreover, being loyal means not complaining whatever happens.　When my father's

company faced a recession few years ago, he could not pay all of his employees. But, they agreed to reduce their salary (→**have their salary lowered**), because they didn't want someone to be fired.

In conclusion, I think loyal employees are more valuable than skilled employees. It is ideal for employees to have both skills and loyalty, but I still think loyalty is more important.

●構成と内容の改善ポイント

★1 エッセイ全体の基本的な立場・展開の流れを示すべき Introduction で，1つの理由のみに言及しています。
  ➡ Introduction で理由に触れる場合は，1つだけではなくすべての理由に簡潔に触れましょう。最初に全体の構成を明確に示すことで，まとまりのよい読みやすいエッセイになります。あるいは内容を述べなくても，「賛成です。その理由は3つあります。」のように「3点あること」を示すと，読み手がその後の構成を読み取りやすくなります。

★2 唐突に「面接で候補者が忠実かどうかを見極める」という話になっており，人事担当者についての話は本筋からそれてしまっています。
  ➡ ここで必要とされるのは，「会社はスキルを教えることはできるが，忠実さを教えることはできない」という主張を支える説得力のある説明です。「従業員が忠実であれば，足りないスキルは会社が補うことができる」という内容に絞って第2段落を構成しましょう。

★3 一般論とは言い難く，説得力のある説明がない限り唐突な印象です。
  ➡ 「有能な（スキルのある）社員」について話を展開しようとすると主張からそれやすいので，「忠実でない従業員」についての話でまとめましょう。

★4 For example（例えば）などと前置きすると，これから具体例を述べることを明確に示すことができます。

★5 例として挙げた従業員の行為が，どのような点で「会社にとって悪い」のかを，具体的に説明していません。
  ➡ 説得力をアップさせるために，従業員の忠誠心を損ねたために会社の金銭的損失につながったという，具体的な説明を加えましょう。

★6 「会社の経営者が従業員に対してより忠実であることを期待する」という内容は，「忠実な従業員は有能な従業員よりも貴重である」と考えた場合の結果と言えるので，主張を支える根拠としては説得力に欠けます。
  ➡ 各段落の第1文では，その段落の要旨となる内容を明確に述べましょう。ここでは後半の具体例を活かして，まず忠実な従業員の好ましい特徴を端的に述べましょう。キーセンテンスから始め，具体例や詳細を述べていくことで，まとまりのある文章になります。

《構成の改善例》

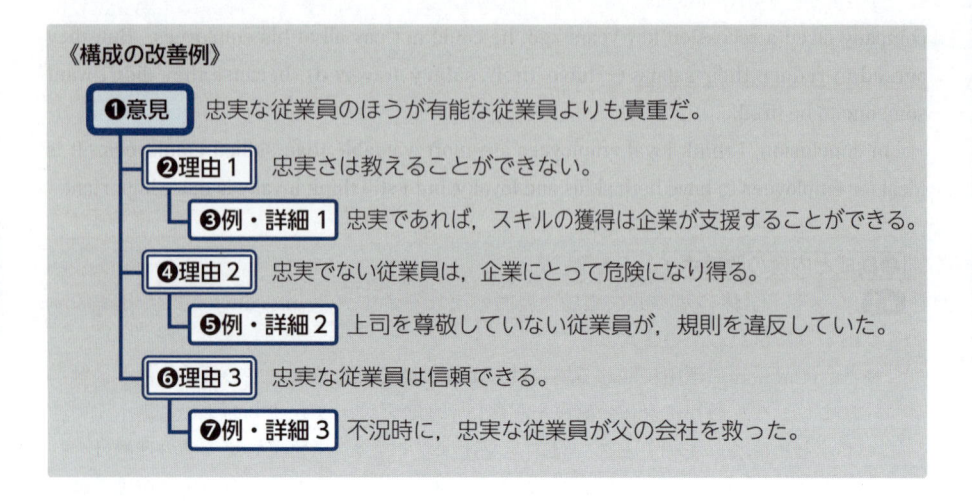

- **❶意見** 忠実な従業員のほうが有能な従業員よりも貴重だ。
  - **❷理由1** 忠実さは教えることができない。
    - **❸例・詳細1** 忠実であれば，スキルの獲得は企業が支援することができる。
  - **❹理由2** 忠実でない従業員は，企業にとって危険になり得る。
    - **❺例・詳細2** 上司を尊敬していない従業員が，規則を違反していた。
  - **❻理由3** 忠実な従業員は信頼できる。
    - **❼例・詳細3** 不況時に，忠実な従業員が父の会社を救った。

適切な解答例

　I totally agree with the opinion that loyal employees are more valuable than skilled employees. ★1 Loyalty cannot be taught in the same way that skills can. Also, employees that are not loyal can be dangerous to a company. Most importantly, loyal employees are more flexible and reliable.

　First, unlike skills, loyalty is not something that a company can "teach" to its employees. ★2 Rather, loyalty is something that a company must earn by providing employees with a helpful, positive, and financially rewarding work environment. If employees are loyal and dedicated, then a company can invest in helping them acquire the skills they need. For example, some companies will pay for long-term employees to attend various schools and classes in order to increase their abilities.

　Second, ★3 employees that are not loyal are often dangerous to a company. ★4 For example, when I was a freshman in high school, I worked at a local coffee shop. Our boss was rude to all of the employees, and none of them respected him. Because of this, many of the employees would give away free food and drinks to friends and family members, even though it was against the rules. ★5 Essentially, they were stealing from the company, because their boss had not got their loyalty.

　Most importantly, ★6 loyal employees are more flexible and reliable. My father, who owns a small construction company, told me that having loyal employees helped his company stay in business during the recession a few years ago. He could not afford to pay all of his employees, but they agreed to have their own salary lowered rather than to have someone fired. Since all of them felt like a family, they made an effort to cooperate, and ultimately it saved the company.

　In conclusion, loyal employees are more valuable than skilled employees. Of course, having an employee that is both loyal and skilled is ideal, but overall loyalty is more important. (317 words)

　（忠実な従業員のほうが有能な従業員よりも貴重であるという意見に，全面的に賛成です。忠実さはスキルと同じようには教えることができません。また，忠実でない従業員は，企業にとって危険になり得ます。最も重要なのは，忠実な従業員のほうが柔軟性があり，信頼できるということです。
　第1に，スキルとは違って，忠実さは企業が従業員に「教える」ことのできるものではありません。むしろ，忠実さとは，有益で，好ましい経済的に報われる労働環境を従業員に与えることによって，企業が獲得しなければならないものです。もし，従業員が忠実で献身的であれば，企業はその従業員が必要とするスキル獲得の支援に投資することができます。例えば，勤続年数の長い従業員に対し，能力を高めさせるために，さまざまな学校や授業に出席する費用を支払う企業もあります。
　第2に，忠実でない従業員は，企業にとって危険であることがよくあります。例えば，私は高校1年生の時，地元のカフェで働いていました。私たちの上司は従業員全員に対して無作法な態度を取り，従業員の誰も彼を尊敬していませんでした。このため，従業員の多くは，規則違反であるにもかかわらず，友人や家族に無料で食事や飲み物を出していました。要するに，上司が従業員から忠誠を得ていなかったために，従業員は会社から盗みをしていたのです。
　最も重要なのは，忠実な従業員のほうが柔軟性があり，信頼できるということです。私の父は小さな建設会社を所有しているのですが，忠実な従業員たちがいてくれたおかげで，数年前の不況時にも事業を継続することができたと私に語りました。父には従業員全員に賃金を払う余裕がありませんでしたが，彼らは誰かを解雇するのではなく，自分たちの給料を下げることに同意してくれました。誰もが家族のように感じていたので，協力するよう努め，最終的にそのことが会社を救うことになりました。
　したがって，忠実な従業員は有能な従業員よりも貴重です。もちろん，忠実で有能な従業員を持つことは理想ですが，全体的に考えると，忠実さのほうが重要です。）

＋別解　「忠実な従業員のほうが貴重である」に反対の場合

　There is no denying that loyal employees are a valuable asset for a company. Even so, loyalty is not as important as skill, and I believe that skilled employees are worth more overall.

　Ideally, skilled employees will also be loyal, but this is not totally necessary. However, a loyal employee without the skills necessary to do his or her job is a burden on a company. Even if an employee cares deeply about her company, without proper training and skills, she will be unable to perform her job adequately. This could potentially lead to failed projects and a serious loss in profits.

　In addition, although most people might avoid admitting it, loyalty can be bought. For example, a "loyal employee" might work longer days, but companies can also get the same results by paying workers overtime. In this way, it could be said that any employee who adequately performs the job she is paid for is "loyal."

　Finally, companies can increase profits by using skilled employees. Companies are always looking for employees that have a wide range of skills, experience, and education. The reason for this is that skilled employees can help in providing products and services that are more valuable. Last year, for example, my father paid his nephew to build a new website for his company. He gave him the job simply because they are family. However, in the end my father had to get a professional to improve the website, because his nephew was not experienced enough to do the job properly. Although he was loyal, his lack of skill cost the company extra money. On the other hand, the revised website resulted in increased profit.

　For these reasons, I have to disagree with the statement. While I do agree that loyalty is something to be valued, it cannot replace the skills that are required to complete various jobs.　　　　　　　　　　　　　　　　　　　　　　　　　　　　　(315 words)

　（忠実な従業員が企業にとって貴重な財産であることは否定できません。それでも，忠実さは能力ほど重要ではなく，概して，有能な従業員のほうが価値が高いと私は思います。

　理想的には，有能な従業員が忠実でもあればよいのでしょうが，それは絶対に必要だというわけではありません。しかし，仕事に必要な能力のない忠実な従業員は，企業にとって負担になります。たとえ，ある従業員が自分の会社に深く思いを寄せているとしても，適切なトレーニングやスキルがなければ，仕事を満足に行うことはできないでしょう。このことは，プロジェクトの失敗や深刻な利益の損失につながる可能性があります。

　それに，ほとんどの人は認めないかもしれませんが，忠誠心はお金で買うことができます。例えば，「忠実な従業員」はより長く働くかもしれませんが，企業は従業員に残業代を支払うことで同じ結果を得ることも可能です。このようにすれば，労賃が支払われている仕事を十分に果たすどんな従業員も，「忠実だ」ということができます。

　最後に，企業は有能な従業員を活用することで利益を増やすことができます。企業は常に，幅広いスキルや経験を持ち，さまざまな教育を受けたことのある従業員を求めています。この理由は，有能な従業員はより価値のある製品やサービスを提供する上で役立つからです。例えば，昨年，私の父は甥にお金を払って，自分の会社の新しいウェブサイトを作らせました。父は，単に家族だからという理由で，その仕事を甥に与えたのです。しかし，父は結局，プロに頼んでウェブサイトを改善させなければならなくなりました。甥にはその仕事をきちんと行うのに十分な経験がなかったからです。甥は忠実でしたが，能力の欠如のせいで，会社に余分なお金をかけさせることになりました。一方，修正されたウェブサイトは，より大きな利益をもたらしました。

　以上のような理由から，私はこの主張には反対せざるを得ません。忠誠心は評価されるべきも

のだということには同意しますが，さまざまな仕事をやり遂げるのに必要とされる能力の代わりにはできないのです。）

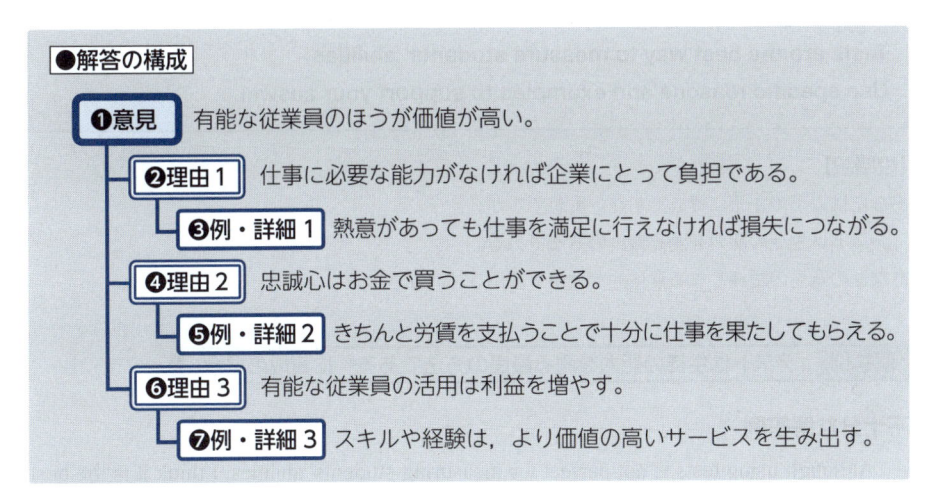

●解答の構成

- **❶意見** 有能な従業員のほうが価値が高い。
  - **❷理由1** 仕事に必要な能力がなければ企業にとって負担である。
    - **❸例・詳細1** 熱意があっても仕事を満足に行えなければ損失につながる。
  - **❹理由2** 忠誠心はお金で買うことができる。
    - **❺例・詳細2** きちんと労賃を支払うことで十分に仕事を果たしてもらえる。
  - **❻理由3** 有能な従業員の活用は利益を増やす。
    - **❼例・詳細3** スキルや経験は，より価値の高いサービスを生み出す。

✓ 重要表現チェック

不十分な解答例	☐ loyalty「忠実，忠誠心」　　☐ personnel「人事部〔課〕」
	☐ give away ~「~を渡す，~を無料であげる」
	☐ recession「不景気，不況」
適切な解答例	☐ trustworthy「信頼できる，信用できる」
	☐ reliable「信頼できる，頼りになる」
	☐ rewarding「報いのある，価値のある」
	☐ dedicated「献身的な，熱心な」
	☐ essentially「本質上，つまるところ」
	☐ ultimately「最終的に」　　☐ overall「全体としては，概して」
別解	☐ asset「資産，財産」　　☐ burden「重荷，負担」
	☐ adequately「十分に，適切に」
	☐ potentially「潜在的に，もしかすると」
	☐ failed「不成功の」
	☐ a wide range of ~「広範囲の~，さまざまな~」

問題 2

Do you agree or disagree with the following statement?
Tests are the best way to measure students' abilities.
Use specific reasons and examples to support your answer.

【設問訳】
あなたは以下の主張に賛成ですか，反対ですか。
「テストは生徒の能力を測る最良の方法である。」
あなたの意見の根拠となる具体的な理由や事例を述べなさい。

解答例 「テストは生徒の能力を測る最良の方法である」に賛成の場合

不十分な解答例

　　Although using tests is not perfect for measuring students' abilities, I think it is the best method for the time being. Specifically, tests are objective, fair, and easily carried out.

　　Although (→不要) people like to think of themselves to be logical, objective thinkers, but they really aren't. Humans have a tendency to include their feelings in almost every decisions (→decision) they make. ★1 One example is that a teacher may have a bias when he or she evaluates a student. If the teacher likes or dislikes the student, such personal feelings may affect the evaluation. Therefore teachers will grade tests without looking at the students' names.

　　★2 Here's another example. I have a friend named Clarence, who is an exchange student from the United States. He told me that they do not have college entrance exams in his country, and instead they use a wide variety of application materials such as personal statements, letters of recommendation, club activities, and work experience. ★3 At first I envied them. I even thought of going to the United States to enter a college there. When I told my idea to my parents though, they said I was wrong. Indeed, how does a school decide if playing for a soccer team is more or less valuable than working part-time at a coffee shop?

　　Finally, testing is a quick way to assess students' abilities. Complicated evaluation systems like the one described above has (→have) to be changed depending on the situation, and it takes a long time to evaluate results. ★4 Moreover, students will stop acting naturally in school. For example, some students may engage themselves in certain activities just for the sake of a better evaluation.

　　I admit that test-based evaluations are not always perfect. It is true that there are many discussions against it. ★5 Some other form of evaluation might become the mainstream in the near future. Therefore it is recommended for students to flexibly behave.

●構成と内容の改善ポイント

★1 「人は自分のことを論理的で客観的に考える人間だと思いたがるがそうではない」と述べ,「教師の個人的な感情が評価に影響する」という具体例を挙げていますが,肝心な「テストは客観的である」ということについての説明がありません。読む側が文の主旨を読み取るには,「対照的にテストは客観的だ」と言いたいのだろう,と類推しなければなりません。
→ Introduction で1番目の理由に「テストは客観的である」を挙げていますので,第2段落はこの詳細説明を意図しているはずです。読み手に主旨が伝わりやすいよう,各段落の中でも核となる内容を端的に示しましょう。

★2 第2段落と同様に,初めから具体例が並べられており,何を伝えたいのかがわかりにくくなっています。
→第3段落は Introduction で2番目に挙げられている「テストは公平である」についての説明なので,これを明確に述べます。

★3 アメリカの入学選考の例を聞いた後の経過について述べていますが,「テストは公平である」という主張を支えるには説得力に欠けています。
→アメリカの入学選考との対比から,「テストは公平である」との考えに至る流れを論理的に述べましょう。

★4 具体例が,この段落で扱っている「テストは迅速な手段である」という内容からずれています。
→エッセイを書き始める前に,1つの理由に関連する具体例,詳細説明を書き出しておき,関連性のない具体例,詳細説明を盛り込まないようにしましょう。

★5 最終段落前半の内容に引きずられて論点がそれ,結論で新しい意見を提示してしまっています。
→最終段落は,これまで述べてきた内容の締めくくりなので,新しい情報や意見を示すのは避けます。冒頭で述べた自分の意見を,表現を変えて結論としてもう一度述べましょう。

《構成の改善例》

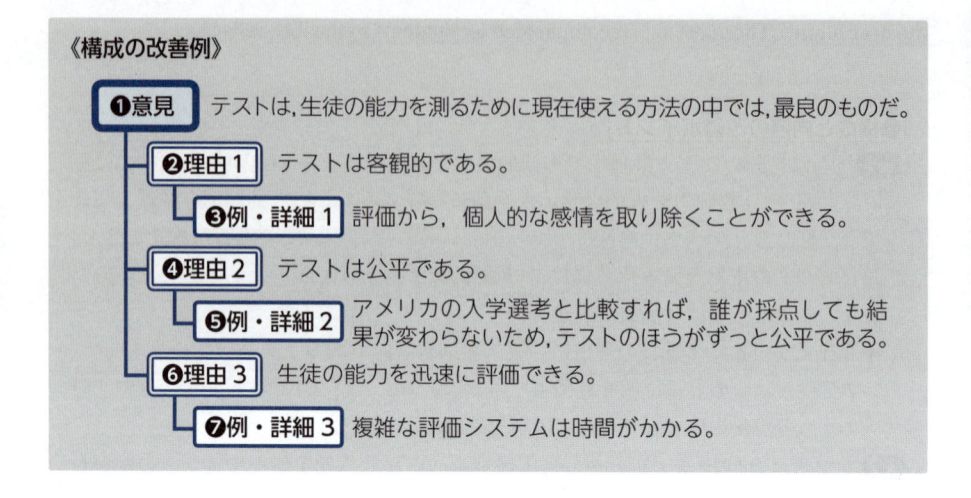

- **❶意見** テストは,生徒の能力を測るために現在使える方法の中では,最良のものだ。
  - **❷理由1** テストは客観的である。
    - **❸例・詳細1** 評価から,個人的な感情を取り除くことができる。
  - **❹理由2** テストは公平である。
    - **❺例・詳細2** アメリカの入学選考と比較すれば,誰が採点しても結果が変わらないため,テストのほうがずっと公平である。
  - **❻理由3** 生徒の能力を迅速に評価できる。
    - **❼例・詳細3** 複雑な評価システムは時間がかかる。

適切な解答例

　　Although using tests is not a perfect method for measuring students' abilities, it is the best method currently available. Specifically, tests are objective, fair, and easily carried out.

　　★1 Using tests allows a teacher to measure students' abilities objectively. People like to claim that they are logical, objective thinkers, but this is far from true. Humans have a tendency to include their feelings in almost every decision that they make. ★1 Tests are a way to remove personal feelings from evaluations. When using a test, it does not matter if a teacher likes or dislikes a student. All that matters is the test score.

　　★2 Because tests are objective, they are also fair. I have a friend named Clarence, and he is an exchange student from the United States. Clarence told me that they do not have college entrance exams in the United States, and instead they use a wide variety of application materials such as personal statements, letters of recommendation, club activities, and work experience. ★3 He seemed to think that it was a good system, but it seems unfair to me, because it is so subjective. How does a school decide if playing for a soccer team is more or less valuable than working part-time at a coffee shop, for example? ★3 In contrast, test scores are fair because they are the same no matter who grades them.

　　Finally, testing is a quick way to assess students' abilities. Complicated evaluation systems like the one described above have to be changed depending on the situation, and it takes a long time to evaluate results. ★4 On the other hand, using tests is not so troublesome.

　　I am not saying that test-based evaluations do not have any flaws. Rather, there are many ways that they could be improved. ★5 **However, it is currently the best method available for measuring students' abilities.** (306 words)

（テストの活用は，生徒の能力を測る完璧な方法ではないものの，現在使える方法の中では最良のものです。具体的に言うと，テストは客観的で公平で，簡単に実施できます。

テストを用いることで，教師は生徒の能力を客観的に測ることができます。人は，自分が論理的で客観的にものを考える人間だと主張したがりますが，これは事実からかけ離れています。人間というものは，自分が下すほぼすべての決断に感情を加える傾向があります。テストは，評価から個人的な感情を取り除く1つの方法です。テストを利用する時，教師が生徒を好きか嫌いかは重要ではありません。重要なのはテストの点数だけです。

テストは客観的なので，公平でもあります。私には，クラレンスという名前の友人がいて，彼はアメリカからの留学生です。クラレンスは，アメリカでは大学入試がないと教えてくれました。代わりに，自己紹介書や他者からの推薦状，クラブ活動，職業経験などのさまざまな応募資料を用いるそうです。彼は，それがよい仕組みだと思っているようでしたが，私にはそれはあまりにも主観的で，不公平に思えます。例えば，サッカーのチームで活動していることと，カフェでアルバイトをしていることのどちらが価値が高いのか，もしくは低いのかを，どうやって学校は決めるのでしょうか。対して，テストの点数は誰が採点をしても変わらないので，公平なものです。

最後に，テストは，生徒の能力を迅速に評価できる手段です。先述のような複雑な評価システムは，状況に応じて変えなければならず，結果を評価するのに長い時間がかかります。それに対して，テストを利用することは，それほど煩雑ではありません。

私は，テストをもとにした評価にまったく欠点がないと言っているのではありません。むしろ，そこには改善の余地がたくさんあります。しかし，現時点では，テストは生徒の能力を測るのに使える一番よい方法です。）

別解 「テストは生徒の能力を測る最良の方法である」に反対の場合

I disagree with the statement. Tests are often praised for measuring abilities with scores, but it isn't useful in practice. Also, test scores are often inaccurate. Finally, test taking decreases the quality of education in general.

First of all, tests measure knowledge, not abilities. For example, getting high scores on a test to become a lawyer does not make someone a good lawyer. Some medical students that do well on tests cannot perform well in hospitals. Many famous geniuses failed at formal education. People try to measure abilities with tests, but we repeatedly fail to value one's actual performance.

Also, even if a test does a good job at measuring knowledge of a certain subject, test-takers' scores can vary based on mood, energy levels, and time of day. A few months ago, my mother had a car accident. Luckily, she was not hurt seriously, but she had to stay in hospital for a few days. During that time, I had to take a history exam. I had studied a lot for the test, and I was definitely prepared for it, but it was hard for me to concentrate because I was worried about my mother. As a result, I got a bad score on the test.

Perhaps my biggest issue with test-taking in general, though, is the negative effect it has on education. For instance, most high school students I know study hard almost every day. However, they do not study because they want to learn or improve themselves. The main reason they study is because they are trying to pass college entrance exams. Even teachers focus on passing tests when they teach, and education is more about passing tests than it is about learning. Overall, I think this decreases the quality of education.

For these reasons, I disagree with the statement. Although tests may be useful in some respects, I still think that they are not the best method of measuring students' abilities.

(324 words)

（私は，この主張に反対です。テストはよく点数で能力を測ることができると評価されていますが，それは実際の場面では役に立ちません。それに，テストの点数はしばしば不正確です。最後に，テストを受けることは，概して教育の質を下げています。

まず，テストは能力ではなく知識を測っています。例えば，弁護士になるための試験で高得点を取っても，よい弁護士になれるわけではありません。テストでよい点を取っても，病院ではうまく力を発揮できない，医学部の学生もいます。有名な天才の多くが，公教育ではつまずいています。人はテストで能力を測ろうとしますが，我々は再三にわたって，人の実際の能力を評価できずにいるのです。

さらに，テストは，ある教科の知識を測る上では役に立っているとしても，テストを受ける人の点数は，気分や活力の度合い，時間帯によって変わることがあります。数か月前，私の母は交通事故に遭いました。運よくひどい怪我はしませんでしたが，2，3日入院しなければなりませんでした。その間に，私は歴史の試験を受けなければなりませんでした。テスト勉強をたくさんして，しっかりと準備をしていたのですが，母のことが心配でなかなか集中できませんでした。その結果，そのテストで悪い点数を取ってしまいました。

おそらく，テストを受けること全般について，私の中で最も重大な問題は，教育への負の影響でしょう。例えば，私の知っているほとんどの高校生は，ほぼ毎日熱心に勉強しています。しかし，彼らが勉強しているのは，学びたいからでも，自分自身を向上させたいからでもありません。彼らが勉強する主な理由は，大学入試に合格しようとしているからです。教師でさえも，教える時にテストに合格することに焦点を当てており，教育は学習よりもテストに合格することが目的になっています。概して，このことが教育の質を減じていると思います。

以上の理由から，私はこの主張に反対します。テストはいくつかの点で有益かもしれませんが，それでも私は生徒の能力を測る最良の方法ではないと思います。）

●解答の構成

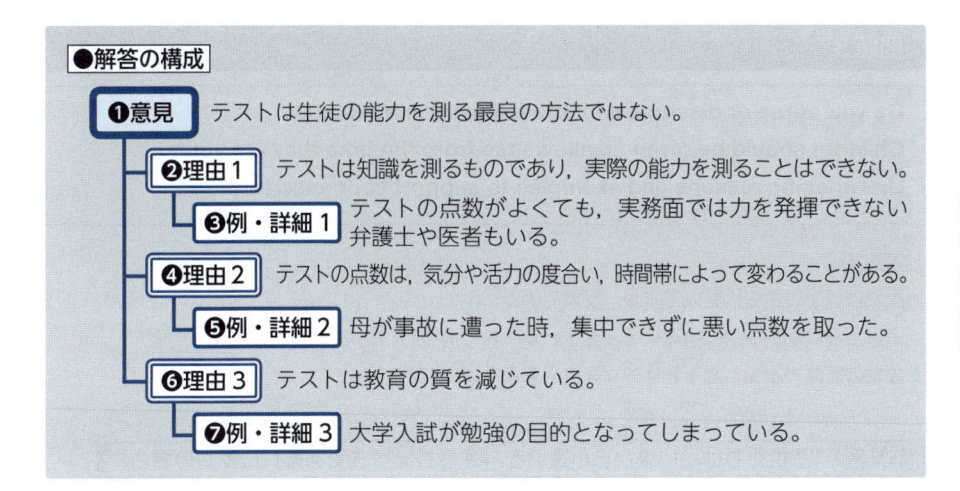

- **❶意見** テストは生徒の能力を測る最良の方法ではない。
  - **❷理由1** テストは知識を測るものであり，実際の能力を測ることはできない。
    - **❸例・詳細1** テストの点数がよくても，実務面では力を発揮できない弁護士や医者もいる。
  - **❹理由2** テストの点数は，気分や活力の度合い，時間帯によって変わることがある。
    - **❺例・詳細2** 母が事故に遭った時，集中できずに悪い点数を取った。
  - **❻理由3** テストは教育の質を減じている。
    - **❼例・詳細3** 大学入試が勉強の目的となってしまっている。

✓ 重要表現チェック

不十分な解答例
- □ specifically「正確に言えば，すなわち」
- □ objective「客観的な」　□ logical「論理的な」
- □ evaluate「～を評価する」　□ application「応募，応募書類」
- □ mainstream「主流」

適切な解答例
- □ available「利用できる」　□ matter「重要である」
- □ subjective「主観的な」

別解
- □ decrease「～を減少させる」　□ in general「概して，一般に」
- □ mood「気分」

問題 3

Do you agree or disagree with the following statement?
Children should be given an allowance from the time they are young.
Use specific reasons and examples to support your answer.

【設問訳】
あなたは以下の主張に賛成ですか，反対ですか。
「子供たちは幼い頃から小遣いを与えられるべきである。」
あなたの意見の根拠となる具体的な理由や事例を述べなさい。

解答例　「子供たちは幼い頃から小遣いを与えられるべきである」に反対の場合

不十分な解答例

　　Today, more and more parents seems (→seem) to be getting interested in financial education. Some people give **an** allowance to children expecting that they learn how to use money and its value from the time they are young.　★1 It is true that the younger the child is, the easier (→**more easily**) he or she masters any skills. However, I think things are different when it comes to the subject of money. If a child is to learn a foreign language, the earlier he starts, the better. The skill of using money sensibly cannot be acquired in the same way as languages.

　　★2 I will explain the first reason with an example. If a young boy is given money, he will buy a toy he has wanted. I know from my own experience that he may be bored with it soon. That's why I think that children should not be given an allowance from the time they are young. It is sure to end up in a waste of money.　★3 He doesn't even realize that he has wasted money. I (→**He**) would never learn the value of money in this situation.

　　Second, giving children an allowance can lead to negative results. For children to have their own money means they can use it when their parents are not with them.　★4 They will buy things which their parents would not want (→**want them to buy**). They will get involved in unexpected accidents such as trouble with other kids or even crime.

　　Last, there are more effective ways of teaching children how to use money. For example, if parents allow their children to use a reasonable amount of money on special occasions, it will give them a good opportunity to learn about how to use money.　★5 I hear that in western countries where the sense of independence is highly valued, parents often give money to their children as a reward for doing some work. In my view, it is a matter of course for children should (→**to**) take on some housework as **a** family member.

In conclusion, I disagree with the idea that children should be given an allowance from the time they are young. Although it is important for children to learn the value of money, giving an allowance will not help.

●構成と内容の改善ポイント

★1 トピックに対して反対であるという立場が，明確に示されていません。
→ 与えられたトピックに賛成なのか，反対なのかをはっきりと述べましょう。Introduction では，トピックに対する自分の立場を明示することが肝心です。その上で，トピックに関する一般論，自分の意見を支える理由を，状況に応じて簡潔に述べましょう。ここで特定の事柄について長々と述べる必要はありません。

★2 何を主張するために例を挙げているのかがわかりにくく，読みにくい印象を与えます。
→ 具体例を述べる時は，その具体例によって裏づけようとしている内容から先に述べると，主旨がより伝わりやすくなります。抽象→具体の順で述べるのが英文の基本と覚えましょう。ここでは，「幼い子供は賢くお金を使えるほど十分に成熟していない」という主張を述べてから，具体例や詳細説明を加えます。

★3 この段落では，自分の考えと幼い男の子の例が整理されないまま次々に述べられており，まとまりのない印象を与えます。また，この文の代名詞 he が離れたものを指しているため，何について話しているのかわかりにくくなっています。
→ ★2 で説明したように，段落内の構成に気をつけながら，代名詞が何を指すのか，読み手が一目でわかるように気を配りましょう。また，「自分だったら…」という最後の一文は，独りよがりな主張に捉えられてしまう可能性があります。ここでは，幼い男の子の例の総括として述べるほうが自然な流れになります。

★4 They will … 「彼らは～だろう」という記述が並んでいますが，各文の論理的なつながりが明確でないため，単なる文の羅列になってしまい説得力に欠けます。
→ 適切な接続表現や構文を使うと，論理の流れが読み手に伝わりやすくなり，説得力が増します。

★5 「子供にお金の使い方を教える，より効果的な方法がある」という段落のトピックから話題がそれています。
→ ここでは最初に示した理由を支える具体例や詳細を述べましょう。「特別な機会に妥当な額のお金を子供に与える」という例を挙げているので，この内容について詳細説明を加えるか具体例を示しましょう。あるいは，さらに別の方法を例示するのもよいでしょう。

《構成の改善例》

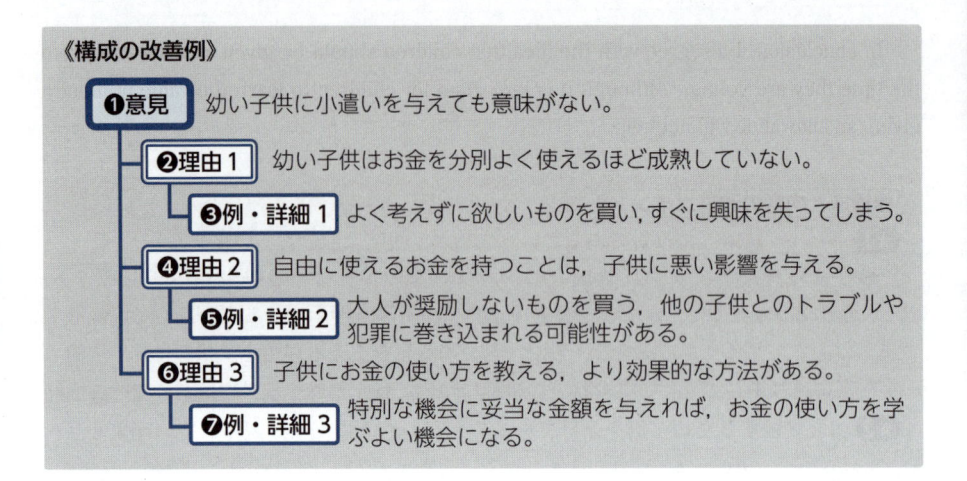

- ❶意見　幼い子供に小遣いを与えても意味がない。
  - ❷理由1　幼い子供はお金を分別よく使えるほど成熟していない。
    - ❸例・詳細1　よく考えずに欲しいものを買い、すぐに興味を失ってしまう。
  - ❹理由2　自由に使えるお金を持つことは、子供に悪い影響を与える。
    - ❺例・詳細2　大人が奨励しないものを買う、他の子供とのトラブルや犯罪に巻き込まれる可能性がある。
  - ❻理由3　子供にお金の使い方を教える、より効果的な方法がある。
    - ❼例・詳細3　特別な機会に妥当な金額を与えれば、お金の使い方を学ぶよい機会になる。

適切な解答例

Today, more and more parents seem to be getting interested in financial education. Some people give an allowance to their children expecting they will learn how to use money and its value from the time they are young. ★1**However, in my opinion, giving an allowance to their children from a very young age does not make sense.** There are three reasons for my opinion.

★2**The first reason is that young children are not mature enough to spend money sensibly.** When they have some money available, they will think they can buy whatever they want with it. They never think things through before buying. For example, a young boy given an allowance wants a toy and buys it immediately. ★3**As is common with little children, he soon loses interest in it. Thus he wastes his allowance. He doesn't even realize that he is wasting money. I don't think he learns the value of money in this situation.**

Second, giving children an allowance can lead to negative results. For children to have their own money means they can use it when their parents are not with them. ★4**In such cases, they might buy things adults would not encourage them to buy. Also there is the risk that they will become involved in unexpected accidents such as trouble with other children or even crime.**

Last of all, there are more effective ways of teaching children how to use money. For example, if parents allow their children to use a reasonable amount of money on a special occasion, it will give them a good opportunity to learn about how to use money. ★5**When I was in elementary school, my parents would give me a certain amount of money on New Year's Day. I was happy and bought things I had really wanted. I tried not to**

waste the money because it was such a special occasion for me.

In conclusion, I disagree with the idea that children should be given an allowance from the time they are young. Although it is important for children to learn the value of money, giving them an allowance will not help. (352 words)

（今日，ますます多くの親がお金の教育に興味を持っているように思われます。子供が小さい頃からお金の使い方やとその価値を学ぶことを期待して，小遣いを与える人もいます。しかし，私の意見では，とても幼い子供に小遣いを与えても意味がないでしょう。私の意見には３つの理由があります。

第１の意見は，幼い子供はお金を分別よく使えるほど成熟していないということです。彼らはいくらか自由にできるお金を持つと，それで何でも好きなものを買えると思うでしょう。何かを買う前によく考えることは決してしません。例えば，小遣いを与えられた幼い男の子がおもちゃを欲しいと思い，それを買います。小さい子供によくあることですが，彼はすぐにそのおもちゃへの興味を失います。こうして，その子は小遣いを無駄にします。自分がお金を無駄にしたことさえ，認識しません。私はこの状況で，彼がお金の価値を学ぶとは思いません。

第２に，小遣いを与えることはよくない結果をもたらす可能性があります。子供たちが自分のお金を持つということは，彼らが，親が一緒にいない時にお金を使えるということを意味します。その場合，彼らは大人が子供に買うことを奨励しないものを買うかもしれません。また，他の子供とのトラブルや，さらには犯罪などの予期しない事件に巻き込まれる恐れもあります。

最後に，子供にお金の使い方を教える，より効果的な方法があります。例えば，親が子供に特別な機会に妥当な額のお金を使うことを許せば，子供がお金の使い方を学ぶよい機会になります。私が小学生の時，両親は元日にある額のお金をくれました。私はうれしくて，本当に欲しかったものを買いました。それは私にとってとても特別な機会だったので，そのお金を無駄遣いしないようにしたのです。

結論として，私は小遣いを子供が幼い時から与えるべきだという考えに反対です。子供がお金の価値を学ぶことは重要ですが，小遣いを与えることは，役に立たないでしょう。）

別解　「子供たちは幼い頃から小遣いを与えられるべきである」に賛成の場合

Children need to learn all kinds of things as they grow. They need to develop language and motor skills, acquire knowledge of how to live in society, and gain a sense of ethical behavior. It is also necessary to learn what money is and how to use it responsibly. Therefore, I think it is good for children to earn an allowance from a young age.

First, getting an allowance will help children appreciate what they have and learn the value of things. One of the first things children must learn is what is theirs and what belongs to another person. This is the first step toward an understanding of the value that people attach to objects. And with an allowance, children can learn the value of money itself, along with the value of the things they buy with that money.

Second, it will teach them how to spend money wisely. If children get a little money every week, they can plan out their purchases, and look forward to getting something they have saved their money for. Of course, it is best if children get only a limited allowance. If they get too much, they may think money will always be easily available, or they may spend it all at once and waste it on something they don't really need.

Finally, it can teach children the value of work. This is possible if the allowance is tied to chores or jobs around the house. This work and the money that comes with it can teach children a lot about the importance of work and how people live in society.

When children make the change from living with their parents to living on their own, they will face the challenge of earning enough money at a job to support themselves. Knowing the value of money and how to use it responsibly early in life would help them immensely. (316 words)

（子供は成長するにつれて，あらゆる種類のことを学ぶ必要があります。言語や運動神経の能力を発達させ，社会生活の仕方についての知識を習得し，道徳的な行動の意識を身につける必要があります。そして，お金とは何かということと，お金を責任を持って使う方法を学ぶことも必要です。したがって，私は子供が幼い時から小遣いを得ることはよいと思います。

第1に，小遣いを得ることで，子供は自分が持っているもののありがたみがわかり，ものの価値を学ぶようになります。子供が最初に学ばなければならないことの1つは，何が自分のもので何が他人のものかということです。これは人がものに付与する価値を理解することへの第一歩です。小遣いによって子供たちは，お金そのものの価値を，そのお金で買うものの価値と同時に学ぶことができます。

第2に，小遣いを得ることは子供にお金の賢い使い方を教えます。もし子供が毎週少しずつお金をもらったら，彼らは買うものについて計画を立て，そのために貯めたお金でものを買うのを楽しみにするでしょう。もちろん，子供は限られた金額だけのお金をもらうのがベストです。もし多くもらいすぎたら，彼らは，お金は常に簡単に手に入ると思うかもしれません。あるいは，一度に全部を使い，本当は必要のないものに無駄遣いをするかもしれません。

最後に，小遣いを得ることは，子供に働くことの価値を教えます。これは小遣いが，家事や家のまわりの仕事と結びついている時に可能になります。こうした仕事やそれにより得られるお金は，子供に仕事の重要性や，人が社会の中でどうやって生活しているかについて多くのことを教えます。

子供は親との生活から1人暮らしに変わる時，自分の生活を支えるために仕事に就き，十分なお金を稼ぐという課題に直面するでしょう。お金の価値とそれを責任を持って使う方法を人生の早いうちに知っていることは，彼らをおおいに助けるでしょう。）

●解答の構成

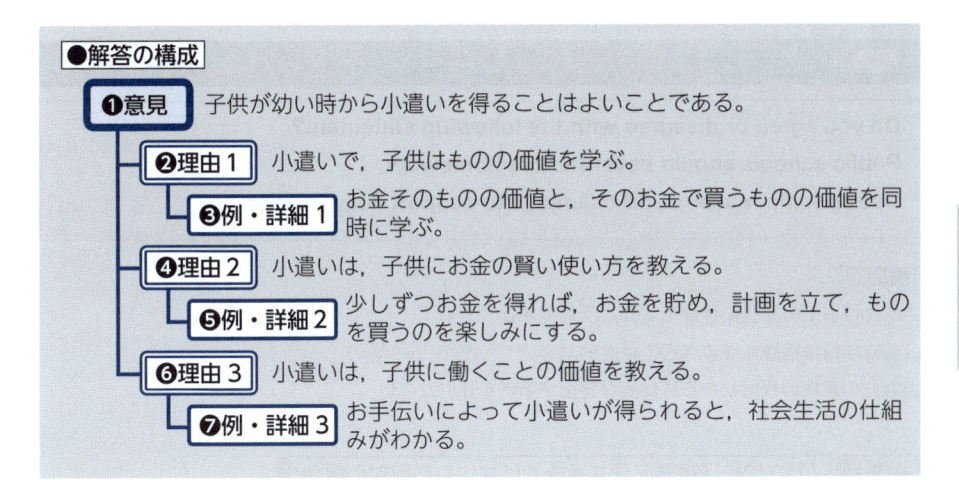

- **❶意見** 子供が幼い時から小遣いを得ることはよいことである。
  - **❷理由1** 小遣いで、子供はものの価値を学ぶ。
    - **❸例・詳細1** お金そのものの価値と、そのお金で買うものの価値を同時に学ぶ。
  - **❹理由2** 小遣いは、子供にお金の賢い使い方を教える。
    - **❺例・詳細2** 少しずつお金を得れば、お金を貯め、計画を立て、ものを買うのを楽しみにする。
  - **❻理由3** 小遣いは、子供に働くことの価値を教える。
    - **❼例・詳細3** お手伝いによって小遣いが得られると、社会生活の仕組みがわかる。

✓重要表現チェック

不十分な解答例
- □ allowance「小遣い」   □ sensibly「分別よく」
- □ be bored with 〜「〜に飽きる」
- □ get involved in 〜「〜に巻き込まれる」
- □ reasonable「妥当な、相応な」
- □ occasion「時、場合」
- □ independence「自立」   □ a matter of course「当然のこと」

適切な解答例
- □ as is common with 〜「〜には普通にあることだが」

別解
- □ ethical「道徳上の」   □ immensely「非常に」

問題 4

Do you agree or disagree with the following statement?
Public schools should never require homework.
Use specific reasons and examples to support your answer.

【設問訳】
あなたは以下の主張に賛成ですか，反対ですか。
「公立学校は宿題を課すべきではない。」
あなたの意見の根拠となる具体的な理由や事例を述べなさい。

解答例 「公立学校は宿題を課すべきではない」に反対の場合

不十分な解答例

　I disagree with the statement. A(→不要) homework is a necessary part of education, because there is simply not enough classroom time to teach everything. ★1 This is partly because Saturday is a whole holiday in many public schools.

　★2 First, homework is useful for teachers who have a very limited amount of time to cover a wide variety of subjects. Students can prepare for lessons before class and review materials after class. Homeworks are (→**Homework is**) helpful especially when teachers run out of time.

　★3 Second, the students' academic levels vary greatly especially in public schools. Nevertheless teachers have limited options for addressing this issue. In contrast, private schools can develop their own teaching methods. For example, some students understand classes and concepts quicker (→**more quickly**) than others. Teachers need to continually stimulate higher-level students' minds without confusing lower-level students. By (→**With**) homework, all students can keep up with the class according to their own learning speed. For example, an assignment that takes thirty minutes for a higher-level student might take over an hour for a lower-level student. In a classroom, this type of time difference causes problems, but it is not an issue when the assignment is given as a(→不要) homework.

　Finally, a (→不要) homework teaches students responsibility. ★4 As an elementary school student, I didn't study at home when the teacher didn't assign homework. At the same time, I was expected to always get good grades at school by my parents. Later, I knew that it was fortunate that my teacher assigned lots of homework. Otherwise, I would have never studied at home. In this way, a (→不要) homework is **a** useful tool for teaching students about responsibility.

For these reasons, I disagree with the opinion that public schools should never require homework. I believe that homework is an essential teaching way (→**tool**), and it helps students to learn quicker (→**more quickly**) and efficiently.

●構成と内容の改善ポイント

★1 全体の方向性を示すべき Introduction で，特定の理由について詳しく述べてしまっています。また，「多くの公立学校では土曜日は丸1日休みである」という事実が，第2段落以降で詳しく意見を述べていく上でどのような役割を持つのかが不明です。
　➡ Introduction は，エッセイ全体の方向性を示すことを意識して書きましょう。意見に対する理由を述べる場合は，それぞれの要点を簡潔に示します。ここに時間をかけすぎて，Body にかける時間が不足しないように注意しましょう。

★2 第2段落のそれぞれの文の間に，論理的つながりが見えません。またどの文も内容の説明が十分でないため，説得力に欠けます。
　➡「宿題によって，生徒が授業の前後に予習・復習できる」ということが，なぜ「時間が足りない教師にとって有益である」のか，因果関係が読み手にわかるように説明を加えましょう。指示語や接続表現を効果的に使い，全体が論理的につながるようにまとめます。

★3 第2段落に対して第3段落の分量が多く，全体のバランスが悪くなっています。また，第1〜3文で公立学校と私立学校の違いについて述べていますが，For example 以降はこの比較に言及せず，生徒の習得の速度の違いに対処するための宿題の効用のみに焦点を当てており，文章の流れに一貫性がなくなっています。
　➡ここでは「宿題は生徒がそれぞれのペースで進めることができる」という特徴が最も重要ですので，公立学校と私立学校の違いについては必要ない情報と判断できます。段落の主旨を伝えるために必要な情報に絞って，文章を展開しましょう。

★4 「先生が宿題を出さなければ家で勉強しなかった」という具体例は，「宿題が責任感を育てる」というトピックを支える根拠になりません。
　➡「宿題」と「責任感」を結び付ける説得力のある具体例を挙げます。その段落で伝えるべきポイントからそれないように，論理のつながりをチェックしましょう。

《構成の改善例》

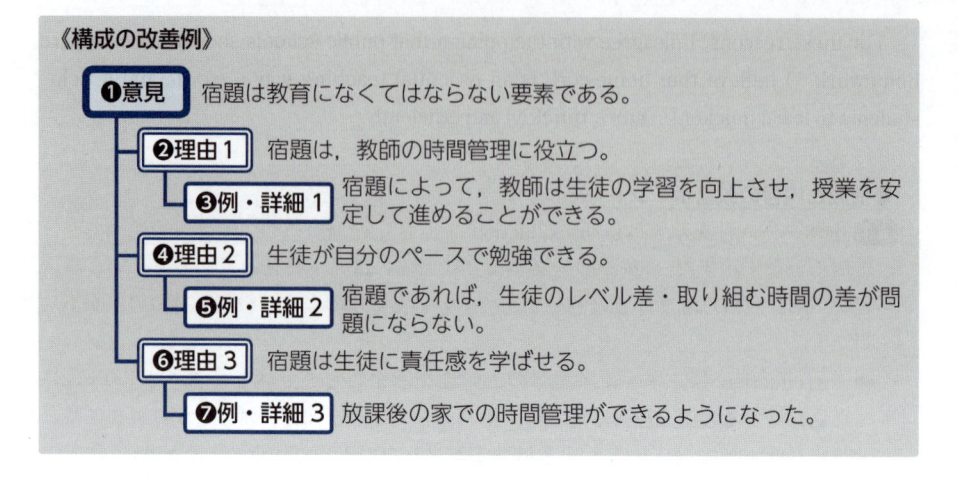

- **❶意見** 宿題は教育になくてはならない要素である。
  - **❷理由1** 宿題は，教師の時間管理に役立つ。
    - **❸例・詳細1** 宿題によって，教師は生徒の学習を向上させ，授業を安定して進めることができる。
  - **❹理由2** 生徒が自分のペースで勉強できる。
    - **❺例・詳細2** 宿題であれば，生徒のレベル差・取り組む時間の差が問題にならない。
  - **❻理由3** 宿題は生徒に責任感を学ばせる。
    - **❼例・詳細3** 放課後の家での時間管理ができるようになった。

適切な解答例

I disagree with the statement. Homework is a necessary part of education, because it is helpful for time management. In addition, ★1 it allows students to learn at their own paces and to develop a sense of responsibility.

First, ★2 homework is useful, because it helps teachers with time management. Teachers have a very limited amount of time to cover a wide variety of subjects. By giving homework, they can let students prepare for lessons before class and review materials after class. This increases students' understanding and learning overall. Also, sometimes teachers run out of time when teaching in class. Using homework, they can ensure that the class is moving forward steadily.

Second, ★3 homework allows students to learn at a comfortable pace. Some students understand classes and concepts more quickly than others. Teachers need to continually stimulate higher-level students' minds without confusing lower-level students. With homework, all students can keep up with the class according to their own learning speed. For example, an assignment that takes thirty minutes for a higher-level student might take over an hour for a lower-level student. In a classroom, this type of time difference causes problems, but it is not an issue when the assignment is given as homework.

Finally, homework teaches students responsibility. When I was in elementary school, ★4 my parents never asked me if I had done my homework. At the same time, I was expected to always get good grades at school. As a result, I knew that I had to give my homework priority, and I learned to manage my time at home after school. In this way, homework is a useful tool for teaching students about responsibility.

For these reasons, I disagree with the opinion that public schools should never require homework. I believe that homework is an essential teaching tool, and it helps students to learn more quickly and efficiently. (309 words)

（私は，この主張には反対です。宿題は時間管理の面で有効なため，教育になくてはならない要素です。それに，宿題のおかげで，生徒たちは自分のペースで勉強をすることができ，さらに責任感を育むことができます。

第1に，宿題は教師の時間管理に役立つという点で有益です。教師には，幅広い教科を教えるのにごく限られた時間しかありません。宿題を与えることで，教師は生徒に，授業前の予習と，授業後の教材の復習をさせることができます。これにより，全体として，生徒の理解と学習が向上します。また，教師は授業で時間がなくなってしまうことがあります。宿題を活用することで，教師は確実に授業を安定して進めていくことができます。

第2に，宿題のおかげで，生徒たちは快適なペースで学んでいくことができます。他の生徒よりも速く授業や概念を理解する生徒もいます。教師は，常にレベルの低い生徒を混乱させることなく，レベルの高い生徒の意識を刺激し続ける必要があります。宿題があれば，すべての生徒がそれぞれの学習スピードで授業についてくることができるのです。例えば，レベルの高い生徒には30分でできる宿題が，レベルの低い生徒には1時間以上かかるかもしれません。授業中は，このような時間の差が問題になりますが，課題が宿題として与えられていれば，これは問題にはなりません。

最後に，宿題は生徒に責任感を学ばせます。私が小学生だった時，両親は私に宿題をやったかどうか聞くことは一度もありませんでした。同時に，私は学校でいつもよい成績を取ることを期待されていました。その結果，私は宿題を優先しなければならないことを悟り，放課後の家での時間を管理できるようになりました。このように，宿題は生徒に責任感を学ばせる有益なツールとなります。

以上の理由から，私は，公立学校は宿題を課すべきでないという意見に反対です。宿題は重要な教育ツールであり，生徒がより速く効率的に学ぶのに役立つと思います。）

別解　「公立学校は宿題を課すべきではない」に賛成の場合

  I agree with the statement. Homework might seem like a necessary addition to every classroom, but in reality it does not improve education very much. Rather, it takes away time from other important activities.

  When children have to do homework, they have less time to play sports, relax, and have fun with their friends. For example, when I was in elementary school, I loved playing basketball with my friends after school. As I got older, though, my teachers started assigning more homework, and I did not have as much free time. Eventually I stopped playing basketball completely, and now I am less active and healthy than I used to be.

  In addition, because children have more free time without homework, parents can have them study things that are not covered in school. For example, if I have children, I want them to speak many languages when they grow up. For this reason, I would like to have them take language lessons after school. If they have a lot of homework, though, then I am worried that this extra burden might be too much for them. Without homework, I can have them study a number of different subjects that I think are valuable and rewarding.

Lastly, although this is not true of all teachers, there are many teachers that assign homework only so that they can grade students more easily. Ideally, homework should be used to increase students' knowledge of various school topics. That said, I can remember many homework assignments from my childhood that felt were meaningless. This type of homework is actually a waste of time, and it does little to improve education.

To summarize, I think that homework is an outdated concept that does not necessarily produce positive results. By removing homework from schools we could enable children to improve themselves in a variety of interesting ways and make learning more rewarding.

(314 words)

(私は，この主張に賛成です。宿題は各授業に必要な追加の学習のように思えるかもしれませんが，実際には，教育をそれほどよくはしていません。むしろ，他の大切な活動の時間を奪います。

宿題をしなければならない場合，子供たちがスポーツをしたり，くつろいだり，友達と楽しんだりする時間は少なくなります。例えば，私は小学生の頃，放課後友達とバスケットボールをするのが大好きでした。しかし学年が上がるにつれて，先生は宿題を多く出し始め，私はこれまでと同じような自由な時間が持てなくなりました。結局，私はバスケットボールをやめてしまい，今では以前よりも活動的でなくなり，健康的ではなくなってしまいました。

さらに，宿題がなくなり，子供がより多く自由な時間を持つことで，親は子供に，学校では扱われないことを学ばせることができます。例えば，もし私に子供ができたら，大人になった時にたくさんの言語を話せるようになってほしいと思います。ですので，私は放課後に，自分の子供を語学のレッスンに通わせたいです。でも，もし宿題がたくさんあったら，このさらなる負担は子供たちにとって重すぎるかもしれないと心配です。宿題がなければ，自分が価値があり有意義だと思うさまざまな科目を子供たちに学ばせることができます。

最後に，すべての教師に当てはまることではありませんが，生徒の評価を簡単にするためだけに宿題を出す教師がたくさんいます。理想的には，宿題は生徒がさまざまな教科の知識を増やすのに使われるべきです。とは言っても，私が思い出せるのは，子供の頃無意味だと思えたたくさんの宿題ばかりです。このような宿題は，実際には時間の無駄で，教育の向上にはほとんど役に立ちません。

つまり，宿題は必ずしも好ましい効果を生むことのない時代遅れの概念だと私は思います。学校からの宿題をなくすことで，私たちは子供たちがさまざまな興味深い方向へ成長できるようにし，学習をもっと有意義にすることができるかもしれません。)

●解答の構成

- **❶意見**　宿題は，必ずしも教育をよくしていない。
  - **❷理由1**　宿題は，子供がスポーツや遊びをする時間を奪う。
    - **❸例・詳細1**　宿題をするためにバスケットボールをやめ，以前より活発でなくなった。
  - **❹理由2**　宿題がなければ，子供に学校では学べない有意義なことを学ばせることができる。
    - **❺例・詳細2**　自分の子供には，放課後に語学のレッスンを受けさせたい。
  - **❻理由3**　成績をつけやすくするためだけに宿題を出す教師もいる。
    - **❼例・詳細3**　無意味な宿題も多く，単に時間の無駄で，教育の向上には役立たない。

✓ 重要表現チェック

不十分な解答例
- □ material「教材，資料」
- □ run out of ～「～を使い果たす」
- □ stimulate「～を刺激する」
- □ keep up with ～「～に遅れずについていく」
- □ assignment「宿題，割り当て」

適切な解答例
- □ ensure「～を確実にする」
- □ steadily「着実に」
- □ priority「優先」
- □ manage「～を管理する」
- □ essential「不可欠の」

別解
- □ addition「追加」
- □ eventually「結局は」
- □ grade「～に成績をつける」
- □ that said「とは言っても」
- □ to summarize「手短に述べると」
- □ outdated「時代遅れの」

問題 5

Do you agree or disagree with the following statement?
Adults should never lie to children.
Use specific reasons and examples to support your answer.

【設問訳】
あなたは以下の主張に賛成ですか，反対ですか。
「大人は子供に決して嘘をつくべきではない。」
あなたの意見の根拠となる具体的な理由や事例を述べなさい。

解答例 「大人は子供に決して嘘をつくべきではない」に賛成の場合

不十分な解答例

  I agree that adults should never lie to children. Like adults, children do not like being told lies. Also, adults can **be** honest with children without telling them everything. Finally, adults can only teach children to be honest by being honest themselves.

  First, children appreciate honesty. I think that many adults do not fully recognize children's ability to understand when someone is lying to them. ★1 I still remember when I was told a lie by adults when I was still little. One time it happened on the train when I asked a question to my aunt. I didn't feel like respecting her when I understood she was lying to me.

  Second, adults can avoid sensitive topics and language without lying directly. ★2 Using the example above, my aunt could have told something different without lying. Instead, she chose to lie to me, which was totally unnecessary. Because adults can withhold information without lying, there is no good excuse **for** lying to children.

  Finally, adults should be good examples for children. As children grow up, adults repeatedly tell them that they must not lie, but then many of those adults lie to those children themselves. Actions teach children more than words do, and children **are** highly aware of the behavior of adults around them. ★3 It is true that there are many situations where you don't want to tell the truth to children. Even in such situations, there is always the option of honestly telling them that they have to keep certain information a secret.

  In conclusion, I can find no good reason for an adult to lie to a child. ★4 When there is something that they cannot tell the child, use this type of honest approach. Then adults can get more respect from children and also **be** models of good behavior that they should follow.

●構成と内容の改善ポイント

★1 「おばに嘘をつかれた」という経験を挙げていますが，どのような場面でどのような嘘をつかれたのかという部分の具体的な説明が不足しており，主張を支える根拠としての説得力に欠けます。
➡ その状況についての最低限必要な情報と，そこで何を感じたのかをまとめて述べましょう。具体例を述べる際は，そこからどのような主張を導きたいのかを意識し，読み手にその例を挙げた意図が伝わるように説明しましょう。

★2 嘘をつく以外に方法があるというこの段落の主張に対し，ただ「嘘をつかずに何か違うことを言うこともできた」と述べるだけでは漠然としており，理由のサポートになっていません。
➡ おばはその時どうするべきだったのかについて，具体的な方法を述べましょう。詳細情報を述べる際は，常に直前の文よりも一歩踏み込んだ説明になるよう心がけましょう。

★3 「情報を秘密にしておかなければならないと正直に告げることができる」という内容は，第3段落で扱った2つ目の理由に関する記述です。この段落では「大人は子供の模範であるべきだ」という3つ目の理由について述べており，段落のトピックからそれているため，読み手が混乱する可能性があります。
➡ この部分を前の段落に組み込むか，適切な解答例にあるように，結論でまとめとして述べましょう。1段落1トピックが英文ライティングの原則です。

★4 this type of honest approach が何を指すのかがあいまいです。
➡ 「嘘をつくことなく，言いたくないことを差し控えるというアプローチ」と簡潔に述べることで，これまで述べてきた主張を再確認し，結論の説得力を高めることができます。

《構成の改善例》

- ❶意見　大人は子供に決して嘘をつくべきではない。
  - ❷理由1　子供は嘘が嫌いであり，大人がついた嘘に気づいている。
    - ❸例・詳細1　おばが嘘をついたことで，尊敬の気持ちを失った。
  - ❹理由2　嘘をつくことなく，微妙な話題や言葉を避けることができる。
    - ❺例・詳細2　秘密にしておかなければならないと正直に伝える方法がある。
  - ❻理由3　大人は子供のよい手本であるべきである。
    - ❼例・詳細3　嘘をついてはならないと子供に教える大人自身が嘘をついてしまっている。

適切な解答例

I agree that adults should never lie to children. Like adults, children do not like being told lies. Also, adults can be honest with children without telling them everything. Finally, adults can only teach children to be honest by being honest themselves.

First, children appreciate honesty. I think that many adults do not fully recognize children's ability to understand when someone is lying to them. ★1**I remember one time when I was still little, and I asked my aunt what a bad word meant, because I had heard it while I was on the train. I forget what she told me exactly, but I remember instantly understanding that she was lying to me, and I lost respect for her.**

Second, adults can avoid sensitive topics and language without lying directly. ★2**Using the example above, my aunt could have simply told me that it was a bad word, and that I should not say it.** Instead, she chose to lie to me, which was totally unnecessary. Because adults can withhold information without lying, there is no good excuse for lying to children.

Finally, adults should be good examples for children. As children grow up, adults repeatedly tell them that they must not lie, but then many of those adults lie to those children themselves. Actions teach children more than words do, and children are highly aware of the behavior of adults around them.

In conclusion, I can find no good reason for an adult to lie to a child. ★3 ★4**Even if there is something that they cannot tell the child, then there is always the option of honestly telling them that they have to keep certain information a secret.** Using this type of honest approach, adults can get more respect from children and also be models of good behavior that they should follow. (302 words)

（私は、大人は子供に決して嘘をつくべきではないと思います。大人と同じで、子供は嘘をつかれるのが嫌いです。また大人は、すべてを伝えずとも、子供に正直であることができます。最後に、大人は自分が正直であることによってのみ、子供たちに正直になることを教えることができるのです。

第1に、子供は正直であることがよいことだとわかっています。誰かが自分に嘘をついていると気づく子供の力を、多くの大人は完全には認識していないと思います。かつて、まだ私が小さかった頃、電車に乗っている時にある悪い言葉を聞き、それがどういう意味なのか、おばに尋ねました。おばが私に何と言ったか正確には覚えていませんが、私に嘘をついていることはすぐにわかったのを覚えています。私はおばへの尊敬の気持ちを失いました。

第2に、大人は直接的に嘘をつくことなく、微妙な話題や言葉を避けることができます。前述の例で言えば、おばは私にただ、それが悪い言葉であり、言ってはいけないと言うこともできました。おばはそうせずに、私に嘘をつくことを選びましたが、それはまったく不必要なことでした。

大人は，嘘をつかずに情報を出さないでおくこともできるのですから，子供に嘘をつく正当な言い訳はないのです。

　最後に，大人は子供のよい手本であるべきです。子供が成長する間，大人は繰り返し，嘘をついてはいけないと教えますが，こうした大人の多くが子供たちに嘘をついています。言葉よりも行動のほうが子供に多くのことを教え，子供はまわりの大人たちの行動がよくわかっています。

　結論として，大人が子供に嘘をつく正当な理由は見つかりません。子供に言えないことがあるとしても，特定の情報を秘密にしておかなければならないと正直に子供に伝える選択肢は常に存在します。このような正直なアプローチをとることで，大人は，子供の敬意を得ることができ，子供が見習うべきよい行いの手本になることもできるのです。）

別解 「大人は子供に決して嘘をつくべきではない」に反対の場合

　I disagree with the statement. I agree that lying is a bad thing, but sometimes lying to children cannot be avoided, as it is necessary to protect them from sensitive information. The purpose of lies can then be explained to children later, when they are older.

　In general, adults do not lie to children for selfish reasons. In almost all cases, adults lie to children to preserve their innocence. Childhood is a delicate time that ends far too quickly, and lying is a tool for making it longer. I remember when I was only five years old, I asked my parents if Santa Claus was real, and they told me that he was not. I was so disappointed, because I actually believed that he existed. Even now, I wish that they had lied to me then, because I would have enjoyed Christmas so much more.

　Also, most lies that adults tell children can be explained later, once they become more mature. If my parents had explained to me that Santa Claus was not real a few years later, I am sure that I would have understood that they were trying to make me happy by lying to me. When adults explain past lies to children as they grow up, it shows the children respect, and it acknowledges that they are becoming adults, which makes them feel good.

　Finally, lying to children is often necessary when talking to other parents' children. Imagine that a child's dog died, but her parents told her that her dog went to visit his family. If the child tells her teacher about this, then asks when the dog will be home, the teacher should probably tell a lie. If not, the child's parents might be angry at the teacher.

　Although it is nice to imagine a world without lying, sometimes it is necessary. In particular, adults often need to lie to children in order to protect their innocence. Also, once children get older, adults can explain their reasons for lying to them. (336 words)

（私は，この主張に反対です。嘘をつくのが悪いことだということには同意しますが，扱いの難しい情報から子供を守る必要があって，子供に嘘をつくことが避けられない場合もあります。嘘をついた理由については，後になって，子供たちが大きくなった時に，子供たちに説明することができます。

概して，大人は自己中心的な理由では子供に嘘をつきません。ほとんどすべての場合，大人が子供に嘘をつくのは，子供の純真さを保つためです。子供時代というのは，あまりにも急速に終わってしまう繊細な時期であり，嘘をつくことは，この期間を長くする手段です。私がまだ5歳だった時，両親にサンタクロースが実在するのかどうかを尋ねると，両親はサンタクロースは実在しないと言ったのを覚えています。私は実は，サンタクロースがいると信じていたので，とてもがっかりしました。今でも，両親があの時，私に嘘をついてくれていたらと思います。そのほうがクリスマスをもっと楽しめただろうと思うからです。

　また，大人が子供につくほとんどの嘘は，後になって，子供が成長したら説明することができます。もし，両親がサンタクロースは実在しないのだと何年か後に説明してくれていたら，私はきっと，両親が嘘をつくことで私を喜ばせようとしていたのだと理解しただろうと思います。子供が成長してから，大人が過去の嘘を説明すれば，それは子供に敬意を示すことになります。また，それは子供が成長して大人になっていることを認めてのことであり，子供たちをよい気分にします。

　最後に，他の親の子と話す時は，子供に嘘をつくことが必要なことが少なからずあります。ある子供の飼い犬が死んでしまい，彼女の両親が，その犬は家族に会いに行ったんだよと彼女に話していたと想像してみてください。もし，その子が先生にこの話をして，いつ犬が家に帰ってくるかと尋ねたとしたら，先生はたぶん嘘をついたほうがよいでしょう。そうでなければ，その子の両親が先生に腹を立てるかもしれません。

　嘘のない世界を思い描くのはよいことですが，時には嘘も必要です。特に，大人は子供の純真さを守るために，子供に嘘をつく必要があることがよくあります。また，子供が大きくなったら，大人は彼らに嘘をついた理由を説明することができるのです。）

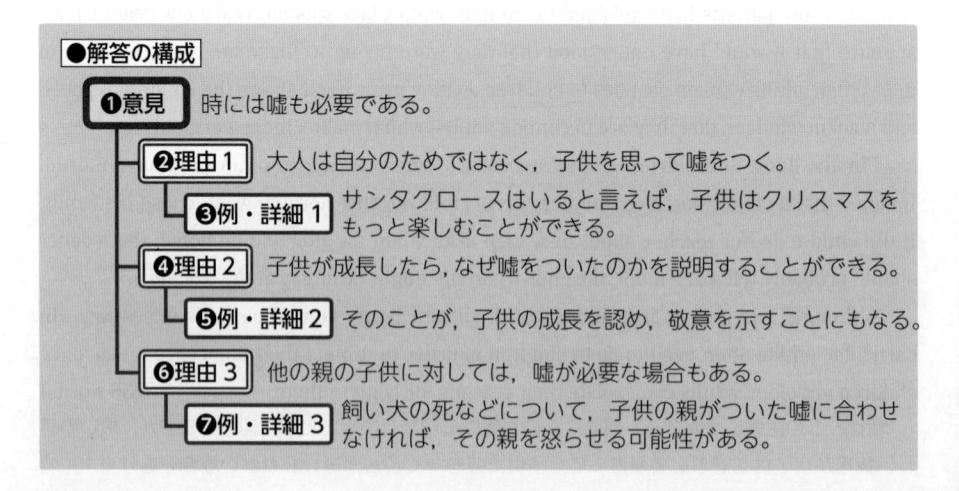

●解答の構成

- ❶意見　時には嘘も必要である。
  - ❷理由1　大人は自分のためではなく，子供を思って嘘をつく。
    - ❸例・詳細1　サンタクロースはいると言えば，子供はクリスマスをもっと楽しむことができる。
  - ❹理由2　子供が成長したら，なぜ嘘をついたのかを説明することができる。
    - ❺例・詳細2　そのことが，子供の成長を認め，敬意を示すことにもなる。
  - ❻理由3　他の親の子供に対しては，嘘が必要な場合もある。
    - ❼例・詳細3　飼い犬の死などについて，子供の親がついた嘘に合わせなければ，その親を怒らせる可能性がある。

✅ 重要表現チェック

不十分な解答例
- □ sensitive「慎重に扱うべき」
- □ withhold「〜を差し控える，〜を与えずにおく」
- □ there is no excuse for 〜「〜に言い訳のしようがない」
- □ repeatedly「繰り返して，何度も何度も」
- □ option「選択肢」　　　□ model「手本，模範」

別解
- □ preserve「〜を保つ」　　□ innocence「純真さ」
- □ delicate「繊細な」　　□ Santa Claus「サンタクロース」
- □ acknowledge「〜を認める」　□ in particular「特に」

問題 6

Do you agree or disagree with the following statement?
Making friends through the Internet is too risky.
Use specific reasons and examples to support your answer.

【設問訳】
あなたは以下の主張に賛成ですか，反対ですか。
「インターネットを通じて友人を作るのは危険が大きすぎる。」
あなたの意見の根拠となる具体的な理由や事例を述べなさい。

解答例 「インターネットを通じて友人を作るのは危険が大きすぎる」に反対の場合

不十分な解答例

　　In the modern world, it appears that the Internet has **become** accepted as a tool for making friends. In my opinion, as far (→**long**) as you are aware that there are some dangers involved in making friends through the Internet, it is not too risky. ★1 To ensure safety, however, I recommend making some rules. I will explain them.

　　First of all, the Internet is no more than a first step to making friends. ★2 The point is the same thing may happen in the real world. When you meet a person for the first time, you don't know anything about him or her. As you gradually learn who (→**what**) he or she is like, a (→不要) friendship deepens. You may follow the same process when you make friends through the Internet. It takes time to develop a friendship.

　　Second, you can avoid most trouble if you behave properly. Children, teens and their parents now face the risk of being involved in deadly serious trouble which no one never (→**ever**) imagined decades ago. ★3 It is essential for you to use your brain, behave in an acceptable manner and find ways not to hurt someone or not to get hurt by someone. In short, there is no problem if you don't do what you wouldn't do in the real world.

　　Finally, the Internet can be a good tool for meeting people if you use it wisely. For example, when it is difficult for you to find friends to share your interests, such as viewing operas, climbing mountains, stargazing, it is great to find it (→**one**) through a trustworthy website. The Internet has now become an essential part of our daily life. Not a little (→**few**) young people are already making friends online. ★4 We need to take measures against this issue.

　　In conclusion, as far (→**long**) as you are well prepared for the risks, it is not too risky to make friends on the internet.

●構成と内容の改善ポイント

★1 論点が,「インターネットで友人を作るのは危険が大きすぎるかどうか」ではなく「安全を保証するためのルールを説明する」ことに変わってしまっています。
  ➡ これから展開するのはあくまで「インターネットで友人を作るのは危険すぎるという意見には反対である」という議論です。ここでは,「インターネットは適切に使えばよいツールとなる」というエッセイ全体に共通する立場を示しましょう。」

★2「現実世界でも同じことが起こるかもしれない」と述べていますが,何と何が「同じ」なのかがわかりにくくなっています。
  ➡「同じこと」とはどのようなことかを具体的に示して説明します。読み手が文の意図を読み取るのに類推を必要とするような漠然とした表現は避けます。

★3 前の文の内容との論理的なつながりが見えないため,説得力に欠けます。
  ➡ 適切な接続語句を用いて,前の文で述べたインターネットの危険性に対処するための方法を述べていることを明確にしましょう。

★4 ネット上で友人を作る若者がいることに「対処する必要がある」と述べていますが,これは自分と反対の立場をサポートすることになり得る内容です。
  ➡ インターネットで友人を作ることに問題があることを認めるとしても,危険すぎるという考え方には反対であるという立場はぶれないようにします。具体例を展開しているうちに自分の立場が曖昧にならないようにしましょう。

《構成の改善例》

- **❶意見** インターネットは,その危険性を認識している限り,危険すぎるということはない。
  - **❷理由1** インターネットは友人を作る第一歩にすぎない。
    - **❸例・詳細1** 友情を深めるのに時間がかかるのは,現実世界で友人を作るのと同様である。
  - **❹理由2** 適切に振舞えば,ほとんどのトラブルを回避できる。
    - **❺例・詳細2** 現実世界ではしないであろうことをしなければ問題はない。
  - **❻理由3** 賢く使えば人々と出会うのによいツールとなる。
    - **❼例・詳細3** 趣味を共有できる友人を探すのが難しい時,ウェブサイトを通じて見つけることがてきる。

適切な解答例

In the modern world, it appears that the Internet has become accepted as a tool for making friends. In my opinion, it is not too risky as long as you are aware of its dangers. ★1 **Rather, it is a good tool if you use it properly.**

First of all, the Internet is no more than a first step to making friends. ★2 **The point is you may be taking similar steps whether you make friends with someone through the Internet or in the real world.** When you meet a person for the first time, you don't know anything about him or her. As you gradually learn what he or she is like, friendship deepens. You may follow the same process when you make friends through the Internet. It takes time to develop a friendship.

Second, you can avoid most trouble if you behave properly. Children, teens and their parents now face the risk of being involved in deadly serious trouble which no one ever imagined decades ago. ★3 **However, if you behave in an acceptable manner, you will find ways not to hurt other people or not to get hurt.** In short, there is no problem if you don't do what you wouldn't do in the real world.

Finally, the Internet can be a good tool for meeting people if you use it wisely. For example, when it is difficult for you to find friends to share your interests, such as watching operas, climbing mountains or stargazing, it is great to find one through a trustworthy website. The Internet has now become an essential part of our daily life. Not a few young people are already making friends online. ★4 **It doesn't seem sensible to ignore the fact just because it seems too risky.**

In conclusion, as long as you are well prepared for the risks, it is not too risky to make friends on the Internet. (312 words)

（現代社会において，インターネットは友人を作る手段として受け入れられるようになったように見えます。私の意見では，その危険性を認識している限り，危険すぎるということはありません。むしろそれは，適切に使えばよいツールとなります。

まず第1に，インターネットは友人作りの第一歩にすぎません。要は，インターネットで友人を作ろうと，現実世界で友人を作ろうと，同じ手順を踏んでいるかもしれないということです。初めて人に会う時，その人について何も知りません。その人がどんな人であるかを徐々に知るにつれ，友情が深まります。インターネットで友人を作る時にも同じプロセスを経験するでしょう。友情を発展させるのには時間がかかるのです。

第2に，適切に振舞えば，ほとんどのトラブルを回避することができます。子供，10代の若者，そしてその親は今，数十年前には誰も想像しなかったひどく深刻なトラブルに巻き込まれる危険性に直面しています。しかし，好ましい態度で振舞えば，誰かを傷つけたり，傷つけられたりしない方法を見つけることができるでしょう。要するに，現実世界でしないであろうことをしなけ

れば，何も問題はありません。

　最後にインターネットは賢く使えば人々と出会うのによいツールとなり得ます。例えばオペラ鑑賞，登山，天体観測のような趣味を共有する友人を探すのが難しい時，信頼できるウェブサイトを通じて友人を見つけられるのは素晴らしいことです。インターネットは今，私たちの日常生活に欠かせないものとなっています。多くの若い人たちがすでにオンラインで友人を作っています。この事実をただ危険すぎるようだからと無視するのは賢明には思えません。

　結論として，リスクに対する備えが十分であれば，インターネットで友人を作るのは危険が大きすぎることはありません。）

別解 「インターネットを通じて友人を作るのは危険が大きすぎる」に賛成の場合

　It can be great to find other people online who share our interests. However, people should be aware that there are many risks involved in looking for friends on the Internet. Therefore, I agree with the topic statement.

　First, many people do not tell the truth about themselves on the Internet. Even if they provide a photograph and some biographical information, it may not be correct. They may be trying to remain anonymous, or they may be taking on an entirely different identity to fool people. There is no way to make sure that they have not hidden some information about themselves.

　Second, many people may go onto the Internet with a dishonest purpose. Sometimes, they want to get money illegally from people. Others are looking for personal contacts that might be dangerous. People get involved in trouble when they meet people through the Internet. You may meet someone who seems friendly and trustworthy, but they may try to use you in some way, such as taking your personal information to commit a crime.

　Finally, the Internet can take our attention away from our real lives. When we get too involved in talking to people online, we often find our normal social lives suffer. Instead of putting efforts into the friends and family around us, we are likely to withdraw to cyber-space. For example, I have seen people who were once very social and outgoing at school become quiet and withdrawn after getting involved in social networks. People can lose their sense of balance from spending too much time in cyber-space.

　It is all right to make friends over the Internet, but it is best if the Internet is used only as a place for introductions, not a place to spend time together. Regular life is different from life in cyber-space and regular life is better.　　　　　　　　　　　　　　　　(306 words)

　（自分と同じことに興味を持つ人をインターネット上で見つけるのは素晴らしいことかもしれません。しかし人々はインターネットで友人を探すことには多くの危険が含まれることに気づくべきです。そのため私はこの主張に賛成です。

　第1に，多くの人々はインターネット上で自分について本当のことを言いません。たとえ彼ら

が，写真や自分の情報を提供したとしても，それは本当ではないかもしれません。彼らは匿名でいようとしているかもしれないし，人々をだますためにまったく別の人になりすましているかもしれません。彼らが自分について何らかの情報を隠していないと確信する方法はありません。

　第2に，多くの人が不正な目的でインターネット上に来ているかもしれません。人々から非合法的にお金を取ろうとする人たちもいます。危険につながり得る個人的付き合いを求める人もいます。インターネットを通じて人と出会う時，人々は問題に巻き込まれます。友好的で信頼できるように見える人に出会うかもしれませんが，彼らは，例えばあなたの個人情報を得て罪を犯すというような方法で，あなたを利用しようとするかもしれません。

　最後にインターネットは私たちの興味を現実の生活から引き離すことがあります。インターネット上で人々に話しかけることに熱中しすぎて，通常の社会生活に支障をきたしていることがしばしばあります。私たちの周りの友人や家族に気持ちを注ぐ代わりに，インターネット上の仮想空間に閉じ込もりがちになるのです。例えば，以前は学校でとても社交的で外向的だった人が，ソーシャルネットワークに熱中した後,寡黙になり引きこもってしまったのを私は見てきました。人々はインターネット上の仮想空間で多くの時間を過ごしすぎたことによりバランス感覚を失うことがあるのです。

　インターネットによって友人を作ることは構いませんが，インターネットは一緒に時間を過ごす場ではなく，きっかけの場としてのみ使われるのが最善です。日常生活は仮想空間とは別のもので，日常生活のほうがよりよいものなのです。)

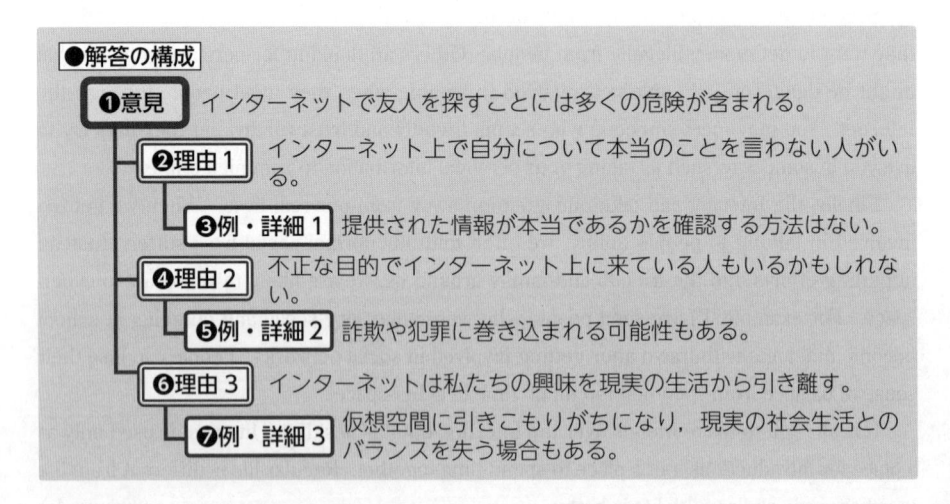

●解答の構成

- ❶意見　インターネットで友人を探すことには多くの危険が含まれる。
  - ❷理由1　インターネット上で自分について本当のことを言わない人がいる。
    - ❸例・詳細1　提供された情報が本当であるかを確認する方法はない。
  - ❹理由2　不正な目的でインターネット上に来ている人もいるかもしれない。
    - ❺例・詳細2　詐欺や犯罪に巻き込まれる可能性もある。
  - ❻理由3　インターネットは私たちの興味を現実の生活から引き離す。
    - ❼例・詳細3　仮想空間に引きこもりがちになり，現実の社会生活とのバランスを失う場合もある。

✓ 重要表現チェック

不十分な解答例	☐ decade「10年間」
	☐ acceptable「好ましい，受け入れられる」
適切な解答例	☐ sensible「賢明な，分別のある」
別解	☐ biographical「伝記的な，自伝的な」
	☐ anonymous「匿名の」　　☐ identity「本人であること，身元」
	☐ fool「～をだます，～をあざむく」　☐ dishonest「不正な，不正直の」
	☐ withdraw「閉じ込もる」
	☐ cyber-space「サイバースペース，インターネット上の仮想空間」
	☐ outgoing「外向的な」

問題 7

Do you agree or disagree with the following statement?
Teachers should make more money than movie stars.
Use specific reasons and examples to support your answer.

【設問訳】
あなたは以下の主張に賛成ですか，反対ですか。
「教師は映画スターよりも多くの収入を得るべきである。」
あなたの意見の根拠となる具体的な理由や事例を述べなさい。

| 解答例 | 「教師は映画スターよりも多くの収入を得るべきである」に賛成の場合 |

不十分な解答例

★1 Whether teachers should make more money than movie stars or not is a difficult question to answer. There may be a wide variety of income levels among movie stars. Also, I don't really know how much a movie star earns a year. Let's say he or she earns at least more than one hundred million yen. I can hardly imagine an ordinary person like a teacher earning that much. Still I believe teachers are much more valuable to society than movie stars. ★2 In addition, education should not be neglected because income levels are a representation of what a society cares about.

First, teaching is one of the most important professions in the world, because they give children important guidance for their futures. If you ask someone to name about (→不要) a good teacher from their childhood, they can mostly (→almost) always give you an answer. Quite often that answer will follow by (→with) examples of how that teacher gave valuable lessons about life. One of my favorite teachers from childhood was named Mr. Uehara. ★3 He taught me so many things about life, and I am very thankful to him.

In addition to general life guidance, teachers also equip students with practical knowledges (→knowledge) and skills that they will need once they become adults. For example, in order to be highly succeeded (→successful) at a company, it is very helpful to have good problem-solving skills. Although this is not the focus of most classes, almost all teachers help students to develop these skills by giving them new challenges every day. This is such a valuable service.

★4 Finally, paying teachers high salaries may improve the quality of teachers. By paying movie stars more money than teachers, we are showing that entertainment is more important than education. As a result, many children do not dream of becoming teachers that change students' lives. Instead, they dream of becoming famous and appearing in movies. Society teaches them to have these dreams.

　In conclusion, I agree that teachers should make more money than movie stars. I doubt that this will ever happen, but it would be so nice to see this noble profession get more respect. ★5 I hear the environment surrounding teachers is stressful. If their salary were lower, how could they provide good education?

●構成と内容の改善ポイント

★1 Introduction で「この質問は答えるのが難しい」という内容を長々と述べていますが，設問で求められていることに答える上で，必要のない情報です。
　➡ Introduction ではまず，自分の立場をはっきり示さなければなりません。トピックについての一般論を述べる時は，あくまで自分の意見を導入することを目的として，1〜2文にとどめましょう。

★2 「収入のレベルは社会が何を大切に考えているかを表しているので，教育は軽視されるべきでない」となっており，because で結んだ節同士が適切な因果関係になっていません。
　➡「収入のレベルは社会が何を大切に考えているかの表れである。そして，教育はもっと大事にされるべきである。（しかし現状では軽視されている。）」としたほうが，自然な流れになります。適切な接続詞を用いて論理の流れを作りましょう。

★3 教師は最も重要な職業の1つであると主張し，具体例として自分の先生について述べていますが，彼がどのようによい先生だったかという説明に終始しています。
　➡「教師は映画スターよりも多くの収入を得るべきだ」という意見を支える根拠として，価値に見合った収入を得ているかどうかという観点の記述を加えると，説得力が増します。

★4 第1文の「高い収入を払うことで教師の質が上がる」という主張と，具体例の内容がかみ合っていません。
　➡エッセイ全体の論理の一貫性を意識しましょう。Introduction や具体例の内容を加味すると，この段落の主旨は，「教師に高い収入を払うことで，子供たちが教職の重要性を認識する」ということです。この内容を第1文で述べると，読みやすい展開になります。

★5 結論で自分の意見を締めくくった後に，論点から外れた余分な情報を述べています。
　➡結論では，これまで述べてきたことをまとめ，自分の意見を再度明示して結びます。新しい話題を持ち出したり，脇道にそれることがないようにしましょう。

《構成の改善例》

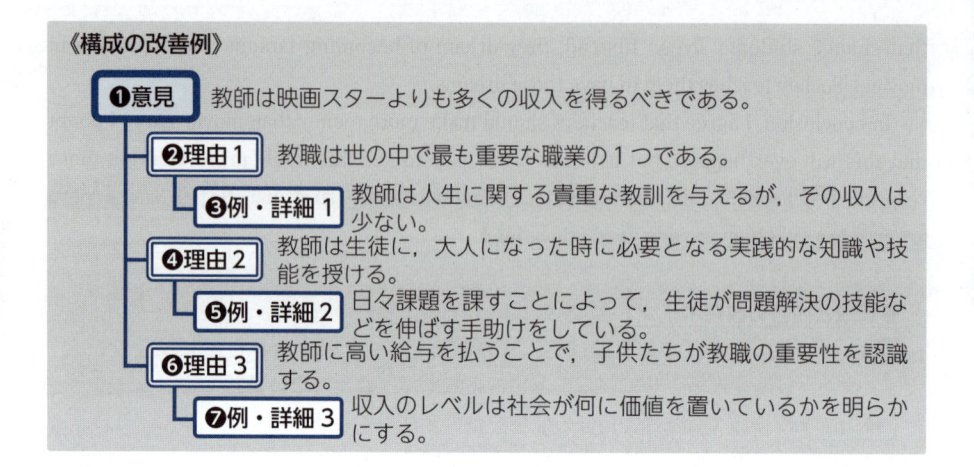

- ❶意見　教師は映画スターよりも多くの収入を得るべきである。
  - ❷理由1　教職は世の中で最も重要な職業の1つである。
    - ❸例・詳細1　教師は人生に関する貴重な教訓を与えるが，その収入は少ない。
  - ❹理由2　教師は生徒に，大人になった時に必要となる実践的な知識や技能を授ける。
    - ❺例・詳細2　日々課題を課すことによって，生徒が問題解決の技能などを伸ばす手助けをしている。
  - ❻理由3　教師に高い給与を払うことで，子供たちが教職の重要性を認識する。
    - ❼例・詳細3　収入のレベルは社会が何に価値を置いているかを明らかにする。

適切な解答例

*1 **I agree that teachers should make more money than movie stars.** For one thing, teachers are much more valuable to society than movie stars. In addition, *2 **income levels are a representation of what a society cares about, and education should be valued more.**

First, teaching is one of the most important professions in the world, because they give children important guidance for their futures. If you ask someone to name a good teacher from their childhood, they can almost always give you an answer. Quite often that answer will follow with examples of how that teacher gave valuable lessons about life. One of my favorite teachers from childhood was named Mr. Uehara. *3 **He taught me so many things about life, and I am very thankful to him, but I am sure that he does not make much money, which is unfortunate.**

In addition to general life guidance, teachers also equip students with practical knowledge and skills that they will need once they become adults. For example, in order to be highly successful at a company, it is very helpful to have good problem-solving skills. Although this is not the focus of most classes, almost all teachers help students to develop these skills by giving them new challenges every day. This is such a valuable service.

*4 **Finally, by paying teachers high salaries, more children would realize how important teachers' jobs are. This is because income levels reveal the true values of a society.** By paying movie stars more money than teachers, we are showing that entertainment is more important than education. As a result, many children do not dream of becoming teachers that change students' lives. Instead, they dream of becoming famous and appearing in movies. Society teaches them to have these dreams.

In conclusion, I agree that teachers should make more money than movie stars. I doubt that this will ever happen, but it would be so nice to see this noble profession get more respect.
(326 words)

（私は，教師は映画スターよりも多くの収入を得るべきだという意見に賛成です。1つには，教師は映画スターよりもはるかに社会にとって価値ある存在だからです。そして，収入のレベルは社会が何を大切に考えているかの表れであり，教育はもっと重視されるべきです。

　第1に，教職は世の中で最も重要な職業の1つです。なぜなら彼らは子供たちに将来に向けての重要な指導を行うからです。誰かに，子供の頃に出会ったよい先生を挙げるように尋ねれば，ほとんどの場合回答が得られます。多くの場合そうした回答には，その先生がどのように人生に関する貴重な教訓を与えてくれたかについての具体的な実例が続くでしょう。私が子供時代に出会った好きな先生の1人は，上原先生という方でした。上原先生は人生についてとてもたくさんのことを教えてくれて，私は先生にとても感謝していますが，先生はあまりたくさん収入を得ていないことは確かで，これは残念なことです。

　一般的な生活指導に加えて，教師は生徒に大人になった時に必要となる実践的な知識や技能を授けることもします。例えば会社で高い成功を収めるためには，高い問題解決の技能を持つことがとても役に立ちます。たとえ，これがほとんどの授業で焦点となっていないとしても，ほぼすべての教師が日々新たな課題を与えることによって，生徒たちがこれらの技能を伸ばす手助けをしているのです。これはそのような価値のある奉仕なのです。

　最後に，教師に高い給与を払うことで，より多くの子供たちが，教職の重要性を認識するでしょう。なぜなら，収入のレベルは，社会の真価を明らかにするからです。私たちは，映画スターに教師よりも多くのお金を払うことで，エンターテイメントのほうが教育よりも重要だということを示しているのです。その結果，多くの子供たちは，生徒の人生を変えるような教師になることを夢見ません。それよりも，有名になることや映画に出ることを夢見ます。社会が子供たちにこうした夢を持つように教えてしまっているのです。

　結論として，私は，教師は映画スターよりも多くの収入を得るべきだという意見に賛成します。こうしたことが起こることはないと思いますが，この尊い職業がもっと敬意を得るようになればと思います。）

別解 「教師は映画スターよりも多くの収入を得るべきである」に反対の場合

　I disagree with the opinion that teachers should make more money than movie stars. High incomes would give the wrong incentive to teachers and send the wrong message to children. In addition, it is simply not possible to pay teachers movie-star salaries.

　First, if teachers were offered giant salaries, the number of teachers only interested in making money would increase. All of the great teachers that I have ever met cared deeply about education. In addition to teaching school subjects, they also provided students with advice about life in general. It was clear that they became teachers because they wanted to help children grow into successful adults. Teachers should not do their jobs just to make lots of money.

　Second, paying teachers more money than movie stars might send the wrong message to children. Many good teachers are almost like close friends or family to their students, but if teachers made a lot of money, then this might not be possible. Children might start to respect teachers for their large incomes, but not for their knowledge and kindness. Similarly, children might feel that their teachers do not really care about teaching, but only about making more money.

　Finally, it makes more sense for movie stars to get paid higher salaries, because they provide value to a much larger number of people. There is a limit to how many people can benefit from the services of one teacher, but movie stars are involved in creating mass media products that are distributed to millions of people. Economically, this means that it is much easier for movie stars to receive large incomes.

　For these reasons, I disagree with the statement. While I do think that society should respect and value teachers more, giving them more money is not the way to do so.

(300 words)

　（私は，教師は映画スターよりも多くの収入を得るべきだという意見に反対します。高収入は教師に誤ったインセンティブを与え，子供たちに間違ったメッセージを送ることになります。それに，教師に映画スターほどの給料を払うことは絶対に不可能です。

　第1に，もし教師に巨額の給料が提示されたら，金儲けにしか興味のない教師が増加するでしょう。私が出会った優れた教師は皆，教育に深い関心がありました。学校の教科を教えるのに加えて，彼らは生徒に一般的な人生についてのアドバイスも提供しました。彼らが教師になったのは，子供たちが立派な大人になる手助けをしたいと思ったからだというのは明らかです。教師たちは，金儲けだけのために仕事をすべきではありません。

　第2に，教師に映画スターよりも多くのお金を払うことは，子供たちに誤ったメッセージを送ることになるかもしれません。多くのよい教師たちは，生徒たちにとって親しい友人や家族同様ですが，もし教師がたくさんお金を稼いでいたら，これは不可能かもしれません。子供たちは教師を，知識や優しさではなく，収入が多いからという理由で尊敬し始めるかもしれません。同様に，子供たちは，教師が本当は教えることを大事に思っているのではなく，単に金儲けにしか関心がないと感じるかもしれません。

　最後に，映画スターがより高い収入を得ていることのほうが理にかなっています。なぜなら，彼らはより多くの人々に価値を提供しているからです。1人の教師の仕事から利益を受ける人の数は限られていますが，映画スターは，何百万人もの人々に提供するマスメディアの商品の製作に関わっています。経済的に見ても，これは，映画スターが高い収入を得るのが非常に容易であることを意味しています。

　以上の理由から，私はこの主張に反対します。社会はもっと教師を尊敬し，価値を認めるべき

だとは思いますが，もっと多くのお金を教師に与えることは，そうするための手段ではありません。）

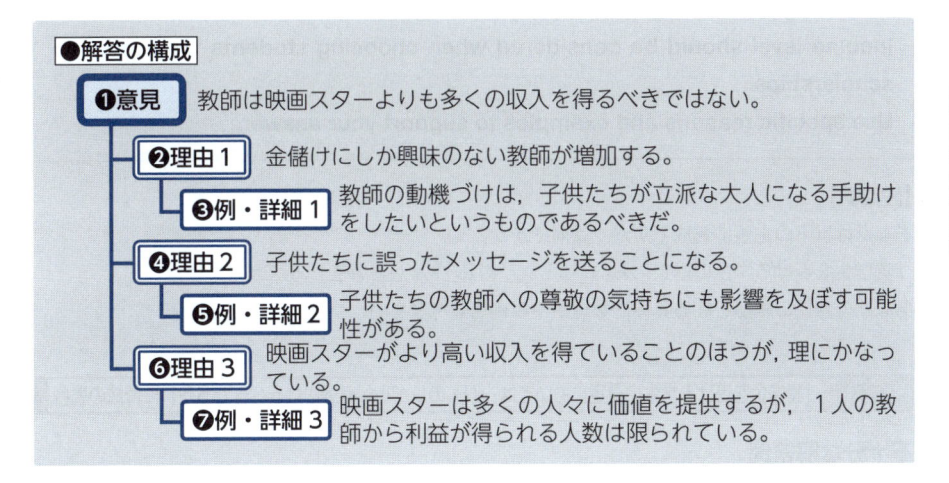

●解答の構成

- **❶意見** 教師は映画スターよりも多くの収入を得るべきではない。
  - **❷理由1** 金儲けにしか興味のない教師が増加する。
    - **❸例・詳細1** 教師の動機づけは，子供たちが立派な大人になる手助けをしたいというものであるべきだ。
  - **❹理由2** 子供たちに誤ったメッセージを送ることになる。
    - **❺例・詳細2** 子供たちの教師への尊敬の気持ちにも影響を及ぼす可能性がある。
  - **❻理由3** 映画スターがより高い収入を得ていることのほうが，理にかなっている。
    - **❼例・詳細3** 映画スターは多くの人々に価値を提供するが，1人の教師から利益が得られる人数は限られている。

✓重要表現チェック

不十分な解答例
- □ representation「表現，表れ」
- □ guidance「指導」
- □ appear「出演する」
- □ profession「職業」
- □ problem-solving「問題解決の」
- □ noble「立派な，尊い」

適切な解答例
別解
- □ for one thing「1つには」
- □ incentive「励みとなるもの，刺激」
- □ similarly「同様に」
- □ benefit「利益を得る」
- □ reveal「〜を示す」
- □ make sense「道理にかなう」
- □ distribute「〜を分配する」

問題 8

Do you agree or disagree with the following statement?
Income level should be considered when choosing students for academic scholarships.
Use specific reasons and examples to support your answer.

【設問訳】
あなたは以下の主張に賛成ですか，反対ですか。
「奨学金を受ける学生の選定においては，収入のレベルが考慮されるべきである。」
あなたの意見の根拠となる具体的な理由や事例を述べなさい。

解答例 「奨学金を受ける学生の選定においては，収入のレベルが考慮されるべきである」に賛成の場合

⚠ 不十分な解答例

I agree that income level should be considered when choosing students for academic scholarships. ★1 Scholarships provide a (→不要) greater value to low-income students and get (→motivate) them to study more than high-income students. Otherwise, the disparity between both groups will become wider. Opportunities should be equally given to all students.

The main purpose of scholarships are (→is) to enable students with less (→fewer) opportunities to excel academically. For example, imagine that there are two students with almost identical academic records. However, one of them comes from a wealthy family, and the other one comes from a poor family. ★2 We feel it unfair if a scholarship is given to the former.

Furthermore, scholarships motivate students in low-income families to focus on their studies. If a low-income student has only a small chance of receiving a scholarship, then there is very few (→little) reason to study hard. It is difficult for a student like this to have hope for an academic future, because his or her family will not be able to provide with (→不要) support without a scholarship. Conversely, if there are many scholarships for low-income students, then there is more motivation to work hard, succeed academically, and get funding to continue studying. ★3 On the other hand, if many scholarships are offered students from a wealthy family, the chance for low-income students will be smaller. As a result, many of the academically brilliant students whose parents' incomes are low get discouraged.

Finally, using income as a factor when giving out scholarships makes the student selection process much simpler. ★4 The process should ideally be fair. At my university, for example, large scholarships usually have hundreds of applicants, but only a very little (→**small**) percentage of students can be chosen. Selection committees are under a lot of pressure to choose the correct (→**right**) candidates. ★5

In conclusion, I think that income level is an important point to consider when selecting students for scholarships.

●構成と内容の改善ポイント

★1 全体の構成を示すべき Introduction で,「機会の不平等」という1つの論点についてしか触れられていません。
   ➡ Introduction では, 各段落で扱う論点の概略を述べるにとどめ, 詳細説明は Body の各段落で展開します。Introduction で各段落の論点を一目瞭然にすることで, 読みやすいエッセイになります。

★2 「私たちは不公平に感じるだろう」という総括の仕方だと,「低所得層の学生が奨学金を与えられるべきだ」という主張を支える根拠として説得力に欠けます。
   ➡低所得層の学生とそうでない学生では, 学習面でどのように事情が異なっているのか, なぜ低所得層の学生が奨学金を受け取るべきなのかを読み手にわかるように説明しましょう。

★3 On the other hand と前置きしていますが, この段落の前半と内容が重複しています。読み手は前に述べたことの逆の場合を想定して読み進めるため, 混乱する恐れがあります。
   ➡メインの主張を言葉を変えて繰り返し述べることは, 説得力を高める効果がありますが, 同じ内容の繰り返しでは冗長になるだけで説得力にはつながりません。そのため, ここでは該当部分は削除します。また, 接続表現は適切なものを用いましょう。

★4 「選考過程は, 理想的としては公平であるべきだ」という内容は,「収入のレベルを考慮することが選考過程を簡略にする」というこの段落の主旨に, 直接関係がありません。後に続く具体例とも関連性が薄いです。
   ➡ここでは該当部分は削除します。段落の趣旨や, 文と文のつながりを意識しましょう。

★5 「選考委員会は候補者を選ぶのにプレッシャーを抱えている」という内容で段落が終わっており, この情報が何を示唆するのかが曖昧です。
   ➡選考委員のこのような事情を踏まえて, 収入のレベルを考慮することがどのように有益なのかをまとめましょう。

《構成の改善例》

- **❶意見** 奨学金を受ける学生の選定においては，収入のレベルが考慮されるべきだ。
  - **❷理由1** 奨学金は，低所得層の学生が学問を修めるのを可能にする。
    - **❸例・詳細1** 貧しい家庭出身の場合，奨学金がなければ学校へ行けないかもしれない。
  - **❹理由2** 奨学金は，貧しい家庭の学生に，勉学に集中する意欲を与える。
    - **❺例・詳細2** 彼らは家族の経済的支援を得ることができない。
  - **❻理由3** 収入のレベルを考慮することは，選考過程を簡略にする。
    - **❼例・詳細3** 多くの候補者から学生を選ばなければならない選考委員会にとって有益な指標になる。

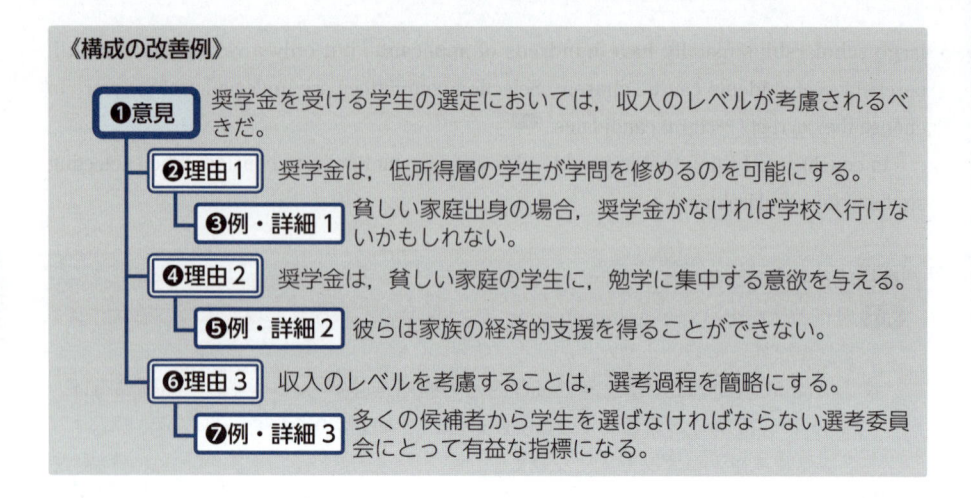

適切な解答例

　I agree that income level should be considered when choosing students for academic scholarships. ★1<u>Scholarships provide greater value to low-income students and motivate them to study more than others. In addition, considering income makes the selection process much simpler.</u>

　The main purpose of scholarships is to enable students with fewer opportunities to excel academically. ★2<u>In other words, scholarships are designed for low-income students in particular. This is because low-income students have a greater need for scholarships.</u> For example, imagine that there are two students with almost identical academic records. However, one of them comes from a wealthy family, and the other one comes from a poor family. ★3<u>Even if the student in the wealthy family does not receive a scholarship, he will still be able to study. However, the low-income student may not be able to go to school at all without a scholarship. Scholarships are made to help students like this one.</u>

　Furthermore, scholarships motivate students in low-income families to focus on their studies. If a low-income student has only a small chance of receiving a scholarship, then there is very little reason to study hard. It is difficult for a student like this to have hope for an academic future, because his or her family will not be able to provide support without a scholarship. Conversely, if there are many scholarships for low-income students, then there is more motivation to work hard, succeed academically, and get funding to continue studying.

　Finally, using income as a factor when giving out scholarships makes the student selection process much simpler. At my university, for example, large scholarships usually have hundreds of applicants, but only a very small percentage of students can be chosen. Selection committees are under a lot of pressure to choose the right candidates. ★5**Income level is a useful way for them to determine a student's need in addition to their academic performance.**

　In conclusion, I think that income level is an important point to consider when selecting students for scholarships. (332 words)

（私は，奨学金を受ける学生の選定においては，収入のレベルが考慮されるべきだと思います。奨学金は，低所得層の学生により大きな価値を与え，他の人よりももっと勉強をしようという意欲を与えます。それに，収入を考慮することで，選考過程はずっと簡略になります。

　奨学金の主な目的は，機会の少ない学生が，学業面で秀でることができるようにすることです。言い換えれば，奨学金は，特に低所得層の学生のために作られたものです。なぜなら，低所得層の学生のほうが奨学金をより必要としているからです。例えば，学業成績がほとんど同じ２人の学生がいたと仮定します。ただし，そのうちの１人は裕福な家庭の出身で，もう１人は貧しい家庭の出身です。たとえ裕福な家庭の学生が奨学金を得られなかったとしても，彼は勉強をすることができるでしょう。しかし，低所得層の学生は，奨学金がなければ，まったく学校へ行くことができないかもしれません。奨学金は，このような学生を助けるために作られています。

　さらに，奨学金は低所得層の家庭の学生に，勉学に集中する意欲を与えます。もし，低所得層の学生に，奨学金を受けるチャンスが少ししかなければ，熱心に勉学に励む理由がほとんどなくなってしまいます。奨学金がなければ，家族では支援できないので，このような学生は学業面での未来に希望を持ちにくいのです。逆に，低所得層の学生のための奨学金がたくさんあれば，勉学に励み，学問で成功し，学業を続けるための資金を獲得する意欲が増すでしょう。

　最後に，奨学金を与える際の要素として収入を考慮することは，学生の選考過程をずっと簡略にします。例えば，私の大学では高額の奨学金には何百もの応募がありますが，ごくわずかな割合の学生だけしか選ばれません。選考委員会は，適切な候補者を選ぶのに多くのプレッシャーを抱えています。収入のレベルは，学生の学業成績に加え，選考委員が学生の奨学金の必要性を判断するのに有益な方法です。

　結論として，私は，収入のレベルは奨学金を受ける学生を選定する際に考慮すべき重要なポイントだと思います。）

別解　「奨学金を受ける学生の選定においては，収入のレベルが考慮されるべきである」に反対の場合

　Personally, I believe that income should not be considered when choosing scholarship recipients. Aside from the fact that income has no relation to academic ability, it also is a poor measure of financial need. In addition, it can discourage hard work.

　First, income and academic ability are not related. Scholarships are meant to be incentives for hard-working students that are serious about taking their education to the next level. Considering income when choosing students for a scholarship changes its true purpose, making it more like charity. Students should believe that their hard work will be appreciated, and that is why scholarships should be based on academic achievement, accomplishments in sports, and so on.

Second, income level does not always give a clear picture of financial need. For example, I have a friend that got a full scholarship to study at a university in Tokyo. Although he did not have impressive academic records, he still got a scholarship due to his financial situation. His application said that his family did not have much money, because his mother was supporting them by herself. However, he actually has quite a lot of money, because his rich grandparents help him and his mother financially. So even though his family appears to have a low income, they are not actually in a difficult financial situation.

Lastly, I believe that using income to choose scholarship recipients discourages students in middle-class families from studying. Scholarships are extremely competitive nowadays, and most middle-class students feel that even if they study a lot, they still will not be able to get a scholarship, because students in low-income families will always get them instead. It is unfortunate that so many scholarships are based on financial situations rather than on academic achievements.

For these reasons, I do not agree with the statement. Scholarships should encourage learning and hard work more than anything else. (312 words)

（個人的には，奨学金の受給者を選ぶ際に，収入は考慮するべきではないと思います。収入は学力と関係がないという事実に加え，経済的な困窮度合いを測るには不十分な指標です。それに，勉学に励む意欲を削ぐことにもなり得ます。

第1に，収入と学力は関係がありません。奨学金は，自分たちの教育を次のレベルへ真剣に進めようとする勤勉な学生への動機づけになるように作られたものです。奨学金を受ける学生の選定において収入を考慮することは，奨学金の本来の目的を変えてしまい，慈善活動のように変えてしまいます。学生は，自分たちの努力がきちんと評価されると信じられるようでなければいけませんし，だからこそ，奨学金は学業成績，スポーツでの功績などをもとにするべきです。

第2に，収入のレベルは，経済的な困窮度合いを必ずしも明確に示すわけではありません。例えば，私には，東京の大学で勉強するために全額支給の奨学金を受給している友人がいます。彼の学業成績は素晴らしいものではありませんでしたが，経済状況を理由に奨学金を受給していました。彼の応募書類によると，母親1人が家族を養っているため，家庭にはあまりお金がないと書かれていました。しかし，彼は，実際にはかなりのお金を持っていました。裕福な祖父母が，彼と母親を経済的に支援していたからです。というわけで，彼の家族は収入が少なく見えますが，実際には，経済的に困難な状況には置かれていません。

最後に，奨学金の受給者を選定するのに収入を考慮すると，中流階級の家庭の学生が勉強をする意欲をなくすと，私は思います。最近では，奨学金はかなり競争率が高くなっており，ほとんどの中流階級の学生は，自分たちではなく，低所得層の家庭の学生がいつも奨学金を得るので，

いくら勉強しても奨学金を得ることはできないと感じています。あまりにも多くの奨学金が，学業成績よりも経済的状況に基づいているのは残念なことです。

　以上の理由から，私は，この主張に反対します。奨学金は，何よりも学習と勤勉の励みとなるべきです。）

●解答の構成

- **❶意見** 奨学金の受給者を選ぶ際に，収入は考慮するべきではない。
  - **❷理由 1** 収入と学力は関係がない。
    - **❸例・詳細 1** 奨学金は勤勉な学生への動機づけであり，学生の努力がきちんと評価されるべきである。
  - **❹理由 2** 収入のレベルは，経済的な困窮度合いを必ずしも明確に示すわけではない。
    - **❺例・詳細 2** 祖父母に経済的支援を受けているにもかかわらず，奨学金を受給している友人がいる。
  - **❻理由 3** 収入を考慮すると，一部の学生が勉強をする意欲をなくす可能性がある。
    - **❼例・詳細 3** 中流階級の学生は，いくら勉強しても奨学金を得ることはできないと感じる。

✓重要表現チェック

不十分な解答例
- excel「秀でる」
- identical「同一の」
- conversely「逆に言えば」
- motivation「動機づけ」
- funding「資金」
- applicant「応募者」
- committee「委員会」

適切な解答例
- be designed for ～「～を意図している」

別解
- recipient「受領者」
- aside from ～「～に加えて」
- be meant to do「…することを意図されている」
- charity「慈善」
- achievement「成績」
- competitive「競争的な」

問題 9

Some people recommend changing jobs many times to acquire new skills. Other people say it is better to work at one company for one's entire career. Which of these two positions do you agree with? Use specific reasons and examples to support your answer.

【設問訳】
新しいスキルを獲得するために，何度も転職することを勧める人もいれば，生涯１つの会社に勤め上げるほうがよいと言う人もいます。
あなたはこれら２つの立場のうち，どちらに賛成しますか。あなたの意見の根拠となる具体的な理由や事例を述べなさい。

解答例　「新しいスキルを獲得するために，何度も転職するほうがよい」と答える場合

不十分な解答例

　When I was growing up, my parents and teachers always told me that I should stay at one company for **my** entire career. As I got older, I slowly realized that I disagree with them. ★1 Now I think their view seems outdated.

　The main reason they advised (→**recommended**) this is for a stable career. If an employee stays with one company, then that company is unlikely to fire him or her. There is one huge problem with this idea, though —— most companies are not loyal to employees. ★2 Things are different from decades ago. When companies get into financial trouble, it is likely (→**common**) for them to lay off highly-paid, dedicated employees.

　Because employees can never be sure that their jobs are safe, they should try to develop a wide range of useful skills. This can be done by having a variety of different jobs. ★3 For example, there are a person who works in one company's marketing department for 20 years and another person who worked in four different companies' marketing departments for 5 years each. If both of them lose their jobs, the latter will find a new job more easy (→**easily**).

　Last but not least, having many different jobs is more interesting. ★4 When I was at university, I experienced various part-time jobs. From this experience, working at many different companies sounds a lot more fun than only working at one company for my whole life.

　In conclusion, my opinion is that it is better to change jobs many times in one's career. ★5 Although there may be some dangers involved in changing jobs, I will take advantage of every opportunity.

●構成と内容の改善ポイント

★1 自ら例に挙げた「親や先生の助言」に対して「時代遅れのように思える」と述べており,「何度も転職するほうがよい」という立場が間接的に示されています。
　➡ Introduction では,問われていることに対する自分の立場を明確にすることが大切です。間接的に示すこともテクニックの1つですが,論理関係をきちんと示さなければ,伝わりにくくなってしまう恐れがあります。ここでは「何度も転職するほうがよい」とはっきり述べ,より伝わりやすいエッセイにします。

★2 「数十年前とは事情が異なる」という説明だけでは,何がどのように異なるのかが不明であり,説得力に欠けます。
　➡「会社は社員に義理立てしない」という背景にある,現在の状況を具体的に説明しましょう。

★3 「後者(何度か転職を経験している人)のほうが新しい仕事を簡単に見つけられる」という主張の根拠が述べられていません。
　➡「異なる会社で働いた経験のある人のほうが多様なスキルを身につけている」という説明を加えましょう。前後の文に論理的飛躍がないように意識しましょう。

★4 漠然と「さまざまなアルバイトを経験したため,多くの異なる会社で働くことはおもしろそうだ」と述べるだけでは,「スキルの獲得のために何度も転職をする」というトピックから離れる印象を与えます。
　➡ここでは,さまざまな職場を経験することから得られる利点に焦点をあて,それがスキルの獲得につながることを示すと,説得力が増します。

★5 「転職にはリスクがある」という新しい観点が述べられています。
　➡結論部分で新しい観点を持ち出すと,読み手が混乱します。結論では,これまで述べてきたことをまとめ,自分の立場を再提示しましょう。

《構成の改善例》

- **❶意見** 職業人生中に何度も転職するほうが,ずっとよい選択肢である。
    - **❷理由1** 今日,ほとんどの会社は社員に義理立てしない。
        - **❸例・詳細1** 会社が経済的な問題を抱えた場合,献身的で給料の高い社員を解雇することがある。
    - **❹理由2** さまざまな異なる仕事を通してスキルを伸ばすべきである。
        - **❺例・詳細2** 多様なスキルを持っていると,新しい仕事を見つける可能性は高くなる。
    - **❻理由3** さまざまな仕事を経験するほうがおもしろい。
        - **❼例・詳細3** 新しい人々と出会い,新しい考えを聞き,自分を成長させることができる。

適切な解答例

When I was growing up, my parents and teachers always told me that I should stay at one company for my entire career. As I got older, I slowly realized that I disagree with them, and *1 **I now believe that changing jobs many times in one's career is a much better option.**

The main reason they recommended this is for a stable career. If an employee stays with one company, then that company is unlikely to fire him or her. There is one huge problem with this idea, though — most companies are not loyal to employees. *2 **In today's modern society, it is difficult to know which companies will continue to make a steady profit for many years.** When companies get into financial trouble, it is common for them to lay off highly-paid, dedicated employees.

Because employees can never be sure that their jobs are safe, they should try to develop a wide range of useful skills. This can be done by having a variety of different jobs. *3 **For example, a person who works in one company's marketing department for 20 years will have less skills than another person who worked in four different companies' marketing departments for 5 years each. If both of them lose their jobs, then the second person has a better chance of getting a new job, because he has more diverse skills.**

Last but not least, having many different jobs is more interesting. *4 **I want to meet new people, hear new ideas, and develop myself into a highly skilled, intelligent professional, and I think working at multiple companies is a great way to do this.** For me, working at many different companies sounds a lot more fun than only working at one company for my whole life.

In conclusion, my opinion is that it is better to change jobs many times in one's career. *5 **This option is more interesting, teaches more useful skills, and makes people into more desirable, valuable employees.** (325 words)

（子供の頃，両親と先生はいつも私に，生涯1つの企業に居続けるべきだと言っていました。大人になるにつれて，私はだんだん，彼らの意見に反対だということがわかってきて，今は，職業人生中に何度も転職するほうが，ずっとよい選択肢だと思っています。

両親と先生たちが，私に1つの会社で働くように言った主な理由は，職業の安定のためです。ある社員が1つの会社に居続けるなら，会社がその社員を解雇する可能性は低いでしょう。しかし，この考えには1つ，大きな問題があります。ほとんどの会社は，社員に義理立てしないということです。今日の社会では，どの会社が何年も安定した利益を出し続けるかを判断することは，難しくなっています。会社が経済的な問題を抱えた場合，給料が高く，献身的な社員を一時解雇するのはよくあることです。

社員は，自分の仕事が安泰だと確信することは決してできないので，役に立つあらゆるスキルを伸ばす努力をするべきです。これは，さまざまな異なる仕事をすることで実現可能でしょう。例えば，1つの会社のマーケティング部で20年間働いていた人は，4つの異なる会社のマーケティング部で5年ずつ働いた人よりもスキルが少ないでしょう。もし，2人とも職を失ったとしたら，2人目の人のほうが，多様なスキルを持っているので，新しい仕事を得る可能性は高くなります。

最後ですが，何と言っても，さまざまな仕事を経験するほうがおもしろいです。新しい人々と出会い，新しい考えを聞き，能力の高い知的なプロフェッショナルへと自分を成長させたいと思いますし，複数の会社で働くことが，こうするための素晴らしい方法だと思います。私には，さまざまな異なる会社で働くほうが，一生1つの会社で働くよりも，ずっとおもしろそうに思えます。

結論として，私は，生涯に何度も転職するほうがよいという意見です。この選択肢のほうがおもしろく，有益なスキルをより多く与え，人々をより望ましい，価値の高い社員にします。)

別解 「生涯1つの会社に勤め上げるほうがよい」と答える場合

I agree with the opinion that it is better to work at one company for one's entire career. Changing jobs often looks bad to employers, and working at a single company is a great opportunity to master valuable skills and advance one's career.

First, I have heard many people say that companies do not like to hire employees that change companies often. Finding and hiring new employees costs time and money, so companies want as much as possible to avoid going through this process. For this reason, they are less likely to hire job applicants that have a history of changing companies. Human resources managers assume that these types of job applicants will just quit as soon as they find another opportunity.

Second, working at a single company is one of the best ways to master a single type of job. For example, my father has been working in the sales department of a large company for over twenty years. Over that time, he has gradually moved up in the company. Each time he was promoted, he learned new, valuable skills. He now knows more about running the sales department of a large company than any person I have ever met. Eventually, I want to master a profession in the same way that he has.

Finally, staying at one company increases the chances of getting promotions. If there are two employees that have similar experience and skills, then the employee that has worked at the company for a longer period will have a better chance of getting promoted. I am sure that companies appreciate loyalty, and they are more likely to reward employees for it by giving them more responsibilities and higher wages.

For these reasons, I believe that it is not good to change jobs many times throughout one's career. Working at a single company has more advantages overall. (310 words)

（私は，1つの会社で生涯働くほうがよいという意見に賛成です。何度も転職をすることは，雇用主に悪い印象を与えることがよくありますし，1つの会社で働くことは，価値のあるスキルに熟練し，キャリアを高める素晴らしい機会です。

第1に，企業は頻繁に転職をしている社員を雇いたがらないと，多くの人々が言うのを聞いたことがあります。新しい社員を見つけて雇うのには時間とお金がかかるので，企業はできるだけこの過程を避けたいと思っています。このため，転職した経歴のある応募者を雇う可能性は低くなるでしょう。人事部長は，こうしたタイプの応募者は，別の就職の機会を見つけたらすぐに辞めるだろうと考えるのです。

第2に，同一の会社で働くことは，1種類の仕事に熟練する最良の方法の1つです。例えば，私の父は，大企業の営業部で20年以上働いています。その間，父は会社の中で徐々に昇進していきました。昇進するたびに，父は新しい貴重なスキルを身につけました。今では，父は私が知っている誰よりも，大企業の営業部を運営することについてよく知っています。いずれは，私も父と同じようにして1つの職業に熟練したいです。

最後に，1つの会社に居続けると，昇進の可能性が高まります。似たような経験とスキルを持つ2人の社員がいるとしたら，その会社での勤務期間の長い社員のほうが昇進する可能性が高いでしょう。会社は忠誠心を大切に思うもので，社員にさらに多くの責任と高い賃金を与えることによって，社員の忠誠心に報いようとします。

以上の理由から，私は，生涯に何度も転職することはよくないと思います。1つの会社で働くことのほうが，概して利点が多いです。）

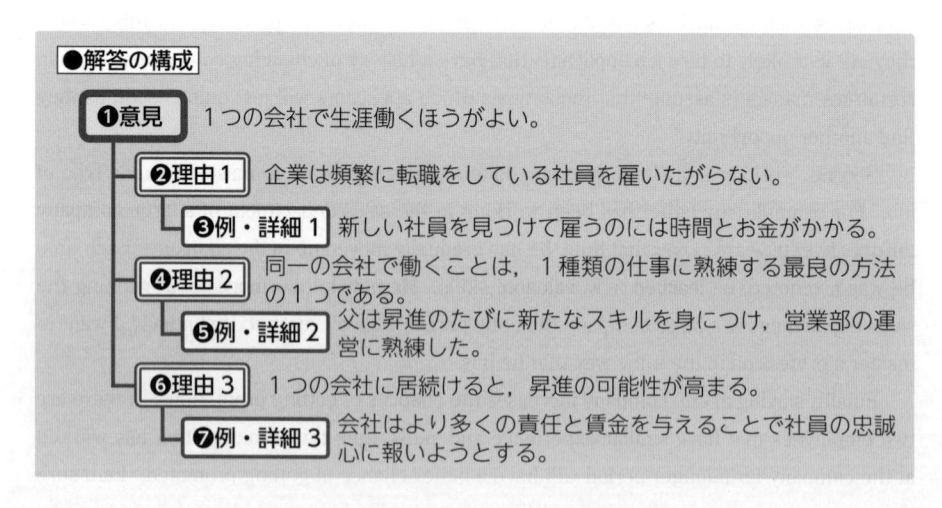

●解答の構成

❶意見　1つの会社で生涯働くほうがよい。

　❷理由1　企業は頻繁に転職をしている社員を雇いたがらない。

　　❸例・詳細1　新しい社員を見つけて雇うのには時間とお金がかかる。

　❹理由2　同一の会社で働くことは，1種類の仕事に熟練する最良の方法の1つである。

　　❺例・詳細2　父は昇進のたびに新たなスキルを身につけ，営業部の運営に熟練した。

　❻理由3　1つの会社に居続けると，昇進の可能性が高まる。

　　❼例・詳細3　会社はより多くの責任と賃金を与えることで社員の忠誠心に報いようとする。

✓ 重要表現チェック

不十分な解答例	☐ stable「安定した」	☐ fire「〜を解雇する」
	☐ lay off 〜「〜を一時解雇する」	
	☐ a wide range of 〜「幅広い〜, 広範囲の〜」	
	☐ marketing department「マーケティング部」	
	☐ take advantage of 〜「〜を利用する」	
適切な解答例	☐ steady「安定した, 着実な」	☐ diverse「多様な」
別解	☐ go through 〜「〜を経験する,（手続き）を踏む」	
	☐ history「履歴, 経歴」	
	☐ human resources manager「人事部長」	
	☐ sales department「営業部」	☐ move up「昇進する」
	☐ promote「〜を昇進させる」	☐ run「〜を管理する」

問題 10

Some people like to live in a big city. Other people like to live in the quiet countryside.
Which do you prefer to live in? Use specific reasons and examples to support your answer.

【設問訳】
大都市に住むのが好きな人もいます。静かな田舎に住むのが好きな人もいます。
あなたはどちらに住みたいと思いますか。あなたの意見の根拠となる具体的な理由や事例を述べなさい。

解答例 「大都市に住みたい」と答える場合

不十分な解答例

*1 Some people might say it is not a good idea to live in a big city. For example, they point out that a city is so polluted that many people suffer from lung diseases. Also, a city is very crowded with people and dangerous. In my opinion, however, these disadvantages are outweighed by the advantages. I would therefore prefer to live in a big city.

First, I love the excitement a big city can offer. In Tokyo, Japan, where I currently live in (→不要), there are various types of entertainment available. *2 There are, for example, movie theaters, baseball stadiums, game arcades, concert halls, night clubs, bars, and so on. In a big city such as mine, I can always find something exciting to do. It is almost impossible for me to get boring (→bored).

*3 Second, a city has good public transportation. The train and subway systems in my city is (→are) efficient, and the fares are reasonable. I can go to (→不要) anywhere by using public transportation; I do not need to own a car. Besides, shopping is easy in a big city. In my neighborhood, for example, there are some big supermarkets that stay open until midnight. *4 It is very convenient.

Finally, I can meet a diversity of people in a big city. These include not only people from remote areas of my own country, but also those from distant parts of the world. By meeting and talk (→talking) with people from abroad, I can learn about their cultures and broaden my view. *5 Furthermore, when I talk with them, I use English.

For the reasons stated above, I think it is better to live in a big city than in a (→the) countryside. *6 I have enjoyed life in a big city because it enables me to keep up with the latest trends.

●構成と内容の改善ポイント

★1 自分と反対の立場に言及することは，Introduction の定番の書き出し方の1つですが，非常に具体的な例を挙げて長々と論じると，読み手をかえって混乱させる可能性があります。
  ➡ Introduction で自分とは逆の立場に言及する場合には，1〜2文以内に簡潔にまとめ，自分の立場が明確に伝わるように注意しましょう。

★2 具体例を挙げる際，名詞を列挙しただけでは，議論を発展させたとはみなされず，高得点には結びつきません。
  ➡ 単に名詞をいくつも並べるのではなく，そのうちの1つか2つに絞り込み，その事柄について，文で説明することを心がけましょう。そうすることで，議論に具体性が増し，また語数を増やすこともできます。

★3 この段落のキーセンテンスは「公共交通機関が便利である」となっていますが，同じ段落の後半で買い物の話を出しており，自分が最初に示したトピックからそれてしまっています。
  ➡ この段落は最後まで公共交通機関の話で貫き通し，他の段落で買い物の話題を展開するか，あるいは適切な解答例のように convenient というキーワードを用いて，この段落のキーセンテンスを，「公共交通機関」と「買い物」という両方の事例をカバーできるものにします。段落内での主張の一貫性も意識しましょう。

★4 ただ「非常に便利である」と述べるだけでは，漠然としており，説得力に欠けます。
  ➡ 深夜まで開いているスーパーが近所にあると，どのような場合に便利であるかを具体的に説明します。

★5 「英語を使う」というだけで終わってしまっては，それがどのようなメリットをもたらすのかが伝わらず，ひいては「大都市に住むほうがよい」という主張を十分にサポートしたことになりません。
  ➡ 「英語力を向上させることができる」という説明を補います。さらに，「（外国人と交流し，見識を広め，英語力を磨くことは）自分が国際舞台で活躍する助けになる」という段落のまとめとなるコメントを最後に加えると，全体がより引き締まります。

★6 結論の段落で，これまでに言及していない新しい理由を挙げるのは避けましょう。自分の答えをサポートする理由は，Body の段落で展開しなければなりません。
  ➡ 新たな理由を出すことなく，大都市のほうがよいという自分の立場を強調するコメントでエッセイの最後を締めくくります。

《構成の改善例》

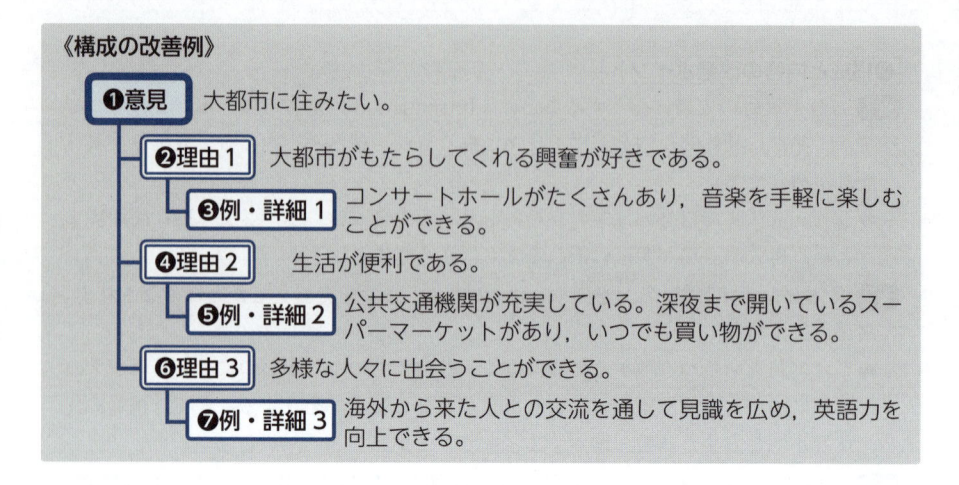

- **❶意見** 大都市に住みたい。
    - **❷理由1** 大都市がもたらしてくれる興奮が好きである。
        - **❸例・詳細1** コンサートホールがたくさんあり，音楽を手軽に楽しむことができる。
    - **❹理由2** 生活が便利である。
        - **❺例・詳細2** 公共交通機関が充実している。深夜まで開いているスーパーマーケットがあり，いつでも買い物ができる。
    - **❻理由3** 多様な人々に出会うことができる。
        - **❼例・詳細3** 海外から来た人との交流を通して見識を広め，英語力を向上できる。

適切な解答例

★1 Some people might say it is not a good idea to live in a big city, pointing out that it is more polluted, crowded, and dangerous. In my opinion, however, these disadvantages are outweighed by the advantages. I would therefore prefer to live in a big city.

First, I love the excitement a big city can offer. In Tokyo, Japan, where I currently live, there are various types of entertainment available. ★2 There are, for example, many concert halls, and famous musicians come from all over the world and hold concerts there. As I am a resident of this city, I can easily attend such superb concerts and enjoy exquisite music. In a big city such as mine, I can always find something exciting to do. It is almost impossible for me to get bored.

★3 Second, life in a big city is convenient. For one thing, a city has good public transportation. The train and subway systems in my city are efficient, and the fares are reasonable. I can go anywhere by using public transportation; I do not need to own a car. Besides, shopping is easy in a big city. In my neighborhood, for example, there are some big supermarkets that stay open until midnight. ★4 This means that even if I work overtime and get back home late, I can walk to one of them and buy whatever I need.

Finally, I can meet a diversity of people in a big city. These include not only people from remote areas of my own country, but also those from distant parts of the world. By meeting and talking with people from abroad, I can learn about their cultures and broaden my view. ★5 Furthermore, when I talk with them, I use English, which provides a good chance for me to improve my English skills. I believe all of this will help me become successful in the international arena.

For the reasons stated above, I would rather live in a big city than in the countryside. **I have enjoyed life in a big city since I moved from a rural area several years ago, and I have no intention to go back to the countryside.** (362 words)

(汚染され，混雑し，危険であるということを指摘して，大都市に住むのはよくないと言う人もいるかもしれません。しかしながら，私の意見では，これらの不利益よりも利益のほうが上回ります。よって，私は大都市に住みたいと思います。

第1に，私は大都市がもたらしてくれる興奮が好きです。私が現在住んでいる日本の東京には，様々な種類の娯楽があります。例えば，コンサートホールがたくさんあり，世界中から有名な音楽家が来て，コンサートを開きます。私はこの都市の住人であるため，そのような素晴らしいコンサートに参加し，見事な音楽を手軽に楽しむことができます。このような大都市では，常にわくわくすることを見つけることができます。退屈することはほとんどありえません。

第2に，大都市での生活は便利です。まず1つ例を挙げると，都市は公共交通機関が優れています。私の都市の電車や地下鉄は効率的で，運賃は手ごろです。公共交通機関を使ってどこにでも行くことができます。車を持つ必要はないのです。加えて，大都市では買い物が簡単です。例えば，私の近所には，真夜中まで開いている大きなスーパーマーケットがいくつかあります。これはすなわち，私が残業をして家に帰ってくるのが遅くなっても，そのうちの1つに歩いて行って，必要なものを何でも買えるということです。

最後に，大都市では多様な人たちに会うことができます。これには国内の遠くの地域から来た人だけでなく，世界の遠い場所から来た人も含まれます。海外から来た人に会い，話をすることで，彼らの文化について学び，見識を広めることができます。さらに，彼らと話をする時には，英語を使いますから，これによって英語力を向上させる絶好の機会が得られます。このことはすべて，私が国際的な場で活躍する助けになると信じています。

上述の理由から，田舎よりも大都市に住むほうがよいと考えます。数年前に地方から引っ越してきて以来，私は大都市での生活を満喫しており，田舎に帰るつもりはまったくありません。)

別解 「田舎に住みたい」と答える場合

In my country, many people move from rural areas to big cities in pursuit of better job opportunities. However, as I have lived in the countryside since I was a child, I am familiar with the benefits of country life. If I can choose where I live, I would like to live in the countryside.

The primary reason is that in the countryside, I can live with nature around me. In the morning, I wake up to the sound of birds singing. When I go for a swim in a river, I can see fish swimming in the clear water. There are wild flowers everywhere. Living in such a beautiful natural environment is good for the soul as well as the physical health. City life, on the other hand, can be unpleasant and harmful to health, considering the noise and pollution resulting from human activity.

Another reason is that there is a strong sense of community in the countryside. Since there are only a limited number of people, everyone knows one another very well. The whole community is like one big family, and people are friendly and kind to other members of the community. Elderly people living alone do not feel lonely or isolated because their neighbors visit them and give them support whenever necessary. In fact, residents are bound by strong ties that would be unthinkable in a city, where people tend to be indifferent to others.

The final reason is that houses are less expensive in the countryside. It would not be difficult for young people like me to own a house. My dream is to live in a house with a big vegetable garden. I would like to grow vegetables without using chemicals so that I can enjoy healthy and tasty vegetables every day. If I lived in a city, this kind of life would be impossible; I would have to live in a tiny apartment with no garden and pay a high rent.

In conclusion, I find it far better to live in the quiet countryside than in a busy city. I believe life in the countryside gives me what I need to live happily.　　　　(359 words)

（私の国では，多くの人々がよりよい就職の機会を求めて，地方から大都市へと移動します。しかしながら，私は子供の頃から田舎に住んでいたので，田舎の生活の利点を熟知しています。もし住む場所を選べるのなら，私は田舎に住みたいと思います。

最初の理由は，田舎では自然に囲まれて暮らせるからです。朝は鳥のさえずりで目を覚まします。川に泳ぎに行くと，澄んだ水の中で魚が泳いでいるのを見ることができます。至るところに野の花があります。そのような美しい自然環境の中で暮らすのは，心にも体の健康にもよいのです。一方，人間の活動によってもたらされる騒音や汚染を考えると，都市での生活は不快で，健康に有害な可能性があります。

もう1つの理由は，田舎には強い共同体意識があることです。限られた数の人しかいないため，誰もがお互いを非常によく知っています。共同体全体が1つの大家族のようで，人々は共同体の他のメンバーに対して友好的で，親切です。1人暮らしの年配者も寂しさや疎外感を抱きません。隣人たちが訪ねて来て，必要な時にはいつでも支援をするからです。実際，住民たちは都会では考えられない強い絆で結ばれています。都会では，人々は他者に対して無関心な傾向があるのです。

最後の理由は，田舎のほうが家が安いからです。私のような若者が家を所有するのも難しくないでしょう。私の夢は，大きな菜園がある家に住むことです。毎日，健康的でおいしい野菜が楽しめるよう，化学物質を使わずに野菜を育てたいと思います。もし都会に住んだら，このような生活は不可能でしょう。庭のない狭いアパートに住み，高い家賃を払わなければならないことでしょう。

結論として，私はあわただしい都会に住むよりは，静かな田舎に住むほうがずっとよいと思います。田舎での生活は私が幸せに生きるために必要なものを与えてくれると思います。）

●解答の構成

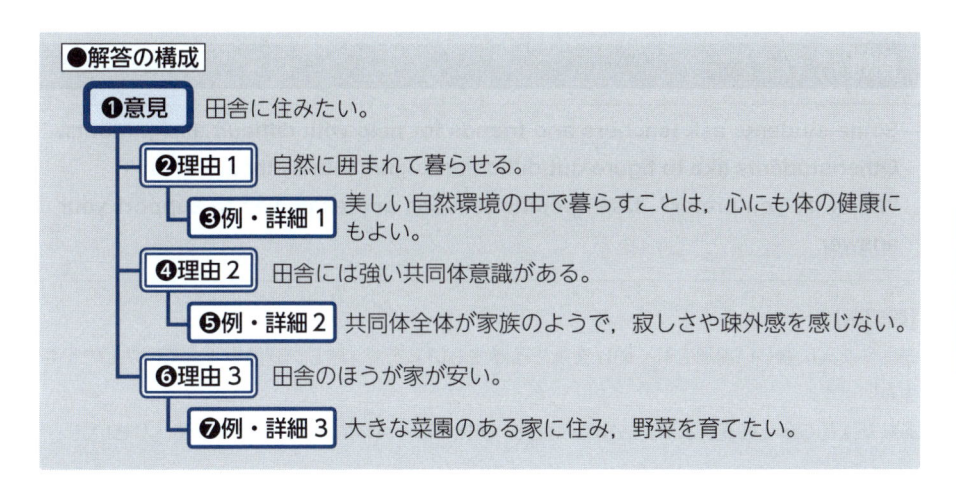

- **❶意見** 田舎に住みたい。
  - **❷理由1** 自然に囲まれて暮らせる。
    - **❸例・詳細1** 美しい自然環境の中で暮らすことは，心にも体の健康にもよい。
  - **❹理由2** 田舎には強い共同体意識がある。
    - **❺例・詳細2** 共同体全体が家族のようで，寂しさや疎外感を感じない。
  - **❻理由3** 田舎のほうが家が安い。
    - **❼例・詳細3** 大きな菜園のある家に住み，野菜を育てたい。

✓ 重要表現チェック

不十分な解答例
- ☐ lung disease「肺疾患」
- ☐ outweigh「～を上回る，勝る」
- ☐ transportation「交通機関，輸送」
- ☐ a diversity of ～「多様な～」
- ☐ broaden *one's* view「見識を広める」
- ☐ keep up with ～「～に遅れずについていく」
- ☐ latest trends「最新の流行」

適切な解答例
- ☐ superb「すばらしい，卓越した」
- ☐ exquisite「見事な，申し分のない」
- ☐ international arena「国際的な場，国際舞台」
- ☐ rural「田舎の，地方の」

別解
- ☐ in pursuit of ～「～を求めて」
- ☐ considering ～「～を考慮すると」
- ☐ sense of community「共同体意識，連帯感」
- ☐ isolated「孤立した，疎外された」
- ☐ bound by strong ties「強い絆で結ばれた」
- ☐ indifferent to ～「～に無関心な」
- ☐ chemical「化学物質」

問題 11

Some students ask teachers and friends for help with difficult assignments. Other students like to figure out difficult assignments by themselves. Which do you prefer? Use specific reasons and examples to support your answer.

【設問訳】
先生や友人に難しい課題を解く助けを求める学生もいますが，難しい課題を1人で解決したい学生もいます。
あなたはどちらを好みますか。あなたの意見の根拠となる具体的な理由や事例を述べなさい。

解答例 「教師や友人に難しい課題を解く助けを求めるほうがよい」と答える場合

不十分な解答例

I prefer to ask friends and teachers for help with difficult assignments. ★1 I think other people have helpful insights and opinions. If you ask people for help without being shy, you can improve yourself. If you get help with assignments, you can avoid mistakes.

The main reason that I prefer to get help with challenged (→**challenging**) assignments is that friends and teachers have different viewpoints and knowledge than me. It is very (→**so**) much easier to understand problems when looking at them by (→**from**) various perspectives. ★2 It would take me ages if I kept thinking about it by myself.

Second, I think that if you are able to ask others for help without hesitation, you will improve yourself. I am (→**It is**) natural to feel shy about asking for help with problems, but I think that I am too shy in general. ★3 I have wanted to overcome my shyness since I was a younger child. The shyness seems to be disappearing recently. Aside from getting interesting information from outside sources, I also improve myself by becoming less hesitate (→**hesitant**) to share my problems with other people.

★4 I will explain another typical example. Last month, I was having a very hard time deciding on a topic for a research paper that I needed to write for my history class. Eventually, I asked a friend to help me, and she told me that the teacher had posted a list of acceptable topics online, which I had not known about. If I didn't ask (→**had not asked**) for help, I would have done the wrong assignment, and I probably would have got a failing grade.

In conclusion, I think it is better to ask for help when facing (→**faced**) with difficult assignments and tasks.

●構成と内容の改善ポイント

★1 Body で展開する理由を3つ挙げていますが，接続語がないのでまとまりが悪く，Introduction として効果的にエッセイの構成を伝えることができていません。
　➡ 3つの理由を，適切な接続語を用いて列挙します。適切な解答例のような客観的な表現を心がけるとよりフォーマルな印象になります。

★2 「1人で考え続けていたら，とても時間がかかる」と述べるだけでは，「教師や友人に頼った方がよい」ことの利点が直接的には伝わらず，説得力に欠けます。
　➡ 「1人で考えているだけでは時間ばかりかかるが，人に相談すれば短時間で解決することがある」という説明を加えます。主張と詳細情報の論理的なつながりを明確に示しましょう。

★3 話の中心が「自分が恥ずかしがりを克服した」という内容に移り，「人に助けを求めるのがよい」という論点からそれてしまっています。
　➡ ここでは，「人に助けを求めることで，恥ずかしがることをやめることができる」という論理関係を示します。主張をサポートするのに必要な情報に絞り，効果的に伝えることを心がけましょう。

★4 「別の典型的な例」では漠然としています。その具体例を挙げることによって伝えたい主張が述べられていないため，段落の主旨がはっきりしません。
　➡ 筆者の主張したいことを，読み手が類推して判断しなければならないような曖昧な表現は避けます。具体例を述べる時は，その具体例によって伝えたい内容を簡潔に示すようにしましょう。

《構成の改善例》

- **❶意見** 友人や先生に難しい課題を解く助けを求めるほうがよい。
  - **❷理由1** 他の人々は常に，役に立つ洞察や意見を持っている。
    - **❸例・詳細1** さまざまな観点から問題を見ると理解しやすく，効率的である。
  - **❹理由2** ためらわずに助けを求めることは自分自身の改善につながる。
    - **❺例・詳細2** 思い切って自分の問題を他者と共有していくことは，恥ずかしがりな性格を変えるよい方法になる。
  - **❻理由3** 助けを求めることで，間違いや誤解を回避できる。
    - **❼例・詳細3** 課題のトピックを決める際，友人に助けを求めたので，誤った課題に取り組まずに済んだ。

適切な解答例

I prefer to ask friends and teachers for help with difficult assignments. ★1 **Other people always have helpful insights and opinions. Also, asking people for help without being shy can lead to self-improvement. Finally, getting help with assignments is a good way to avoid mistakes.**

The main reason that I prefer to get help with challenging assignments is that friends and teachers have different viewpoints and knowledge than me. It is so much easier to understand problems when looking at them from various perspectives. ★2 **But this is extremely difficult to do alone. Sometimes a few minutes talking to someone about a problem can be more effective than hours of thinking about it without any help.**

Second, I think that being able to ask others for help without hesitation leads to self-improvement. It is natural to feel shy about asking for help with problems, but I think that I am too shy in general. ★3 **One great way to stop being so shy is to ask for help when it is needed.** Aside from getting interesting information from outside sources, I also improve myself by becoming less hesitant to share my problems with other people.

★4 **Another benefit of asking for help with difficult assignments is avoiding mistakes and misunderstandings.** Last month, I was having a very hard time deciding on a topic for a research paper that I needed to write for my history class. Eventually, I asked a friend to help me, and she told me that the teacher had posted a list of acceptable topics online, which I had not known about. If I had not asked for help, I would have done the wrong assignment, and I probably would have got a failing grade.

In conclusion, I think it is better to ask for help when faced with difficult assignments and tasks. (302 words)

(私は，友人や先生に難しい課題を解く助けを求めるほうが好きです。他の人々は，常に役に立つ洞察や意見を持っています。また，恥ずかしがらずに助けを求めることは自分自身の改善につながります。最後に，課題を解く助けを得ることは，間違いを避けるよい方法です。

難しい課題を解く助けを得るほうがよいと思う主な理由は，友人や先生は，私と違う視点や知識を持っているからです。さまざまな観点から問題を見てみると，問題がずっと理解しやすくなりますが，これを1人で行うのは極めて困難です。時には，ある問題を解くために誰かと数分話すほうが，まったく助けを得ずにその問題について何時間も1人で考えるよりも，効率的ということもあるでしょう。

第2に，私はためらわずに助けを求めることができるということが自分自身の改善につながると思います。問題解決の助けを求めることを恥ずかしいと感じるのはもっともですが，自分は概して恥ずかしがりすぎるのだと思います。恥ずかしがるのをやめるよい方法の1つは，必要な時に助けを求めることです。外部の情報源からおもしろい情報を得られるだけでなく，自分の問題を他の人々と共有することをあまりためらわないようにすることによって，自分自身の改善にも

なります。

　難しい課題を解く助けを求めることのもう１つの利点は，間違いや誤解を避けられることです。先月，私は，歴史の授業で書かなければならなかった研究論文のトピックを決めるのに，とても苦労していました。最終的に，友人に助けを求めると，先生が望ましいトピックのリストをインターネット上に投稿していたと教えてくれたのですが，私はそのことを知りませんでした。もし，助けを求めていなかったら，誤った課題に取り組んでしまい，もしかすると落第していたかもしれません。

　結論として，私は，難しい課題やタスクに直面したら，助けを求めたほうがよいと思います。)

別解 「難しい課題を１人で解決したい」と答える場合

　There are certainly benefits to getting help with difficult assignments. Other people have interesting ideas and opinions, and they can make challenging work much easier. However, I still prefer to work on difficult assignments without any outside help.

　First, solving difficult problems on my own is a great way to learn new things. When I was in junior high school, I had a math teacher named Mr. Shibata. One day, many of the students were complaining about a difficult assignment, and he said, "If it were easy, then you wouldn't be learning." I realized then that school assignments should be difficult, because difficult challenges make people smarter. Now, whenever I encounter a frustrating problem, I remember his words, and I do everything I can to solve it on my own.

　Second, I only want to ask my friends and teachers for help in very serious situations. If I ask for help every time that I face a difficult challenge, then my friends and teachers might start to think that I am lazy, and they will not want to help me anymore. However, if I very rarely ask them for help, then they will know that I am facing a serious problem when I request their assistance.

　Finally, I do not like asking for help, because it is embarrassing. I know that I probably should not feel embarrassed about asking friends and teachers for help, but I still do. As a result, in many cases, I would rather deal with an unpleasant assignment on my own than feel embarrassed. I am not sure if this is a good thing or a bad thing, but it is one of the reasons why I avoid asking for help with difficult assignments.

　For these reasons, I prefer to work on difficult assignments by myself, without asking for help from friends and teachers. (308 words)

（難しい課題を解く助けを得ることには，確かによい面があります。他の人の中には，おもしろい考えや意見を持っていて，難しい仕事をずっと簡単にできる人もいます。しかし，それでも私は，外部からの助けなしに難しい課題に取り組むほうが好きです。

　まず，自力で難しい問題を解決することは，新しい物事を学ぶ素晴らしい方法です。中学生の時，柴田先生という名前の数学の先生がいました。ある日，生徒たちの多くが難しい課題に文句を言

っていると，柴田先生は「これが簡単だったら，あなたたちの学びにならないでしょう」と言いました。私はその時，難しい課題は人を賢くするので，学校からの課題は難しくあるべきなのだと気づきました。今では，挫折感を抱くような問題に直面するたびに，柴田先生の言葉を思い出し，自力で解決するためにできるあらゆることをしています。

　第2に，私は，非常に深刻な状況にある場合にだけ，友人や先生に助けを求めたいと思います。もし，難しい課題に直面するたびに助けを求めていたら，友人や先生たちは，私が怠惰だと思い始めるかもしれません。そうしたら，私をもう助けたいと思わなくなるでしょう。しかし，私がごくまれにしか助けを求めないとしたら，私が彼らの助けを求める時は，深刻な問題に直面しているのだとわかってくれるでしょう。

　最後に，私は助けを求めるのが気まずいので，好きではありません。おそらく，友人や先生に助けを求めることを気まずく感じるべきではないのだろうと思いますが，それでもそう感じてしまいます。その結果，多くの場合，私は気まずい思いをするよりは，むしろ嫌な課題に1人で取り組むほうがよいと思います。これがよいことか悪いことかはわかりませんが，これも私が難しい課題を解く助けを求めることを避けている理由の1つです。

　以上のような理由から，私は，友人や先生に助けを求めることなく，難しい課題に自力で取り組むほうが好きなのです。）

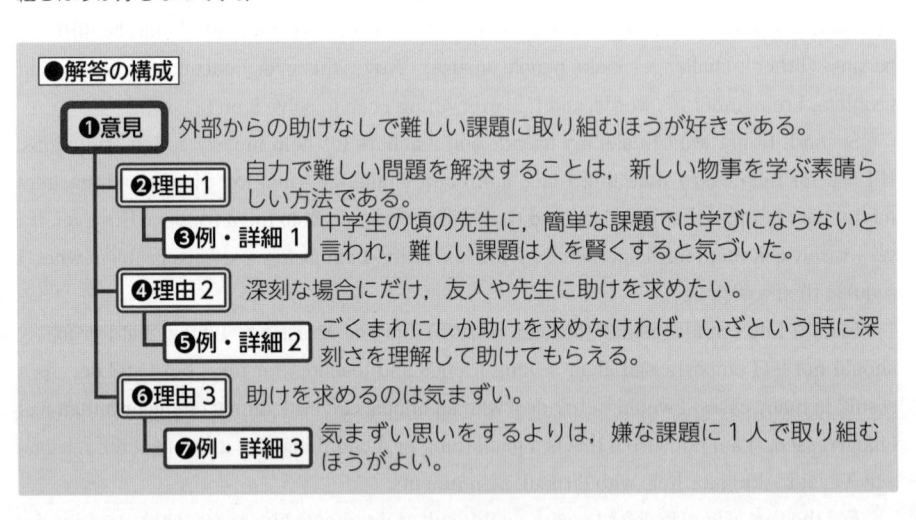

●解答の構成

- **❶意見**　外部からの助けなしで難しい課題に取り組むほうが好きである。
  - **❷理由1**　自力で難しい問題を解決することは，新しい物事を学ぶ素晴らしい方法である。
    - **❸例・詳細1**　中学生の頃の先生に，簡単な課題では学びにならないと言われ，難しい課題は人を賢くすると気づいた。
  - **❹理由2**　深刻な場合にだけ，友人や先生に助けを求めたい。
    - **❺例・詳細2**　ごくまれにしか助けを求めなければ，いざという時に深刻さを理解して助けてもらえる。
  - **❻理由3**　助けを求めるのは気まずい。
    - **❼例・詳細3**　気まずい思いをするよりは，嫌な課題に1人で取り組むほうがよい。

✓ 重要表現チェック

不十分な解答例
- ☐ insight「洞察，見識」
- ☐ challenging「やりがいのある，骨の折れる」
- ☐ perspective「観点」　　☐ hesitation「ためらい」
- ☐ post「〜を掲示する，掲載する」　☐ failing grade「落第点」

適切な解答例
- ☐ self-improvement「自己改善」　☐ misunderstanding「誤解」

別解
- ☐ frustrating「がっかりさせる，挫折感を与える」
- ☐ rarely「めったに〜ない」　☐ embarrassing「気まずい」

問題 12

Some people prefer to live alone when they become old. Others want to live with their children or relatives.
Which do you prefer? Use specific reasons and examples to support your answer.

【設問訳】
老後は1人暮らしをしたい人もいれば，子供や親戚と暮らしたい人もいます。
あなたはどちらを好みますか。あなたの意見の根拠となる具体的な理由や事例を述べなさい。

解答例 「老後は子供や親戚と暮らしたい」と答える場合

不十分な解答例

　Whether elderly people live alone or live with their family can be a big decision for everyone involved. ★1 It may be ideal for me to live with my children and get on well with them. On the other hand, I can imagine how stressful it will be if I am not getting along with my daughter-in-law, for example. Nevertheless I would prefer to live with family when I become old. I have three reasons of (→**for**) this preference.

　Firstly, ★2 if I live with the family of one of my children and I am healthy, I will try not to be dependent on them. I will help them in many ways. As people become older, they may tend to feel left out or unwanted by society. ★2 Living with their family helps them stay fit mentally and physically.

　Secondly, living with family can be more economic (→**economical**) than living alone. It is obvious that living separately will cost more than living together under one roof. ★3 If I live with my child's family, I can do housework and take care of their children. It will be good for both the parents and the children.

　Finally, living with family will benefit society. ★4 Elderly people who choose to live alone are not actually independent. They wouldn't like to depend on neighbors or friends even if they have an accident, become sick, or something unpleasant happens. Then they have no choice but to rely on public services. In today's society where welfare costs are becoming a heavy burden, it would be best for the elderly to be supported by their families.

　In conclusion, I would prefer living with my children or relatives than (→**to**) living alone. It is more beneficial not only for me but also for other family members and for society.

●構成と内容の改善ポイント

★1 Introduction で自分の立場を表明するまでの説明が長くなっています。
➡ Introduction で自分の意見を表明する際,「マイナス面もあるが,やはり〜がよい」と述べることは,自分の意見の客観性を強調する効果があります。しかし,長々と述べると議論に一貫性のない印象を与えるため,1〜2文程度にとどめましょう。

★2 「子供の家族と暮らしたら彼らに頼らないようにし,彼らを助けるつもりだ」という内容と,同じ段落後半の「年をとると疎外感を抱きやすく,家族と暮らすことは精神的にも肉体的にも健康でいることに役立つ」という内容との関連性が読み取れません。
➡ 「お互いに助け合うことは家族の一員として尊重されることであり,それが精神的・肉体的な健康につながる」という論理展開が伝わるような説明を加えましょう。また,段落の主旨を「他の世代の人と一緒に暮らすことは,家族のそれぞれのメンバーに利点がある」とまとめ,第1文で述べることで,読みやすいエッセイになります。

★3 「1つの家に住むほうが経済的だ」という主張との関連が不明瞭であり,具体例が主張を支える根拠としての役割を果たしていません。
➡ 1つの家に住むことがどのようにお金の節約につながるのかについて,具体例や詳細説明を加えます。

★4 1人暮らしを選ぶ高齢者について,「実際には自立していない」と述べ,「近所の人や友人に頼りたがらない」「公的サービスを受けるより他ない」と,非難ともとれる強い主張が続いています。
➡ 1人暮らしを選ぶ高齢者が必ずそうであると言い切ることは難しい内容であり,このような極端に強い主張は,客観性に欠ける印象を与える場合があります。ここでは might / may / in some cases などを用いて,誰が読んでも違和感のない表現にすることで,説得力が増します。

《構成の改善例》

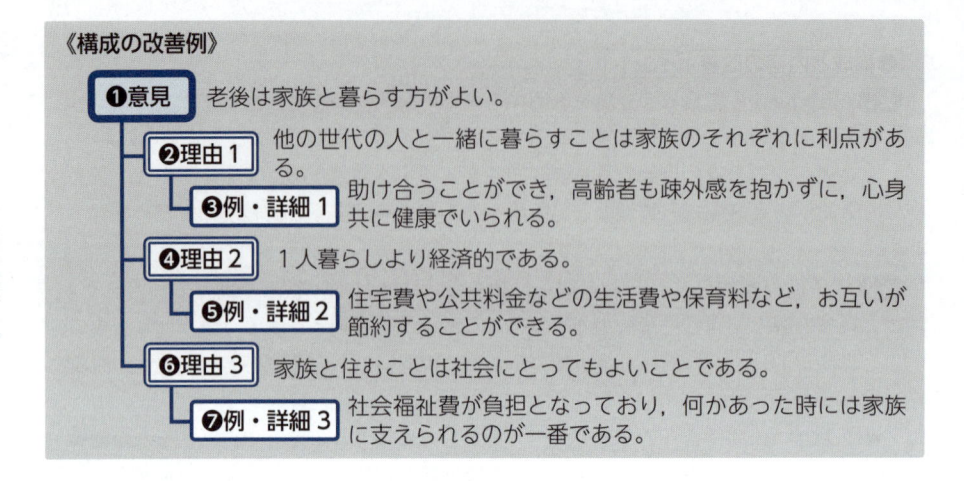

- **❶意見** 老後は家族と暮らす方がよい。
  - **❷理由1** 他の世代の人と一緒に暮らすことは家族のそれぞれに利点がある。
    - **❸例・詳細1** 助け合うことができ，高齢者も疎外感を抱かずに，心身共に健康でいられる。
  - **❹理由2** 1人暮らしより経済的である。
    - **❺例・詳細2** 住宅費や公共料金などの生活費や保育料など，お互いが節約することができる。
  - **❻理由3** 家族と住むことは社会にとってもよいことである。
    - **❼例・詳細3** 社会福祉費が負担となっており，何かあった時には家族に支えられるのが一番である。

適切な解答例

　　Whether elderly people live alone or live with their family can be a big decision for everyone involved.　★1 Although living with other family members may require some effort, I would prefer to live with family when I become old.　I have three reasons for this preference.

　　Firstly,　★2 having different generations living together will benefit each member of the family.　If I live with the family of one of my children and I am healthy, I can do some housework for them when they are busy working or looking after their children.　In other words, we can help each other.　As people become older, they may tend to feel left out or unwanted by society.　★2 Living with their family and being respected as a family member may help them stay fit mentally and physically.

　　Secondly, living with family can be more economical than living alone. It is obvious that living separately will cost more than living together under one roof.　★3 If I live with my child's family and share the living expenses such as housing costs and utilities, it will be good for both of us.　Moreover, when they need someone to take care of their children, I can be there. That will can save on childcare costs, too.

　　Finally, living with family will benefit society.　★4 Elderly people who choose to live alone might think they are independent.　However, even if they are not living with their family, they may need to be supported by someone else.　Whether they like it or not, they may need to depend on neighbors or friends if they accidentally have an accident or become sick, or if something unpleasant happens.　In some cases, they may have no choice but to rely on public services.　In today's society where welfare costs are becoming a heavy burden, it would be best for the elderly to be supported by their families.

In conclusion, I would prefer living with my children or relatives to living alone. It is more beneficial not only for me but also for other family members and for society.

(344 words)

（高齢者が１人で暮らすか，家族と暮らすかは関係するすべての人にとって大きな決断となり得ます。他の家族のメンバーと暮らすのは何らかの努力を要するかもしれませんが，私は老後は家族と暮らすほうがよいです。この選択には３つの理由があります。

第１に，他の世代の人と一緒に暮らすことは家族のそれぞれに利点があります。もし私が子供のうちの１人の家族と暮らし，健康でいたら，子供たちが仕事や子育てで忙しい時に彼らのために家事をすることができます。つまり，私たちは助け合えるということです。人々は年を取るにつれて，社会から疎外されていたり，必要とされていないと感じがちになるかもしれません。家族と暮らし，家族の一員として尊重されることは，彼らが精神的，肉体的に健康でいることに役立つかもしれません。

第２に，家族と一緒に暮らすことは１人暮らしより経済的です。別々に暮らす方が１つ屋根の下で一緒に暮らすより明らかに多くお金がかかります。私が子供の家族と一緒に暮らし，住宅費や公共料金などの生活費を分担するなら，私たち両方にとってよいでしょう。さらに，彼らが子供たちの世話をする人が必要な時は，私ができます。彼らは保育料も節約することができます。

最後に，家族と住むことは社会にとってもよいことです。１人暮らしを選ぶ高齢者は，自分たちは自立していると思っているかもしれません。しかし，たとえ彼らが家族と住んでいないとしても他の誰かに支えてもらわなければならないかもしれません。彼らが好もうが好むまいが，たまたま事故に遭ったり，病気になったり，または何か不快なことが起きたら，近所の人や友人を頼らなければならないかもしれません。時には公的サービスを受けるより他ない場合もあるかもしれません。社会福祉費が重い負担となっている今日の社会では，高齢者は家族に支えられるのが一番です。

結論として，私は１人暮らしより自分の子供や親戚と暮らすほうがよいです。それは自分にとってだけでなく，他の家族や社会にとってもより有益なのです。）

別解 「老後は１人暮らしをしたい」と答える場合

Many elderly people all over the world live alone. Some of them might prefer living apart from other family members. For others, living alone might not be their preference, but they do so because they do not have any close relatives who can support them. As for me, I would like to live by myself as long as I am healthy and not bed-ridden.

The first benefit of living alone is the freedom. As long as I am healthy, I would be happy to cook for myself and do other housework. I would also enjoy being able to go anywhere I wanted to go and coming home anytime without having to tell my family. And if I wanted to stay home all day and do nothing, I could do that, too.

Second, I would be able to make friends more easily. It's important for the elderly to have others around. If I depended only on my family, I may not meet anyone else. But if neighbors or friends stopped by to call on me every day, I would enjoy contact with a wide variety of people. And by staying in touch with them, if something goes wrong, we can help each other.

Finally, living separately from relatives is the best way to keep a good relationship with them. Speaking from my experience, my mother and grandmother lived together for several years. They fought often and it was very stressful for everyone involved. If relatives have distance between them, they will appreciate each other more and feel more relaxed when they get together.

Living alone, I may feel lonely sometimes. But if I had many friends nearby, and if my children and their families came to visit occasionally, I think my life would be very fulfilling. Therefore, I would prefer to live alone for as long as I can. (308 words)

（世界中で多くの高齢者が1人で暮らしています。彼らの中には家族と離れて住むのを好んでいる人もいるかもしれません。1人暮らしを好んでしているのではなく，支えてくれる近い親族がまったくいないからそうしている人もいるかもしれません。私に関しては，自分が健康で寝たきりでない限り，1人で暮らしたいです。

1人暮らしの第1の利点は自由です。私が健康でいる限り，自分で料理をしたり，他の家事を喜んでするでしょう。行きたいところにどこへでも行き，家族に伝える必要なくいつでも帰宅できることを楽しみたいです。また，もし1日中家にいて何もしたくないなら，そうすることもできるでしょう。

第2に，私はより容易に友人を作ることができるでしょう。周りに人がいることは高齢者にとって重要です。もし私が家族だけに頼っていたなら，他の誰にも会わないかもしれません。しかし，もし近所の人や友人が毎日私を訪ねに来てくれるとしたら，さまざまな人々との付き合いを楽しむでしょう。そして，その人たちと連絡を取り合い続けることで，何か問題が起きたらお互いに助け合うことができます。

最後に親族から離れて暮らすことは，彼らとよい関係を保つのに一番よい方法です。私の経験から言うと，私の母と祖母は数年間一緒に暮らしました。彼女たちはしばしば喧嘩をしましたが，それは周りの皆にとって非常にストレスの多いものでした。もし親類同士の間に距離があれば，よりお互いに感謝し，集まった時によりくつろげるでしょう。

1人暮らしをしていると時には寂しく感じるかもしれません。しかし近くに多くの友人がいて，子供たちやその家族が時々訪ねに来るなら，私の人生はとても充実したものになるでしょう。したがって，私はできるだけ長く1人で暮らしたいです。）

●解答の構成

- **❶意見** 老後は1人で暮らしたい。
  - **❷理由1** 1人暮らしは自由である。
    - **❸例・詳細1** 行きたいところに行って好きな時間に帰宅でき，何もしたくなければしなくてもよい。
  - **❹理由2** 容易に友人を作ることができる。
    - **❺例・詳細2** 家族に頼らず1人暮らしをすれば，人付き合いを楽しみ，助け合うこともできる。
  - **❻理由3** 家族と離れて暮らすことで，よい関係を保つことができる。
    - **❼例・詳細3** 一緒に暮らすと喧嘩も起きるが，離れているとお互いに感謝し合える。

✓重要表現チェック

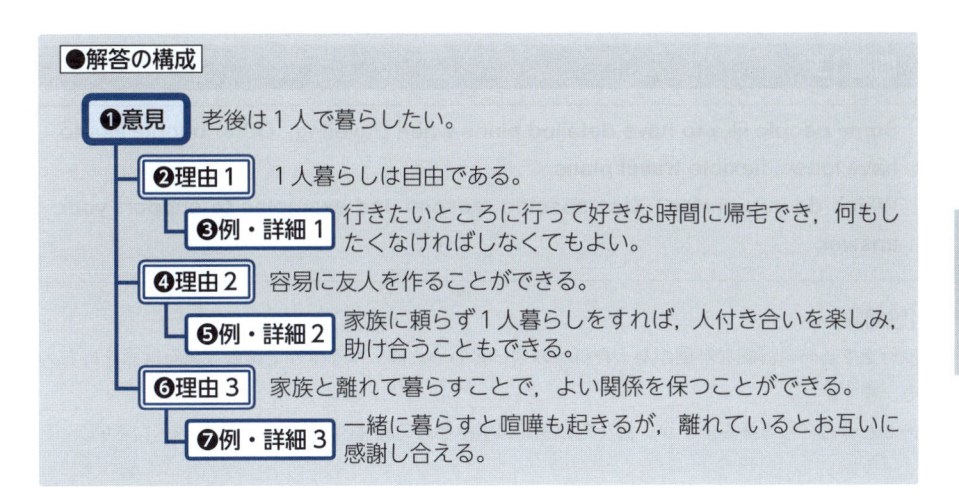

不十分な解答例	☐ daughter-in-law「義理の娘」	☐ leave out ～「～を除く，締め出す」
	☐ unwanted「必要とされていない」	☐ economical「経済的な」
	☐ separately「離れて，別々に」	☐ welfare「福祉」
適切な解答例	☐ utilities「公共料金」	☐ childcare「育児の，保育の」
別解	☐ bed-ridden「寝たきりの」	☐ stay in touch「連絡を取り合う」
	☐ fight「喧嘩する，口論する」	
	☐ fulfilling「達成感を与える，充足感のある」	

問題 13

Some people like to have detailed plans when traveling. Other people like to have loose, flexible travel plans.
Which do you prefer? Use specific reasons and examples to support your answer.

【設問訳】
旅行をする時に詳細な計画があったほうがよい人もいれば，ゆるやかで柔軟な旅行計画を好む人もいます。
あなたはどちらを好みますか。あなたの意見の根拠となる具体的な理由や事例を述べなさい。

解答例 「旅行をする時に詳細な計画があったほうがよい」と答える場合

不十分な解答例

　I like to have detailed plans when traveling.　**★1** The most important thing in making plans for a trip is good time management. You should make sure that your schedule is realistic. Also, without plans you might miss opportunities to see interesting places. Finally, having a plan makes traveling <u>more easily</u> (→**easier**) and stress-free.

　First of all, most people have busy work schedules, and <u>they</u> (→**it**) can be difficult to take long vacations. **★2** They have to pack lots of interesting travel experiences into a short period of time. However I carefully plan out trips in detail. Last summer, I went to Europe with my family for one week. **★3** Because we had just one week, we had a very busy itinerary. Without the detailed plan, we wouldn't have enjoyed the trip.

　<u>Additional</u> (→**Additionally**), building a detailed travel plan is also a great chance to learn about interesting travel spots. My sister and I read many travel guides about Europe. **★4** For example, we saw famous castles in Germany and beautiful seaside towns in Italy. We also visited local theaters, art galleries, markets and so on.

　Most <u>important</u> (→**importantly**), having detailed plans makes traveling <u>more easily</u> (→**easier**) and more relaxing. Trying to learn about public transportation, local restaurants, and sightseeing spots after arriving can be very stressful and <u>exhausted</u> (→**exhausting**). **★5** However I usually relax and enjoy my trip without these troubles.

　In conclusion, I believe that it is better to have detailed plans when traveling. I am looking forward to <u>create</u> (→**creating**) detailed travel itineraries for all of my trips in the future.

●構成と内容の改善ポイント

★1 旅行の計画を作る際に大切なこと・注意点を説明し,「柔軟な計画よりも詳細な計画があったほうがよい」という論点からそれてしまっています。
　➡ここでは,詳細な計画を作ることの利点として「時間の管理がうまくできること」を示すと,論点からそれません。

★2 前後の文が論理的につながらなくなってしまっています。
　➡適切な接続語を用いて,「長い休みを取るのが難しい。その結果,短い期間に旅行の経験を詰め込まなければならない。その方法として慎重に詳細な計画を立てる。」という流れを作りましょう。伝わりやすさを常に意識しましょう。

★3 ヨーロッパ旅行についての説明が漠然としていて,なぜ「詳細な計画がなければ旅を楽しめなかっただろう」と思うのかが読み手に伝わりません。
　➡詳細な計画がどのように役立ったのかを具体的に説明しましょう。

★4 訪れた観光地を列挙することに終始しています。
　➡具体的な観光地を挙げるのは2,3カ所に絞り,「詳細な旅行の計画を立てることでおもしろい旅行スポットを知り,訪れることができた」という説明を加えましょう。**★3** と同様に,その具体例から何を主張したいのかが読み手に伝わるように意識しましょう。

★5 なぜ「自分はこのようなトラブルなしに旅行を楽しむことができる」のかについての説明が不足しています。
　➡「詳細な旅行の計画を立てると,こうしたトラブルを避けることができる。そのため自分はリラックスして旅行を楽しむことができる。」という論理の流れを明確に示しましょう。

《構成の改善例》

- **❶意見** 旅行をする時は詳細な計画があったほうがよい。
    - **❷理由1** 多くの人は長期休暇が取りにくく,おもしろい経験を短期間に詰め込む必要がある。
        - **❸例・詳細1** 詳細な計画を慎重に立てたことで,たくさんの目的地に行くことができた。
    - **❹理由2** 詳細な計画を立てることは,おもしろい旅行スポットを知る好機である。
        - **❺例・詳細2** 事前に詳細な計画を立てたことで,ガイドブックで見つけた城や町を見逃すことなく訪れることができた。
    - **❻理由3** 詳細な計画は,旅行をより楽でリラックスできるものにする。
        - **❼例・詳細3** 交通機関やレストラン,観光スポットを事前に調べておくとストレスが減る。

適切な解答例

I like to have detailed plans when traveling. ★1 Good time management can make trips more exciting. Also, without plans you might miss opportunities to see interesting places. Finally, having a plan makes traveling easier and stress-free.

First of all, most people have busy work schedules, and it can be difficult to take long vacations. ★2 As a result, it is necessary to pack lots of interesting travel experiences into a short period of time. The only way to do this effectively is by carefully planning out trips in detail. Last summer, I went to Europe with my family for one week. ★3 There were so many things that we wanted to see, and we had a very busy itinerary. Luckily, since we had planned it so carefully, we were able to see almost everything on our list of travel destinations.

Additionally, building a detailed travel plan is also a great chance to learn about interesting travel spots. My sister and I read many travel guides about Europe, ★4 and we learned about a huge variety of interesting places, some of which we were able to see on our trip. For example, we saw famous castles in Germany and beautiful seaside towns in Italy. I am sure that we would have missed many places like these if we had not planned our trip in detail.

Most importantly, having detailed plans makes traveling easier and more relaxing. Trying to learn about public transportation, local restaurants, and sightseeing spots after arriving can be very stressful and exhausting. ★5 By planning ahead, you can eliminate many of these troubles, and this makes it much easier to relax and enjoy your trip with less worries.

In conclusion, I believe that it is better to have detailed plans when traveling. I am looking forward to creating detailed travel itineraries for all of my trips in the future.

(307 words)

（私は，旅行をする時は詳細な計画があったほうがよいです。上手な時間管理は旅行を楽しくします。また，計画がなければ，おもしろい場所を訪れる機会を逃すかもしれません。最後に，計画があるほうが，旅行は楽でストレスのないものになります。

まず，ほとんどの人は忙しい仕事のスケジュールを抱え，長期の休暇は取りにくいかもしれません。その結果，旅行でのおもしろい経験を，短期間にたくさん詰め込む必要があります。効率的にこのことを実行するための唯一の方法は，旅行の詳細な計画を慎重に立てることです。昨夏，私は家族と1週間ヨーロッパへ行きました。見たいものがとてもたくさんあったので，非常にあわただしい旅程でした。幸い，旅行をとても慎重に計画していたので，旅行の目的地のリストにあったほとんどすべてのものを見ることができました。

それから，詳細な旅行計画を立てることは，おもしろい旅行スポットを知る好機でもあります。

姉と私は，ヨーロッパの旅行ガイドブックをたくさん読み，さまざまなおもしろい場所を知りました。そして，そのいくつかは旅行中に訪れることができました。例えば，私たちはドイツの有名な城やイタリアの美しい海辺の町を見物しました。詳細に旅行を計画していなかったら，そのような多くの場所をきっと見逃していたことでしょう。

　最も重要なこととして，詳細な計画を立てることは，旅行をより楽でリラックスできるものにします。到着後に，公共の交通機関や現地のレストラン，観光スポットを知ろうとすると，とてもストレスがかかって疲れてしまうかもしれません。前もって計画しておくことで，こうしたトラブルの多くをなくすことができ，これにより，心配事が少なくなって，リラックスして旅行を楽しみやすくなります。

　結論として，私は，旅行をする時には詳細な計画があったほうがよいと思います。今後のすべての旅行においても，詳細な旅程を作るのが楽しみです。）

別解 「ゆるやかで柔軟な旅行計画を好む」と答える場合

　Personally, I prefer to have loose, flexible plans while traveling. Traveling should be a relaxing experience, but a detailed travel plan is stressful and unrealistic. In addition, surprising experiences are one of the best parts of traveling.

　Most people live life on a schedule. Students have to manage their time effectively and go to classes. Employees have to meet deadlines and get to work on time. Traveling should be a break from this. That is why I never make detailed travel plans. I just want to take it easy when I travel, so I like to go to new places with almost no plans at all. It is so great to have no idea what you are going to do during your free time in a new place.

　In addition to this, accurate travel plans are very difficult to make. For example, my mother loves to have specific plans when she travels, and all of our family vacations always have strict, detailed schedules. It is difficult to schedule activities in a new place, though, and we are almost never able to follow her travel plans exactly. This often causes her to be stressed, and she does not seem to enjoy herself at all.

　Finally, the main reason that I like traveling without plans is that it allows for unexpected adventures. My older sister is just like me, and she never makes detailed plans when she travels. Last summer, she went to Berlin, and she made a lot of new friends at the guest house where she stayed. They invited her to join them on a bus tour around Germany, and she spent the entire week with them. She said it was a great experience. I am sure that she could not have had this type of adventure with a detailed, strict travel schedule.

　For these reasons, I prefer to have loose, flexible plans when traveling. It is more relaxing, more realistic, and more adventurous. (324 words)

（個人的には，旅行中，ゆるやかで柔軟な計画を立てるほうが好きです。旅行はくつろげる経験であるべきですが，詳細な旅行計画はストレスが多く，非現実的です。それに，驚くような経験は，

旅行の一番よいところの1つです。

　ほとんどの人は，スケジュールに沿って人生を送っています。学生たちは，時間を効率よく管理して，授業へ行かなければなりません。会社員たちは，締め切りに間に合わせ，時間通りに出勤しなければなりません。旅行は，こうした日々からの休息であるべきです。このようなわけで，私は，詳細な旅行計画を立てません。旅行をする時は，ただ気楽でいたいので，ほぼまったく計画なしに新しい場所へ行くのが好きです。新しい場所で，自由な時間に，何をするか考えを持たないでおくことはとてもよいものです。

　これに加え，緻密な旅行計画は，立てるのがとても難しいです。例えば，私の母は，旅行をする時に具体的な計画を立てておくのが好きで，家族で行く休暇中の旅行はすべて，いつも厳格で詳細なスケジュールが組まれます。しかし，新しい場所ですることのスケジュールを組むのは難しく，母の旅行計画の通りにいったことは，ほとんど一度もありません。このことは母にストレスを感じさせることが多く，母自身もまったく楽しむことができていないようです。

　最後に，私が計画なしの旅行を好む主な理由は，予期せぬ出来事を経験する余地があるからです。姉は私と同じで，旅行をする時に詳細な計画を立てることがありません。昨夏，姉はベルリンへ行き，滞在したゲストハウスでたくさんの新しい友人を作りました。新しい友人たちは，姉をドイツをめぐるバスツアーへ一緒に行こうと誘い，姉は丸1週間，彼らと一緒に過ごしました。それは素晴らしい経験だったと姉は話していました。姉に詳細で厳格な旅行計画があったら，このような冒険はきっとできなかったでしょう。

　以上の理由から，私は，旅行をする時，ゆるやかで柔軟な計画を立てるほうが好きです。そのほうが，リラックスできて，現実的で，冒険に溢れています。）

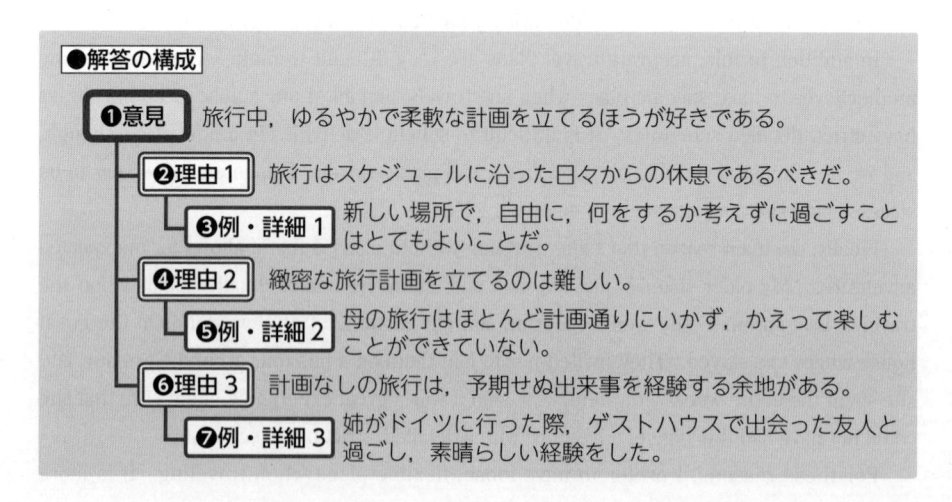

●解答の構成

- **❶意見**　旅行中，ゆるやかで柔軟な計画を立てるほうが好きである。
  - **❷理由1**　旅行はスケジュールに沿った日々からの休息であるべきだ。
    - **❸例・詳細1**　新しい場所で，自由に，何をするか考えずに過ごすことはとてもよいことだ。
  - **❹理由2**　緻密な旅行計画を立てるのは難しい。
    - **❺例・詳細2**　母の旅行はほとんど計画通りにいかず，かえって楽しむことができていない。
  - **❻理由3**　計画なしの旅行は，予期せぬ出来事を経験する余地がある。
    - **❼例・詳細3**　姉がドイツに行った際，ゲストハウスで出会った友人と過ごし，素晴らしい経験をした。

✓ 重要表現チェック

不十分な解答例	☐ realistic「現実的な」	☐ stress-free「ストレスのない」
	☐ pack「〜を詰め込む」	☐ itinerary「旅程」
	☐ additionally「その上，さらに」	☐ exhausting「骨の折れる」
適切な解答例	☐ destination「目的地」	☐ ahead「事前に」
	☐ eliminate「〜を取り除く」	
別解	☐ loose「ゆるい，自由な」	☐ deadline「締め切り」
	☐ specific「明確な，具体的な」	☐ adventurous「冒険的な」

問題 14

Some people prefer to read novels. Other people prefer to read non-fiction books.
Which do you prefer? Use specific reasons and examples to support your answer.

【設問訳】
小説を読むのが好きな人もいれば，ノンフィクションの本を読むのが好きな人もいます。
あなたはどちらを好みますか。あなたの意見の根拠となる具体的な理由や事例を述べなさい。

| 解答例 | 「ノンフィクションの本を読むのが好きである」と答える場合 |

不十分な解答例

　I generally prefer reading non-fiction books to reading fictions because non-fiction books are not only interesting to read but also provide me with practical knowledges (→knowledge). ★1 As the famous proverb goes, fact is stranger than fiction. Non-fiction books are far more interesting to me.

　First of all, a non-fiction book can be useful in our daily lives providing us with practical knowledges (→knowledge). When I was in high school, an autograph (→autobiography) written by a famous athlete was popular among boys. The book was not only amusing but also filled with helpful tips for us improving athletic performance. ★2 We read it through and did the same as he wrote in the book. Thanks to the book, we could practice effectively and overcome the slumps successfully.

　Second, non-fiction books broaden my outlook. Some non-fiction books can act as a guide to a subject which we are unfamiliar with. Non-fiction books interest me more because what these books describe are all real events. These days it is true that you can obtain true stories on various subjects through the Internet. ★3 However you cannot fully trust the information obtained through the Internet. Many of the websites are written by amateurs, so that it is too dangerous to put their idea into practice.

　In addition, ★4 through reading non-fiction books, I gain some knowledges (→knowledge) and thinking on different subjects. They help me in my daily life, and enrich my life mentally.

　For these reasons, I prefer reading non-fiction books to reading fictions because they are not only amusing but also helpful and meaningful.

210

● **構成と内容の改善ポイント**

★1 ことわざに象徴されるような内容は本文で説明されていません。
➡ 本文で展開されている議論との関連性が薄いので省きます。代わりに第4段落で説明されている3つ目の理由を述べましょう。本文で取り上げない内容をIntroductionに盛り込むと、文章の構成上の一貫性が損なわれます。

★2 本に何が書いてあり、それを読んでどう行動したのかが具体的に書かれていないため、次の文で述べられている結果にどのようにつながったのかが不明です。
➡ 「本のおかげで効果的に練習ができ、スランプを乗り越えられた」という内容に論理的につながる説明が必要です。本に書いてあったどのようなことを実践したのかを具体的に述べることで、説得力が増します。

★3 インターネットで得られる情報についての記述になっており、論点がそれています。
➡ 論点は小説（フィクション）とノンフィクションの比較です。インターネットの話はあくまでノンフィクションの本のよさを強調することを目的とし、本筋からそれないように注意します。

★4 「さまざまな題材について知識や考えを得ることができる」と漠然と述べるだけでは、ノンフィクションの本がよいと考える理由として説得性に欠けます。
➡ キーセンテンスの抽象度が高いため、読み手にその主旨が伝わるような具体例や詳細説明を加えましょう。知識や考えを得るのにノンフィクションの本がどのように役立つのか、それによりどのような利点があるのかなどを、具体的に説明します。

《構成の改善例》

- **❶意見** 小説を読むよりノンフィクションを読むほうが好きである。
  - **❷理由1** ノンフィクションの本は、実用的な知識を与える。
    - **❸例・詳細1** 運動選手が書いた自伝書が、運動能力を向上させるのに役立った。
  - **❹理由2** ノンフィクションの本は視野を広げる入門書の役割を果たす。
    - **❺例・詳細2** 現実に起きた出来事について、質の高い情報を提供する。
  - **❻理由3** さまざまな題材についての新しい知識と深い考察を得ることができる。
    - **❼例・詳細3** それらが精神面において人生を豊かにする。

適切な解答例

　I generally prefer reading non-fiction books to reading fictions because non-fiction books are not only interesting to read but also provide me with practical knowledge. ★1 Moreover they broaden my outlook and make me think deeply on a particular subject.

　First of all, a non-fiction book can be useful in our daily lives providing us with practical knowledge. When I was in high school, an autobiography written by a famous athlete was popular among boys. The book was not only amusing but also filled with helpful tips for improving athletic performance. ★2 I learned about how he trained, how he overcame the slumps and so on. The fact that these methods actually worked for the athlete motivated us to put them into practice. Thanks to the book, we could practice effectively and overcome the slumps successfully.

　Second, non-fiction books broaden my outlook. Some non-fiction books can act as a guide to a subject which we are unfamiliar with. Non-fiction books interest me more because what these books describe are all real events. These days it is true that you can obtain true stories on various subjects through the Internet. ★3 However books seem to offer higher quality information than websites, in that in many cases they are written by professionals or experts.

　In addition, ★4 once I have read through this kind of book and become interested in the subject, I am inspired to learn more about it. Then I look for another book which is likely to expand my understanding of it. Through reading, I can gain new knowledge and more insight on a variety of subjects. Such knowledge helps me in my daily life, and the insight enriches my life mentally.

　For these reasons, I prefer to reading non-fiction books to reading fictions because they are not only amusing but also helpful and meaningful. (302 words)

（私は概して，小説を読むよりノンフィクションを読むほうが好きです。ノンフィクションは読むのにおもしろいだけではなく，実用的な知識を与えてくれるからです。さらに，ノンフィクションの本は私の視野を広げ，ある題材についてより深く考えさせてくれます。

　第1に，ノンフィクションの本は実用的な知識を与えてくれるので，日常生活で役立つことがあります。私が高校生の時，ある有名な運動選手が書いた自伝書が男子の間で人気でした。その本はおもしろいだけでなく，私たちが運動能力を向上させるのに役立つ秘訣でいっぱいでした。私は彼がどのようにトレーニングしたか，またどのようにスランプを乗り越えたかなどについて知りました。これらの方法が実際にその運動選手に効果があったという事実により私たちはそれを実行する気になりました。その本のおかげで，私たちは効果的に練習し，スランプをうまく乗り越えることができました。

　第2に，ノンフィクションの本は私の視野を広げてくれます。ノンフィクションの本には，私たちがよく知らない題材について入門書としての役割を果たしてくれるものもあります。ノンフ

イクションの本はすべて現実に起きた出来事を描いているため，より私の興味を引きつけます。最近では，インターネットでさまざまな題材についての実話を知ることができるのも確かです。しかし，本は，多くの場合プロや専門家によって書かれているという点で，ウェブサイトよりも質の高い情報を提供するように思えます。

さらに，いったんこの種類の本を読み終えてその題材に興味を持ったら，私はそれについてもっと知りたくなります。それから，それについての理解を広げてくれそうな別の本を探します。読むことによって私はさまざまな題材についての新しい知識とより深い考察を得ることができるのです。そのような知識は私の日常生活において助けになり，考察は精神面において私の人生を豊かにしてくれます。

これらの理由から，ノンフィクションはおもしろいだけでなく，役に立ち，意義深いため，私はフィクションを読むよりも，ノンフィクションの本を読むほうが好きです。）

別解 「小説を読むのが好きだ」と答える場合

　　In school we sometimes have to read fiction and sometimes non-fiction. I always read whatever is assigned. However, when I read for pleasure, I prefer fiction to non-fiction. I have several reasons for this preference.

　　To begin with, I like the fact that reading fiction does not require any serious thought from me in response. If the book's story has events that are terribly sad, I can remind myself that it is only a story. At the same time, I find that I can enjoy sharing some of the lighter feelings that the characters are experiencing. I'm happy when they are happy, and sometimes, I shed a few tears when they are sad. In contrast, non-fiction often presents serious problems that are taking place in the world, which usually make me sad.

　　Fiction also lets me leave the real world and become absorbed in the lives and activities of the characters. I particularly like it when the circumstances of the characters' lives are much different from my own. Recently I read a novel about a woman who went traveling across Southeast Asia. The author described her adventures so vividly that I felt they were really happening. I felt myself reliving my own travels vicariously through the character in the book.

　　Finally, I also benefit from the rich expressions fiction writers use to describe characters and settings. Writers always fill their books with messages and wonderful writing styles. In many cases, the ideas help to shape my views about people, actions, and the world. Beyond the vocabulary they use, the authors' idioms and metaphors inspire me to learn more and write better. They also make me want to read more books so I can learn even more expressions. The writing styles used in non-fiction books are less inspiring to me. They do not teach me how to weave sentences to create a beautifully written piece.

　　For all of these reasons, I like fiction better than non-fiction. (325 words)

（私たちは学校で小説を読まなければならない時もあれば，ノンフィクションを読まなければならない時もあります。私はいつも割り当てられるものを何でも読みます。しかし，楽しむために読む時はノンフィクションより小説のほうが好きです。この選択にはいくつかの理由があります。

初めに，私は小説に反応する時に深刻に考える必要がないという事実が気に入っています。もしその本の筋の中にひどく悲しい出来事があったら，私はそれがただのお話だと自分に言い聞かせることができます。同時に，登場人物が経験しているより軽い感情を共有するのを楽しむことができると思います。私は彼らが幸せな時に幸せな気持ちになり，彼らが悲しい時は，涙を流すこともあります。対照的に，ノンフィクションはしばしば世界で起きている深刻な問題を紹介しますが，私はたいていそれによって悲しくなります。

小説はまた，私を現実の世界から離れさせ，登場人物たちの生活や活動に夢中にさせます。私は特に登場人物たちの生活の環境が私とかけ離れている場合が好きです。最近，私は東南アジア中を旅行した女性についての話を読みました。作者は彼女の冒険をとても鮮やかに描写していたので，私はそれが本当に起こっていることのように感じました。私はその本の人物を通じて，自分自身が旅行を追体験しているように感じました。

最後に，小説の作者が登場人物や設定を描写するのに使う豊かな表現から得るものもあります。作家は常に，伝えたい教訓と素晴らしい文体で自分の著書を満たします。多くの場合，そのようなアイディアは，人々，行動，世界に対する私の考え方を形成するのに役立ちます。彼らが用いる語彙以上に，作者の熟語や暗喩は，より多くを学び，よりよく書く上で私の刺激になります。彼らはまた，さらに多くの表現を学べるように，もっと多くの本を読みたいと思わせます。ノンフィクションの本で使われる文体は，私にとってあまり刺激になりません。それらは美しく書かれた作品を作るために文章を織り上げる方法を教えてくれません。

これらすべての理由で，私はノンフィクションより小説が好きです。）

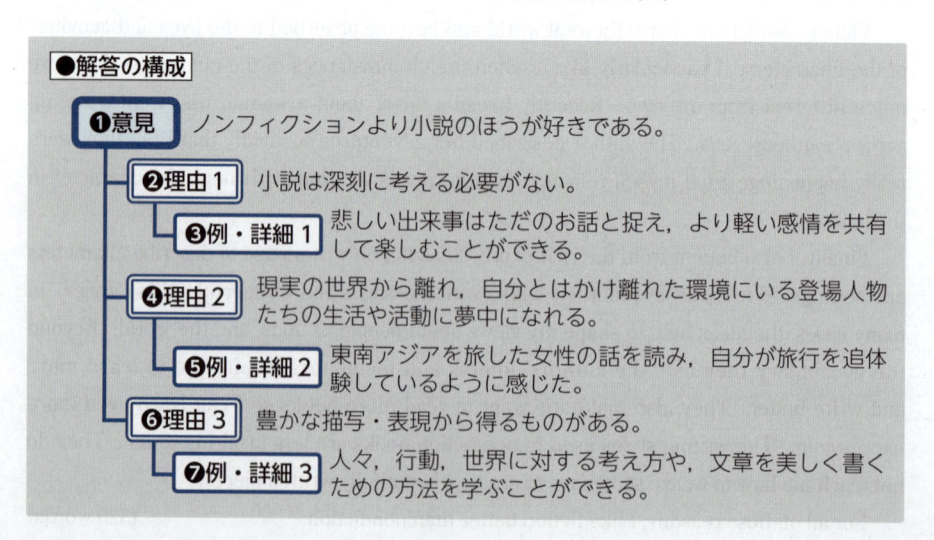

●解答の構成

- **❶意見** ノンフィクションより小説のほうが好きである。
  - **❷理由1** 小説は深刻に考える必要がない。
    - **❸例・詳細1** 悲しい出来事はただのお話と捉え，より軽い感情を共有して楽しむことができる。
  - **❹理由2** 現実の世界から離れ，自分とはかけ離れた環境にいる登場人物たちの生活や活動に夢中になれる。
    - **❺例・詳細2** 東南アジアを旅した女性の話を読み，自分が旅行を追体験しているように感じた。
  - **❻理由3** 豊かな描写・表現から得るものがある。
    - **❼例・詳細3** 人々，行動，世界に対する考え方や，文章を美しく書くための方法を学ぶことができる。

✓ 重要表現チェック

不十分な解答例
- autograph「自筆，サイン」
- autobiography「自伝」
- tip「秘訣」
- slump「スランプ」
- outlook「見解，見通し，視野」
- unfamiliar「未知の，なじみの薄い」
- amateur「アマチュア，素人」
- put ~ into practice「~を実行する」

別解
- preference「好むこと，選択」
- terribly「ものすごく，非常に」
- shed「（涙など）を流す」
- absorb「~を夢中にさせる」
- relive「~を追体験する」
- vicariously「他人の経験を通じて自分のことのように」
- weave「~を織る，編む，作り上げる」

問題 15

> Some people save up money before buying something expensive. Other people like to buy what they want right away with a credit card or an installment plan.
> Which do you prefer? Use specific reasons and examples to support your answer.

【設問訳】
高額のものを買う前に貯金する人もいれば，クレジットカードや分割払いで欲しいものをすぐに買う人もいます。
あなたはどちらを好みますか。あなたの意見の根拠となる具体的な理由や事例を述べなさい。

解答例 「高額のものを買う前に貯金するほうがよい」と答える場合

不十分な解答例

　In the modern world, the use of a credit card or an installment plan are (→**is**) very common. I do have more than one credit cards (→**card**) and use them often. However, if I want to buy something expensive, I would rather saving (→**save**) up money first than buying (→**buy**) it with a credit card or an installment plan. My reasons are personal, social and practical.

　★1 Personally, I sometimes feel uneasy about paying by a (→不要) credit card. Although it is convenient, the use of a credit card has some disadvantages. We should be aware that theft of credit card data is on the increase. Also, once you purchase something with a credit card, you owe a debt. Although it is quicker and more convenient than payment by a (→不要) bank transfer, it's not safe to use a credit card to make payment especially over the Internet.

　★2 Some people purchase expensive things with a credit card or an installment plan, because they believe they will surely earn enough money to pay in the future. But what will happen if they lose their job and cannot pay for the credit card bill? Not only the person who has made the purchase, but also many other people may be affected. I don't think it is socially responsible behavior.

　★3 Finally, the practical reason is that in most cases we are very likely to find a less expensive alternative. I don't agree **with** the idea of getting something very expensive when you don't have enough money. ★4 Another alternative is to save your expenditure.

　In conclusion, although I am not opposing (→**opposed**) to the use of a credit card or an install payment generally, I prefer saving up money before buying something expensive.

●構成と内容の改善ポイント

★1 クレジットカードについて,「個人的には不安を感じる」「便利だが短所がある」「銀行振り込みより早くて便利だが,安全でない」といった記述が続き,根拠となる「データの盗難の危険性」や「借金を負うことになる」という点についての議論が深まっていない印象です。

➡ なぜ「クレジットカードや分割払いで後から支払うより,先にお金を貯めてから買うほうがよい」と思うのか,説得力のある理由を述べる必要があります。適切な解答例では,クレジットカードの短所について,「後から支払うということは実質的には借金を負うことである」という点に絞って記述しています。

★2 唐突に「将来の収入を期待して買い物をする人」の話になっており,この段落で何を伝えたいのかが伝わりにくくなっています。

➡ 具体例を挙げる前に,その段落で伝えたい主張を明確に述べられていると,読みやすいエッセイになります。

★3 「高価でない代わりの品を見つけることができる」という理由を挙げていますが,「高額のものを買う時に,貯金をするか,すぐに買うか」というトピックからそれている印象を与えます。

➡ 「高価でない代わりの品を見つけることができる」→「十分なお金がないのであれば,高価なものをクレジットカード払いや分割払いをしてまで買う必要はなく,収入に見合った暮らしをすべきだ」という論理の流れが,読み手に伝わるように説明を加えましょう。

★4 一見すると前文からの流れに沿っているようですが,**★3**と同様に,「代わりのものを買うことは支出を抑える」という内容は,この問題のトピックからそれてしまっています。

➡ ここでは該当部分は削除します。ブレインストーミングの段階で,各段落で主張する内容と補足説明として述べる内容をきちんと決め,エッセイを書く際はそこで決めた論理展開がぶれないように意識しましょう。書き始めてから新しい話題を盛り込むとトピックからそれる可能性が高いため,注意が必要です。

《構成の改善例》

- **❶意見** 高価なものを買いたいのなら，まずお金を貯めたほうがよい。
  - **❷理由1** クレジットカードで支払うことは，実質的には借金を負うことである。
    - **❸例・詳細1** 支払える額以上に使わないように気をつけなければならない。
  - **❹理由2** 先にお金を貯めるほうがより健全である。
    - **❺例・詳細2** 支払日に十分なお金がなければ，多くの人々に影響が及ぶ。
  - **❻理由3** ほとんどの場合，より安価な代わりの品が見つかる。
    - **❼例・詳細3** 借金を負うよりも安いものを探すほうがよく，収入に見合った暮らしをすることができる。

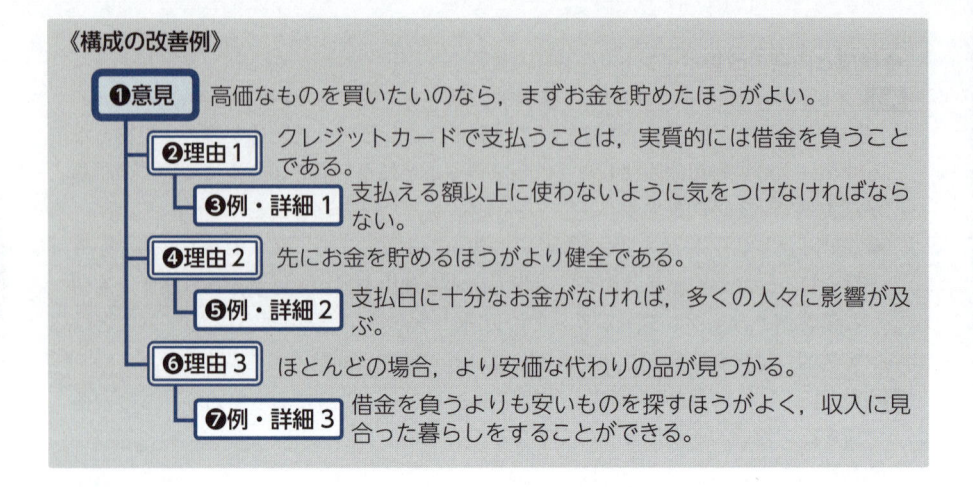

適切な解答例

　In the modern world, purchases by credit card or installments are very common. I have more than one credit card and use them often, too. However, if I want to buy something expensive, I would rather save up the money first than buy it using a credit card or an installment plan. My reasons are personal, social and practical.

　★1 Personally, I don't want to get in debt. Payment by credit card is essentially debt. I mainly use my credit card when I purchase things over the Internet, because it is quicker and more convenient than paying by bank transfer. On the other hand, I keep records of my purchases to see that I don't spend more than I can afford. Therefore I have no reason to buy something which costs more than I have to hand.

　★2 The social reason is that it is healthier to save up money first. No one knows what will happen in the future. In other words, there is no guarantee that your income next month will be as high as you expect. Some people purchase expensive things by credit card or installments, assuming that they will surely have sufficient money on the payment date. But who will suffer if they don't? Not only the person who has made the purchase, but also the shop owner as well as many other people may be affected. I don't think it is socially responsible behavior.

　★3 Finally, the practical reason is that in most cases we are very likely to find a less expensive alternative. I am not in favor of the idea of trying to obtain something very expensive when you don't have enough money. Say, I want to buy a car which seems too expensive. Then, I would rather look for something cheaper than take the risk of going into debt. We can find a way to live within our income.

  In conclusion, although I am not against the use of a credit card or an installment plan as such, I think it more sensible to save up money before buying something expensive.

(347 words)

（現代社会において，クレジットカードや分割払いで買い物をすることは一般的です。私も2枚以上のクレジットカードを持ち，よく使います。しかし，何か高価なものを買いたいのなら，クレジットカードや分割払いで買うよりも，まずお金を貯めたほうがよいです。私の理由は，個人的，社会的，現実的なものです。

　個人的に私は借金を負いたくありません。クレジットカードで支払うことは，実質的には借金を負うことです。私がクレジットカードを使うのは，主にインターネットで買い物をする時ですが，それは銀行振込よりも早くて便利だからです。一方で，支払える額以上に使わないように気をつけるため，自分の買い物を記録しています。だから，私には，持っている以上の金額のものを買う理由がないのです。

　社会的な理由は，先にお金を貯めるほうがより健全だからです。未来に何が起こるかは誰にもわかりません。言い換えれば，次の月に，期待するほど高い収入があるという保証はないのです。支払日に十分なお金が必ずあると見込んで，クレジットカードや分割払いで高価なものを買う人もいます。しかし，もし支払日にお金がなかったら誰が害を被るでしょう。買い物をした人だけではなく，店のオーナーや多くの人々にも影響が及ぶかもしれません。私は，そのようなことは社会的に責任ある行動ではないと思います。

　最後に，実用的な理由は，ほとんどの場合，より安価な代わりの品が見つかるものだということです。私は十分なお金がないのに高価なものを買おうという考えには賛成しません。例えば，あまりに高価だと思われる車が欲しいと思ったとします。その時，私は借金を負うというリスクを冒すよりも，より安いものを探すほうがよいです。私たちは収入に見合った暮らしをする方法を見つけることができます。

　結論として，私はクレジットカードや分割払い自体に反対しているわけではありませんが，何か高価なものを買う前には，貯金をしたほうが賢明だと考えます。）

別解 「クレジットカードや分割払いで欲しいものをすぐに買うほうがよい」と答える場合

  In recent years, the use of credit cards for purchases of all kinds of things has become common. Some people prefer to save up their money for a big purchase, even if they have a credit card. I would prefer to buy what I want first and pay later.

  First, if I save a small amount of money every month, it would take a long time to buy what I want. By the time I have saved enough money to buy it, I might have lost interest in it. For example, I may see a new coat that I think is very fashionable. If it's somewhat expensive, it could take me several years to save enough money to buy it. By that time, the coat will no longer have the same appeal, or it may go out of fashion. By buying what I want first, I can get more enjoyment from the item.

The second reason is inflation. Even if I save money in the bank, the value of the money goes down as inflation continues. The interest the bank gives me may not cover the loss I suffer from inflation. If the rate of inflation is higher than the bank interest rate, I may never be able to buy what I want in the future, so I may as well buy it now.

Third, payments over a long time eventually become more affordable with salary increases. If I buy something on an installment plan, the monthly payments may seem expensive at first. As time goes by, however, my salary will go up and the payments will start to seem relatively smaller. With fixed payments and rising income, a lengthy payment schedule is always a good idea.

Of course, I want to be careful with my money. I won't buy something I don't really need, and I won't make a lot of purchases if I don't think I can pay for them. But given the choice in the question, I would prefer to have an item now and pay for it later. (342 words)

（近年，あらゆるものを購入するためにクレジットカードを使うことは，一般的になってきています。クレジットカードを持っていても，大きな買い物をするために貯金をするのを好む人もいますが，私は，欲しいものを初めに買い，後で支払うことを好みます。

第1に，毎月少額ずつしか貯金しなければ，欲しいものを買うのに長い時間がかかるでしょう。欲しいものを買うのに十分なお金を貯めるまでに，私はそれに対する興味を失ってしまうかもしれません。例えば，私が，とてもおしゃれだと思う新しいコートを見つけたとします。それがいくぶん高価だったとしたら，私がそれを買うのに十分なお金を貯めるのに，数年かかってしまうかもしれません。その間に，そのコートはもはや同じような魅力を持っていないかもしれませんし，流行が過ぎ去ってしまうかもしれません。欲しいものを初めに買うことで，その商品からより楽しみを得ることができるのです。

第2の理由はインフレです。銀行でお金を貯めたとしても，インフレが続けばお金の価値は下がります。銀行が与える利子も，インフレによって被る損失を補うことはできないかもしれません。インフレ率が銀行の利率よりも高くなれば，将来欲しいものを買うことが決してできないかもしれません。だから，私は今買ってしまうほうがよいのです。

第3に，長い期間をかけて支払うと，給料が上がることで，ゆくゆくは支払いやすくなります。分割払いで何かを買うと，初めは月々の支払いが高く思えるかもしれません。しかし，時間が経つにつれて私の給料が上がり，支払い額が相対的に小さく思えるようになります。一定額を支払いながら定期的な収入の増加があるならば，長期間の支払いスケジュールはよい考え方です。

もちろん，お金の取り扱いには注意したいと思います。本当に必要でないものは買いませんし，支払えないと思ったらたくさんの買い物はしません。しかし，質問の選択肢が与えられた場合，私はすぐに商品を買い，後から支払うことを好みます。）

●解答の構成

- **❶意見** 欲しいものを初めに買い，後で支払うことを好む。
  - **❷理由1** 毎月少額ずつしか貯金しなければ，欲しいものを買うのに長い時間がかかる。
    - **❸例・詳細1** 十分なお金を貯めている間に，商品の魅力が失われたり，流行が過ぎ去ってしまう。
  - **❹理由2** お金を貯めたとしても，インフレが続けばお金の価値は下がる。
    - **❺例・詳細2** その場合，お金を貯めても欲しいものが買えないかもしれない。
  - **❻理由3** 長い期間で支払うと，ゆくゆくは支払いやすくなる。
    - **❼例・詳細3** 給料が上がることで，相対的に支払い額が小さくなっていく。

✓ 重要表現チェック

不十分な解答例
- ☐ installment「分割払い」　☐ practical「実用的な」
- ☐ uneasy「不安な」
- ☐ alternative「代わるもの，他の手段」

適切な解答例
- ☐ healthy「健全な」　☐ guarantee「保証」
- ☐ in favor of 〜「〜に賛成して」

別解
- ☐ appeal「魅力」　☐ inflation「インフレーション」
- ☐ interest「利子」　☐ rate「率，割合」
- ☐ affordable「入手しやすい，手ごろな」
- ☐ fixed「固定した」　☐ lengthy「長期間にわたる」

MEMO

確認テスト
第1回

確認テスト 第1回 問題

Question 1 of 2

Reading Time: 3 minutes

Sleep is one of the most important aspects of a healthy lifestyle. Without adequate sleep, humans are shown to suffer both mentally and physically. But have you ever thought about why it is so important?

One of the most important functions of sleep is storing and organizing memories. Throughout the course of the day, our brains process vast quantities of information, and a significant percentage of this information is stored as short-term memories. Then, while sleeping, our brains take small bits of this information and convert them into long-term memories. This is why researchers have found that memory improves with sleep.

A second function of sleep is energy conservation. Thousands of years ago, humans had to fight to survive in nature. Most likely, humans hunted during the daytime, so they needed to save their energy at night. Sleeping decreases metabolism, which made it a useful tool for preserving energy needed during the daytime. Also, a lower metabolism means a lower calorie requirement, so humans had a higher chance of surviving, because they needed less food overall.

Sleep is also necessary for its restorative benefits. In many ways, our bodies heal and improve themselves while we sleep. Scientific research has shown that many important restorative functions occur during sleep, such as muscle growth, tissue repair, and protein synthesis. This explains why health declines drastically without adequate sleep. In fact, humans and other animals will typically lose all immune functions and die after only a few weeks of no sleep.

Now listen to part of a lecture on the topic you just read about. ● CD 19

Directions: You have 20 minutes to plan and write your response. Your response will be judged on the basis of quality of your writing and on how well your response presents the points in the lecture and their relationship to the reading passage. Typically, an effective response will be 150 to 225 words.

Summarize the points made in the lecture you just heard, being sure to explain how they cast doubt on specific points made in the reading passage.

Response Time: 20 minutes

Question 2 of 2

Directions: Read the question below. You have 30 minutes to plan, write, and revise your essay. Typically, an effective response contains a minimum of 300 words.

Do you agree or disagree with the following statement?
Students should be required to take physical education classes throughout their school years.
Use specific reasons and examples to support your answer.

Response Time: 30 minutes

確認テスト 第1回 解説

Question 1　　CD 19

解答例

　The professor talks about how we still do not fully understand why humans need sleep.

　First, scientists still have not completely clarified the relationship between sleep and memory. The professor cites an example of a man in Vietnam, who did not sleep for many years with no negative side effects. This case indicates sleep is not always needed for converting short-term memories to long-term memories. This directly refutes the reading passage, which states that sleep is needed for storing memories.

　Second, scientists still do not understand why some people need less sleep than others. Some people only need a few hours of sleep per night, but they are still healthy. If sleeping conserves energy, then it does not explain why these people are not tired during the day. Again, this contradicts the reading passage, which states that humans need sleep for energy conservation.

　Third, our bodies heal and improve themselves both while we are awake and while we are sleeping. The professor acknowledges that sleeping is beneficial to things like muscle growth and repairing tissues, but he also clarifies that our bodies can do these things without sleep as shown in the case of the man in Vietnam. With this point, the professor opposes the reading's claim that humans need sleep because of its restorative benefits.

　In short, the professor argues that the need for sleep is still not totally understood by scientists.　　　　　　　　　　　　　　　　　　　　　　　　　　(235 words)

　(教授は，私たちはまだ，人間が睡眠を必要とする理由を完全には理解していないということについて話しています。

　第1に，科学者たちはまだ，睡眠と記憶の関係を完全には解明していません。教授は，何年も眠らなくともまったく悪い副作用がない，ベトナム人男性の例を挙げています。この事例は，短期記憶を長期記憶に変換する際に，睡眠は必ずしも必要ではないことを示しています。これは，記憶を蓄積するために睡眠が必要だと述べる課題文に直接的に反論しています。

　第2に，科学者たちには，人と比べて少ない睡眠時間しか必要としない人がいるのはなぜかということについても，まだわかっていません。一晩に数時間の睡眠しか必要としない人もいますが，彼らはそれでも健康です。睡眠によってエネルギーを温存しているのなら，こうした人々が日中に疲れないのはなぜかについて説明できません。ここでも，人間はエネルギー温存のために睡眠を必要とすると述べている課題文に反論しています。

　第3に，私たちの身体は，起きている間も眠っている間も，自らを治癒し，改善しています。教授は，筋肉の成長や組織の修復などに睡眠が有益であることは認めていますが，ベトナム人男性の例でも示されているように，私たちの身体は眠らなくともこれらを行うことができるということも明らかにしています。この点で，教授は，人間はその回復効果のために睡眠を必要とする

という課題文の主張に反対しています。
　つまり，教授は，睡眠の必要性について，科学者たちはまだ完全には理解していないと主張しています。）

解説 講義のポイントを要約しながら，課題文の主張に対して教授がどのような疑問を呈しているかを説明します。解答では，課題文において人間に不可欠なものとされている睡眠の3つの役割に対して，教授がそれぞれ実例や根拠を挙げながら反論し，睡眠の必要性は実のところ完全には解明されていないと主張していることについてまとめます。まず，記憶の蓄積という睡眠の1つ目のポイントについては，何十年も眠らなくとも悪い副作用のない男性の例を挙げて疑問を投げかけています。2つ目のエネルギーの温存というポイントについては，他の人よりも必要とする睡眠時間が少ない人がおり，数パーセントの人は一晩に数時間の睡眠で足りるという研究結果を根拠に，課題文に反論しています。また，3つ目の身体の回復機能を助けるという役割については，起きている間も筋肉の成長や組織の修復などは行われており，前述の男性の例を再び用いて，理論的には必ずしも睡眠は必要ないという持論を述べています。そして最後に，睡眠の必要性は科学者たちもまだ完全には理解していないと締めくくっています。教授の主張が課題文のどのポイントに対するものなのかを整理し，1つ1つ簡潔に書いていきましょう。

▶課題文訳

　睡眠は，健康的なライフスタイルの最も大切な側面の1つです。十分な睡眠がなければ，人間は精神的にも肉体的にも苦痛を感じることが明らかにされています。しかし，なぜ睡眠がそれほど重要なのか，考えてみたことはありますか。

　睡眠の最も重要な役割の1つは，記憶を蓄積して整理することです。私たちの脳は1日中，膨大な量の情報を処理しており，この情報の大部分が短期記憶として蓄積されます。その後，眠っている間に，私たちの脳はこの情報のわずかな部分を取り出し，長期記憶に変換します。研究者たちが睡眠中に記憶が向上することを発見しているのはこのためです。

　睡眠の2つ目の役割は，エネルギーの温存です。何千年も前，人間は自然界で生き延びるために戦わなければなりませんでした。たいていの場合，人間は日中に狩りをしていたので，夜間はエネルギーを温存する必要がありました。眠ることで代謝が低下するため，睡眠は日中に必要なエネルギーを温存する有益な手段となりました。また，代謝が低ければ，必要なカロリーも少ないことから，全体として必要とする食べ物の量が減り，その結果，人間が生き延びる可能性は高くなりました。

　睡眠が必要なのは，その回復効果のためでもあります。私たちの身体は，眠っている間にさまざまな方法で自らを治癒し，改善しています。科学的研究により，筋肉の成長，組織の修復，たんぱく質の合成など，多くの重要な回復機能は睡眠中に働くことがわかっています。十分な睡眠をとらなければ，体調が大きく悪化するのはこのためです。実際，人間やその他の動物は，数週

間でもまったく睡眠をとらなければ，たいていの場合，すべての免疫機能を失って死んでしまうでしょう。

▶ リスニングスクリプト

Now listen to part of a lecture on the topic you just read about.

This article mentions a lot of good theories about the need for sleep in humans. That said, it doesn't really explain the need for sleep... Because the simple truth is that we still don't fully understand why sleep is so important for our health.

There is a lot of scientific evidence supporting this idea that sleep is related to memory function. Usually humans that don't get enough sleep are worse at remembering things... So we know that memory and sleep are related, but we still don't know how they're related ... Yeah, maybe our brains convert short-term memories to long-term memories during sleep, but maybe this is possible without sleep, too. For example, there is one case of a man in Vietnam who stayed awake for 33 years with no negative side effects. He lost his need for sleep after a sickness he had in the 1970's.

The case for energy conservation seems reasonable, too, but it doesn't explain why there are so many people who need less sleep than others. Scientific studies have shown that one to three percent of people only need a few hours of sleep per night. They're awake more than others, which technically means that they're spending more energy. So why aren't they tired during the day?

The author also mentions that sleep helps our bodies to heal and improve themselves, building muscles, repairing tissues, and making protein. But these things happen while we're awake, too. Looking back at the example of the man in Vietnam, he was entirely healthy without any sleep. So bodies are theoretically capable of doing these things without sleep.

Overall, I'm not saying these theories are wrong. They might prove to be true. But we still don't know for sure, because we still don't fully understand why humans need sleep.

▶ リスニングスクリプト訳

今読んだトピックに関する講義の一部を聞きなさい。

　この記事は，人間の睡眠の必要性に関する多くの優れた理論に言及しています。とは言え，睡眠の必要性の説明にはあまりなっていません…。私たちは今でも，睡眠が私たちの健康にこれほど重要なのはなぜかについて，完全には理解していないのが実状だからです。

　睡眠が記憶機能と関連しているという，この考えを裏づける科学的証拠はたくさんあります。人は普通，十分な睡眠をとらなければ記憶力が低下します…。よって，記憶と睡眠に関連性があることはわかるのですが，その関連の仕組みはまだわかっていないのです…。そう，おそらく，

私たちの脳は睡眠中に短期記憶を長期記憶に変換しているのですが、おそらくそれは眠らなくとも可能なのです。例えば、３３年間眠らずにいてもまったく悪い副作用がなかったベトナム人男性の事例があります。１９７０年代に病気を患った後、彼は睡眠の必要がなくなりました。

エネルギーの温存という主張も、もっともなようですが、他の人と比べて必要とする睡眠時間の短い人がとても多く存在する理由は説明されていません。科学的研究により、１％から３％の人は、一晩に数時間の睡眠しか必要としないことがわかっています。こうした人々は、他の人々よりも長時間起きており、厳密に言えば、より多くのエネルギーを消費していることになります。それならば彼らはなぜ、日中疲れないのでしょうか。

著者はまた、私たちの身体が、筋肉を作ったり、組織を修復したり、たんぱく質を合成したりして、自らを治癒し、改善する際にも睡眠が一役買っていると述べています。しかし、これらは起きている間にも起こります。ベトナムの男性の例を振り返ると、彼は眠らなくてもまったく健康だったのです。よって身体は、理論的には眠らずにこれらを行うことが可能なのです。

全体として、私はこれらの理論が間違いだと言っているのではありません。これらは真実だと証明されるかもしれません。しかし、私たちにはまだはっきりとはわからないのです。人間にはなぜ睡眠が必要なのか、私たちはまだ完全には理解していないのですから。

設問訳

指示：20 分間で解答を計画し、書きなさい。解答は、文章の質や、講義の論点と課題文との関係をいかに表しているかに基づいて評価されます。通常、効果的な解答は 150 ～ 225 語です。

今聞いた講義の論点を要約しなさい。その際、課題文で挙げられているどの論点にどのように疑問を投げかけているかを必ず説明してください。

✓ 重要表現チェック

課題文
- ☐ process「～を処理する」
- ☐ vast「膨大な」
- ☐ quantity「量」
- ☐ significant「（数・量が）かなりの」
- ☐ conservation「保存、温存」
- ☐ metabolism「（新陳）代謝」
- ☐ restorative「（体力を）回復させる」
- ☐ tissue「（細胞の）組織」
- ☐ synthesis「合成」
- ☐ immune function「免疫機能」

解答例
- ☐ cite「～に言及する、～を引き合いに出す」
- ☐ side effect「副作用」

リスニングスクリプト
- ☐ technically「厳密に言えば」
- ☐ theoretically「理論上は」

Question 2

設問訳

指示：下記の問題を読みなさい。30分間で解答を計画して書き，修正を行いなさい。通常，効果的な解答は300語以上です。

あなたは以下の主張に賛成ですか，反対ですか。
「学生時代には体育の授業が必修とされるべきだ。」
あなたの意見の根拠となる具体的な理由や事例を述べなさい。

解答例

When I was younger, I wasn't much of an athlete. In fact, I was terrible at sports, and I hated physical education (PE) class. But now I'm really glad that I was required to take it, and I think all students should take it. This is because PE has clear benefits for students.

First, PE is beneficial for physical health. The time spent stretching, running, exercising and playing is extremely valuable for students. For many, especially students who live in the city or who are very busy with schoolwork, it's the only physical activity they get throughout the day. Nowadays we see health problems, such as excess weight and back pain, that were not nearly as common in the past. Time spent exercising at school can help prevent these problems, and can also teach students good habits they will keep for the rest of their lives.

Second, PE helps students in their other classes, too. Research has shown that students who exercise also do better in their studies. I know that after I've spent some time moving around, I can focus better on my lessons and my homework. It's also a great way to relieve stress, which helps with schoolwork and in other aspects of your life.

Finally, PE is important for social skills. In addition to health problems, students of today spend more time alone than students of previous generations. In PE, you have to play with other students, form teams, and compete. These are skills that are good for much more than sports. Working and living in society requires cooperation and teamwork. PE is a great place to learn those skills.

PE may be embarrassing for a lot of young people. It was embarrassing for me, too. However, the purpose of school is to prepare students for adulthood and society. Therefore I think PE should be required for all students. (313 words)

（私は幼い頃，運動があまり好きではありませんでした。実のところスポーツは苦手で，体育の授業は大嫌いでした。しかし今は，体育の授業が必修で本当によかったと思っていますし，すべての学生が受けるべきだと考えます。それは，体育の授業は学生にとって明らかなメリットがあるからです。

第1に，体育は身体の健康に役立ちます。柔軟やランニング，運動や競技に費やす時間は，学生にとって極めて価値があります。とりわけ都市部に住む学生や学業で大変忙しい学生など，多くの学生にとって，体育は1日のうちで唯一体を動かす活動なのです。最近では過剰体重や腰痛など，かつてはそれほどなかったような健康問題があります。学校で運動する時間を持つことでこのような問題を予防し，またその後の人生でも継続できるよい習慣を学生に教えることができます。

　第2に，体育は他の授業でも学生の役に立ちます。研究から，運動をしている学生は学業でもよい結果を出すことがわかっています。しばらく動き回った後には授業や宿題への集中力が増すことは，私にもわかります。体育はストレス解消にもよく，学業や人生の他の場面でも役立ちます。

　最後に，体育は社交性を身につけるためにも重要です。健康問題に加えて，今日の学生は前の世代の学生より1人で過ごす時間が長くなっています。体育では，他の学生とともに競技し，チームを作り，競争しなければなりません。これらは，スポーツよりはるかに役立つ技術です。社会で働き暮らしていくには，協力やチームワークが必要です。体育はこういった技術を学ぶ素晴らしい環境です。

　体育は多くの若者にとって恥ずかしいものかもしれません。私自身もそう感じていました。しかし，学校の目的は学生に成人期や社会に備えて準備をさせることです。よって，私は，体育がすべての学生に必修とされるべきだと思います。)

解説 学生時代には体育の授業が必修とされるべきだというトピックに対し，賛成か反対かを問う問題です。まずは自分の立場を決め，Introductionで明確に示しましょう。解答例では，自分はスポーツが苦手で体育の授業も嫌いであったが，必修の授業として受けていたことでメリットがあったとして，トピックに賛成の立場を取っています。Bodyの3つの段落では，その理由を説明します。体育は「健康に役立つ」「他の授業にも役立つ」「社交性を身につけるためにも重要である」というキーセンテンスをそれぞれの段落の冒頭で明示し，続けて複数の事例とともに詳細な情報を盛り込んでいます。Conclusionでは，体育について一般的にイメージされているマイナスの側面を挙げた後，それを上回るプラスの側面があることを述べ，「よって体育をすべての学生に必修とすべきだ」と再度自分の意見を明確にして締めくくっています。各段落のはじめに First / Second / Finally を用い，最終のまとめは Therefore で締めくくるなど，ディスコース・マーカーを効果的に使うことで論点をわかりやすく提示しましょう。また，各段落内の文と文のつながりや論理構成にも気を配りましょう。

✓ 重要表現チェック

- □ athlete「運動選手，運動好きな人」
- □ physical education (PE)「体育」
- □ embarrassing「気まずい，恥ずかしい」
- □ terrible at ～「～が苦手な」
- □ relieve stress「ストレスを解消する」

MEMO

確認テスト
第2回

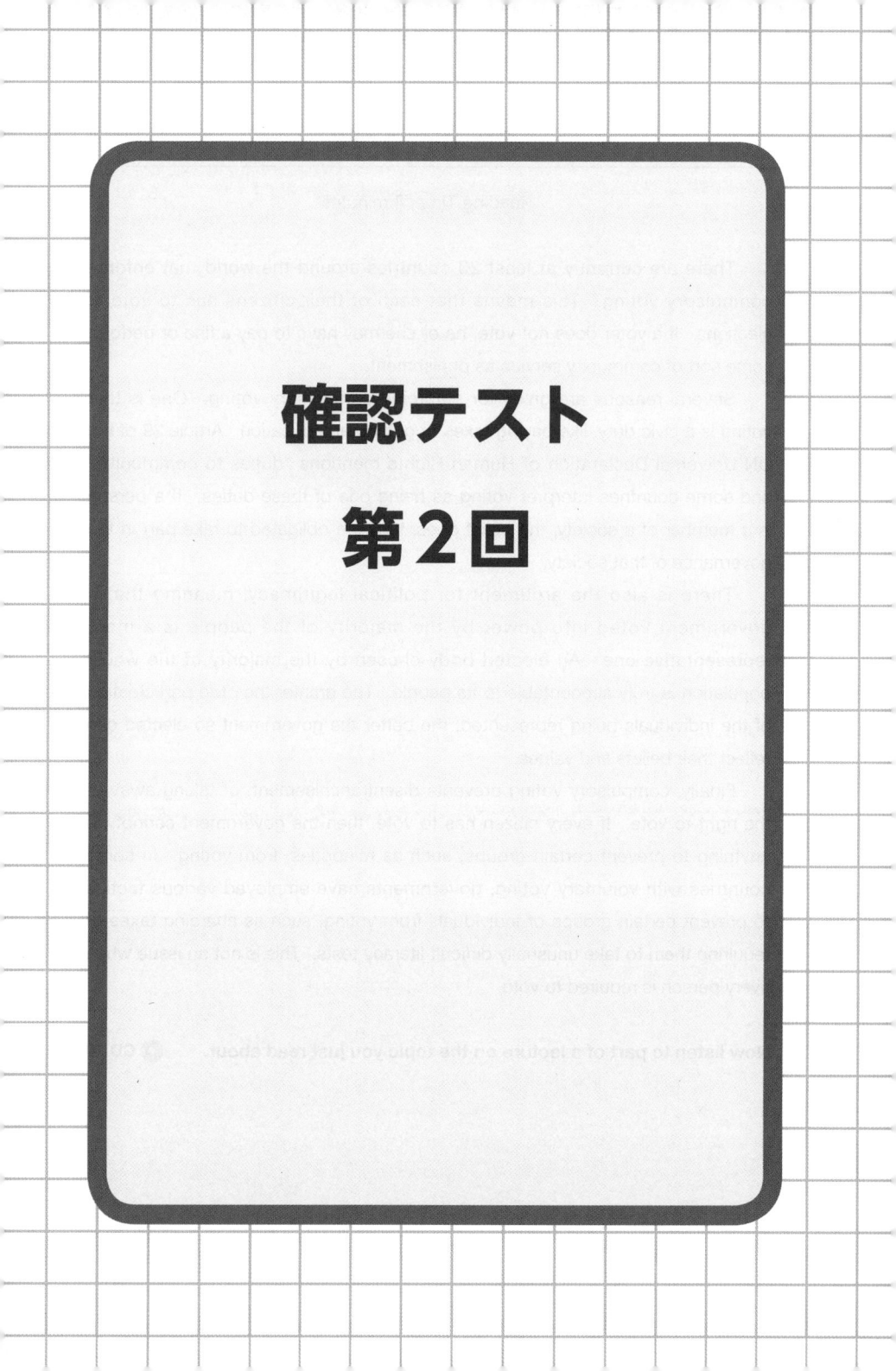

確認テスト 第2回 問題

Question 1 of 2

Reading Time: 3 minutes

There are currently at least 20 countries around the world that enforce compulsory voting. This means that each of their citizens has to vote in elections. If a voter does not vote, he or she may have to pay a fine or perform some sort of community service as punishment.

Several reasons are given for enforcing compulsory voting. One is that voting is a civic duty, like paying taxes or getting an education. Article 29 of the UN Universal Declaration of Human Rights mentions "duties to community," and some countries interpret voting as being one of these duties. If a person is a member of a society, the belief goes, they are obligated to take part in the governance of that society.

There is also the argument for political legitimacy, meaning that a government voted into power by the majority of the people is a more representative one. An elected body chosen by the majority of the whole population is truly accountable to its people. The greater the civic participation of the individuals being represented, the better the government so elected can reflect their beliefs and values.

Finally, compulsory voting prevents disenfranchisement, or taking away of the right to vote. If every citizen has to vote, then the government cannot do anything to prevent certain groups, such as minorities, from voting. In some countries with voluntary voting, governments have employed various tactics to prevent certain groups or individuals from voting, such as charging taxes or requiring them to take unusually difficult literacy tests. This is not an issue when every person is required to vote.

Now listen to part of a lecture on the topic you just read about.　　● CD 20

Directions: You have 20 minutes to plan and write your response. Your response will be judged on the basis of quality of your writing and on how well your response presents the points in the lecture and their relationship to the reading passage. Typically, an effective response will be 150 to 225 words.

Summarize the points made in the lecture you just heard, being sure to specifically explain how they support the explanations in the reading passage.

Response Time: 20 minutes

Question 2 of 2

Directions: Read the question below. You have 30 minutes to plan, write, and revise your essay. Typically, an effective response contains a minimum of 300 words.

Do you agree or disagree with the following statement?
Optimistic people are more likely to succeed.
Use specific reasons and examples to support your answer.

Response Time: 30 minutes

確認テスト 第2回 解説

Question 1   CD 20

解答例

The reading passage introduces the concept of compulsory voting. It offers three main reasons for which compulsory voting is enforced: civic duty, political legitimacy, and the prevention of disenfranchisement. The professor expands on each of these ideas.

First, compulsory voting encourages people to learn more about the issues in their country. According to the reading passage, voting is considered a civic duty. Without being required to vote, people may ignore politics altogether, but the requirement to vote at least forces people to make a decision, and probably pushes them to learn more about what's going on.

Second, the professor mentions the low voter participation in the United States as an example of how compulsory voting results in a more representative government stated in the reading passage. Only about 40% of those eligible to vote turned out in the 2014 election, which means that less than a majority of the people chose the government. The professor questions whether such a government could really be representative.

Finally, there is the point of disenfranchisement. The reading passage gives the examples of taxes and literacy tests, while the professor says those aren't practiced so much anymore but other methods of keeping minorities and poor people from voting are used. The professor mentions the voter ID laws in the United States, and how poor people may simply decide not to vote because they don't have the time or money to get an ID.

(238 words)

（課題文では義務投票制の概念が紹介されています。義務投票の施行には3つの大きな理由があります。国民の義務，政治的合法性，そして選挙権剥奪の防止です。教授はこれらの意図についてさらに詳しく述べています。

第1に，投票が義務であれば人々は国内の問題について知りたいと思うようになります。課題文によれば，義務投票制は，国民の義務であると考えられています。投票する必要がなければ，人々は政治に全く見向きもしないかもしれませんが，投票の義務があれば少なくとも決断をしなければならず，現状を知ろうという気にさせられるでしょう。

第2に，教授はアメリカ合衆国の低い投票率を例に挙げ，課題文で述べられているより民意を反映する政府を，義務投票制がどのように実現するのかについて述べています。2014年の選挙ではわずか約40パーセントの有権者が投票したのみで，これは過半数に満たない人で政府を選んだということなのです。教授は，そのような政府が真に国民の代表と言えるのかと疑問を呈しています。

最後に，選挙権剥奪のポイントがあります。課題文では税金と読み書き試験の例が挙げられています。これに対し教授はそのようなことは今日あまり行われていないが，マイノリティーや貧

困層が投票できないように別の方法が取られていると言っています。教授はアメリカ合衆国の有権者 ID 法について述べ，貧しい人々は ID を受け取るための時間とお金がないことから，投票に行くのをたやすく諦めてしまうと話しています。）

解説 課題文ではまず，義務投票制の概要が説明され，施行の理由として，国民の義務，政治的合法性，選挙権剥奪の防止，という3点が挙げられています。講義では，これらの意図を，具体例を交えながらさらに詳しく説明しています。解答では，課題文のポイントに対する教授のコメントをまとめて記述していきましょう。教授は，1点目の国民の義務に対しては，国の問題を十分理解していない人も適当に投票するのではないかという意見を紹介した上で，投票の義務があれば選挙を無視することはできず，人々は情報収集をするだろうと述べています。2点目の政治的合法性については，投票率が低かったアメリカ合衆国の選挙を例に挙げ，過半数に満たない人に選ばれた政府は国民の真の代表とは言えないと述べています。さらに3点目の選挙権剥奪の防止については，アメリカ合衆国の有権者 ID 法に触れ，貧困層の投票を保障できる点からも義務投票制は公平な制度であると説明しています。解答例は，First / Second / Finally / Thus といったディスコース・マーカーを用いて，これらの要点を整理しながらまとめています。

▶ 課題文訳

今日少なくとも世界で20の国において義務投票制が施行されています。つまり，国民の1人1人が選挙で投票しなくてはなりません。有権者は，投票しなければ，罰金を払うか，罰として何らかの社会奉仕活動をしなければなりません。

投票の義務を課す理由はいくつかあります。1つは，投票は税を納めることや教育を受けることと同様に，国民の義務であるということです。国連の世界人権宣言第29条は「社会に対する義務」に言及しており，投票をこういった義務の1つと解釈する国もあります。社会の一員であれば，その社会の統治に参加する義務がある，という考えなのです。

また，政治的合法性，つまり国民の大多数による投票で政権を認められた政府のほうが，より国を代表している，という議論もあります。全住民の大多数に選ばれた団体が，国民に対して真に責任を持つのです。代表される個々人たちの市民参加が大きければ大きいほど，そのようにして選ばれた政府は国民の考えや価値観をよりよく反映することができるのです。

最後に，義務投票制は選挙権の剥奪，つまり投票権を取り上げることを防ぐということです。全国民が投票しなければならないのであれば，政府は少数派などの特定の集団の投票を阻むことは何もできなくなります。任意投票の国では，政府が税金を課したり，異常なほど難しい読み書きの試験を受けさせたりといったさまざまな方策を取って，特定の集団や個人の投票を阻むこともあります。全員の投票が義務とされるのであれば，このようなことは問題になりません。

▶リスニングスクリプト

Now listen to part of a lecture on the topic you just read about.

Compulsory voting is controversial, more so than the reading passage would have you believe. But all in all it's the best way to run a democracy.

A lot of people argue that people who vote just because they are forced to do so may not fully understand the issues faced by the country, or may simply choose a candidate at random. But I argue that compulsory voting actually makes people more involved in politics. If you have the option of not voting at all, then you can just ignore the election and pretend it has nothing to do with you. But if you're forced to make a choice, then you'll probably do a little research, and learn more about the issues. There's a certain amount of shame in just choosing a candidate at random.

Legitimacy is also a major issue. Countries in which people can choose not to vote sometimes have quite low voter turnout in elections. Voter turnout in the 2014 elections in the United States was the lowest since World War II, roughly 40% overall and even less in some areas. That's hardly a representative democracy, when only a minority of the population is even making a choice.

And the prevention of disenfranchisement, meaning the protection of the right of everyone to vote —— that's a really important point. In some major democracies today, even though there aren't taxes or tests involved, it's not 100% guaranteed that even eligible voters will be able to make it to the polling place without undue burden. I'm thinking of the recent voter ID laws that have been passed in the United States. For some working people and poor people, taking time off work to go and get an ID for voting is nearly impossible. They're more likely to just give up and not vote at all. If it's compulsory, then the system is fairer.

▶リスニングスクリプト訳

今読んだトピックに関する講義の一部を聞きなさい。

義務投票制については意見が分かれますが、課題文を読んだ皆さんが思う以上に、この制度は議論の的となっています。しかし結局のところ、民主主義国家を運営するには最良の方法なのです。

多くの人が、義務だからというだけで投票する人は、国が直面している問題を十分理解していない、あるいはただでたらめに候補者を選んでいるだけかもしれないと言います。ですが、実際は、義務投票の場合、人々はより政治に関わるようになると私は言いたいのです。もし投票する選択肢がまったくなかったら、選挙をただ無視して自分には関係ないふりができます。しかし選択を強いられるなら、あなたはおそらく少しばかり情報収集をして、その争点について知識を深めるでしょう。候補者をただでたらめに選ぶということは、少し恥ずかしいものです。

政治的合法性も大きな問題です。人々が投票しないことを選べる国では、選挙の投票率がかなり低いこともあります。アメリカ合衆国の２０１４年の投票率は、第二次世界大戦以降で最低で

した。全体では約４０パーセントで，さらに低い地区もありました。これでは議会制民主主義とはとても言えません。人口のほんの少数が下した選択なのですから。

選挙権剥奪の防止は，すべての人の投票権を守ることを意味するわけですが，これは実に重要なポイントです。今日の主要な民主主義国家の中には，税金や試験が課せられていないとしても，有権者が不当な負担なく投票所へ行けることが１００パーセント保障されてはいない国もあります。最近アメリカ合衆国で通過した有権者ID法がその例です。労働者や貧困層の人々の中には，仕事の休みを取って投票に必要なIDをもらいにいくことがほとんど不可能な人もいます。彼らはおそらくただ諦めて，投票などしないでしょう。投票が義務であれば，それはより公平な制度です。

[設問訳]

指示：20分間で解答を計画し，書きなさい。解答は，文章の質や，講義の論点と課題文との関係をいかに表しているかに基づいて評価されます。通常，効果的な解答は 150 〜 225 語です。

今聞いた講義の論点を要約しなさい。その際，課題文で挙げられているどの説明をどのようにサポートしているかを必ず説明しなさい。

[✓重要表現チェック]

課題文	□ compulsory「義務的な，強制的な」	
	□ be obligated to *do*「…する義務がある」	
	□ legitimacy「合法性」	□ representative「代表した」
	□ disenfranchisement「権力剥奪」	
解答例	□ eligible to *do*「…する資格がある」	
リスニングスクリプト	□ turnout「投票者数，投票率」	□ undue「不当な」

Question 2

設問訳

指示：下記の問題を読みなさい。30 分間で解答を計画して書き，修正を行いなさい。通常，効果的な解答は 300 語以上です。

あなたは以下の主張に賛成ですか，反対ですか。
「楽観的な人のほうが成功しやすい。」
あなたの意見の根拠となる具体的な理由や事例を述べなさい。

解答例

　When faced with decisions or challenges in life, we cannot always choose the outcome, but we can choose how we think about them. A positive attitude can benefit us in so many ways, while being negative has almost no benefits at all. That is why I agree that optimistic people are more likely to succeed.

　First, being optimistic means that you have passion for something. If you believe that a new job you're applying for or a new business you're trying to start is going to go well, that means you really want it to go well. And wanting something is the first step toward getting it. On the other hand, if your attitude is negative, then it may be because you aren't passionate enough about getting what you want.

　Second, optimistic people are more fun to be around. Success almost never happens without the help of other people. If you want people to help you, you should have a pleasant personality. Most people are more attracted to a positive, optimistic person than a person who is negative and pessimistic. Whether you're trying to succeed in business, in studying, or just in making friends and enjoying life, it's best to have a personality that makes others enjoy being with you.

　Finally, optimism can help you bounce back from failure. Taking a long-term view of any goal you have, there will surely be some troubles along the way. Even the biggest companies and most successful entrepreneurs fail at some time on the road to success. Sometimes they fail many times. However, the key to success is to overcome those failures and keep trying. Being optimistic means believing you can succeed, and that's the attitude that will guide you to actual success.

　In conclusion, a positive attitude gives you much a better chance for success than a negative one. (307 words)

（人生で決断や試練に直面した時，私たちは常に結果を選べるわけではありませんが，その結果をどう捉えるかは選ぶことができます。前向きな態度は私たちに実にさまざまな形で恩恵をもた

らしますが，否定的な態度にはたいていまったく利点がありません。よって，私は楽観的な人のほうが成功しやすいという考えに賛成です。

　第1に，楽観的であるということは，何かに熱意を持っているということです。応募した新しい仕事や，始めようとしている新しい仕事がうまくいくと信じているということは，成功を切に求めているということです。そして，何かを求めることが，それを手に入れるための第一歩なのです。一方で，あなたの態度が否定的ならば，それは，目的を達成することにそれほど熱意を持っていないからかもしれません。

　第2に，楽観的な人のほうが一緒にいて楽しいです。成功は，他人の助けがなければなかなか実現しません。人からの助けが必要ならば，快活でなければなりません。たいていの人は否定的で悲観的な人よりも，前向きで楽観的な人に惹かれます。仕事や勉強で成功しようとするのであれ，単に友人を作って人生を楽しもうとするのであれ，一緒にいる人を楽しい気持ちにするような性格であることが一番です。

　最後に，楽観主義のおかげで失敗から立ち直ることができます。あなたが持つどんな目標も，長い目で見ると，途中で必ず何かしら問題が起きるでしょう。巨大企業や大成功している起業家でも，成功までの道のりの中で時には失敗をします。何度も失敗することもあります。しかし，成功の鍵は，その失敗を克服して挑戦し続けることなのです。楽観的でいることは自分が成功できると信じることであり，その態度があなたを実際に成功に導くでしょう。

　要するに，否定的な態度よりも，前向きな態度のほうが成功する可能性はずっと高いのです。)

解説　「楽観的な人のほうが成功しやすい」という考えに，賛成か反対かを問う問題です。まずは Introduction で自分の立場を明確に示しましょう。解答例では，結果は選べないが，その結果をどう捉えるかは選ぶことができ，悲観的であるよりは楽観的であるほうがメリットは多いとして，賛成の立場を取っています。続く Body では，3つの理由を挙げています。それぞれの理由を端的に表したキーセンテンスを述べた後，より詳細で具体的な説明を加えてその理由をサポートしていくと，論理展開に深みがでます。この時，論理的飛躍があったり，話が重複したりしないように注意しましょう。解答例では，「楽観的な人は熱心である」，「一緒にいて楽しい」，「失敗から立ち直りやすい」という理由を挙げています。それぞれについてまずポイントが簡潔に示され，次にいくつかの詳細な情報が順に盛り込まれていることで，説得力のある裏づけとなっています。Conclusion では再度トピックに対する自分の意見を述べて締めくくります。書き終わったら必ず読み返し，相手を納得させる論理的な展開になっているか確認しましょう。

✓ 重要表現チェック

- □ optimistic「楽観的な」
- □ passionate about ～「～に夢中の」
- □ pessimistic「悲観的な」
- □ entrepreneur「起業家」

MEMO

MEMO

MEMO

【音声収録時間】
47 分 58 秒

【音声吹き込み】
Howard Colefield（アメリカ），Jack Merluzzi（アメリカ），
Rachel Walzer（アメリカ）

【執筆・校閲協力】
（問題執筆）Kevin Glenz，日本アイアール㈱
（解説執筆）中尾千奈美，岡崎恭子，
　　　　　　日和加代子，戸田由美子，
　　　　　　山下友紀，上田雅美
（校閲）　　中尾千奈美，豊田佐恵子

書籍のアンケートにご協力ください
抽選で図書カードをプレゼント！
Z会の「個人情報の取り扱いについて」はZ会Webサイト(https://www.zkai.co.jp/home/policy/)に掲載しておりますのでご覧ください。

TOEFL iBT® TEST ライティングのエッセンス

初版第1刷発行……2015年11月10日
初版第4刷発行……2023年4月10日
著者………………Z会編集部
発行人……………藤井孝昭
発行………………Z会
　　　　　　〒411-0033　静岡県三島市文教町 1-9-11
　　　　　　【販売部門：書籍の乱丁・落丁・返品・交換・注文】
　　　　　　TEL 055-976-9095
　　　　　　【書籍の内容に関するお問い合わせ】
　　　　　　https://www.zkai.co.jp/books/contact/
　　　　　　【ホームページ】
　　　　　　https://www.zkai.co.jp/books/
装丁………………末房志野
DTP………………株式会社 デジタルプレス
録音・編集………一般財団法人 英語教育協議会（ELEC）
印刷・製本………日経印刷株式会社

© Z会 CA 2015　★無断で複写・複製することを禁じます
定価はカバーに表示してあります
乱丁・落丁はお取替えいたします
ISBN978-4-86290-185-9　C0082

別冊 スクリプト・和訳

TOEFL iBT® TEST ライティングのエッセンス

TOEFL is a registered trademark of ETS. This publication is not endorsed or approved by ETS.

論理性×表現力を高めるトレーニング

Z会編集部 編

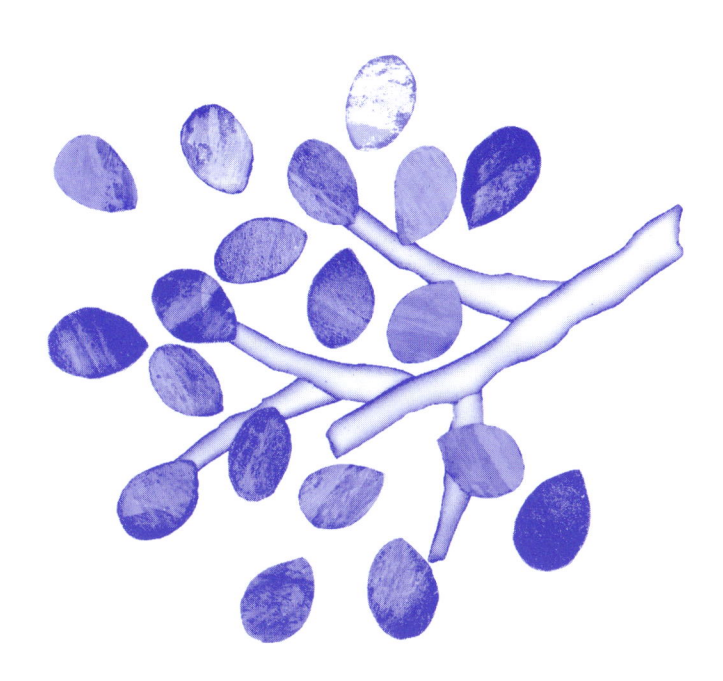

目次

集中トレーニング　Question 1

問題 1 ……………………………………………… 2
問題 2 ……………………………………………… 5
問題 3 ……………………………………………… 7
問題 4 ……………………………………………… 10
問題 5 ……………………………………………… 13
問題 6 ……………………………………………… 15
問題 7 ……………………………………………… 18
問題 8 ……………………………………………… 21
問題 9 ……………………………………………… 24
問題 10 …………………………………………… 27
問題 11 …………………………………………… 29
問題 12 …………………………………………… 32
問題 13 …………………………………………… 35
問題 14 …………………………………………… 38
問題 15 …………………………………………… 40

Integrated Task　Question 1

集中トレーニング

問題 1　　　　　　　　　　　　　　　　　　　　　　　　　　　　問題→本体 p.46

【課題文訳】

　アメリカ政府は，海洋探査と研究の3倍以上の研究費を宇宙探査とその研究に与えています。しかし，現実的な観点から考えると，海洋探査と研究への資金提供のほうがずっと意味があります。なぜなら，気候変動やエネルギー創出，食糧生産のような国内の懸念に関連する発見につながるかもしれないからです。

　気候変動は現在，大きな問題となっています。世界の科学界は，地球温暖化が現実に起きていることであり，政府は地球の気候を保全するための行動を取り始める必要があると警告し続けています。海洋のさらなる探査と研究は，この問題への解決策を生むのに役立つかもしれません。例えば，過剰な二酸化炭素排出量が，気候変動の主たる原因であると言われており，地球の海はこうした二酸化炭素の大部分を吸収しています。さらに研究が進むことで，大気中の二酸化炭素をさらに減らすために海を活用することができるかもしれません。

　海洋研究は，エネルギー創出に関する問題への解決策も生み出すかもしれません。核エネルギーの生成と利用に反対する人々は増えていますが，環境にやさしいエネルギー源はまだ世界中の都市に完全には電力を供給することができません。科学者の中には，まだ実用化されていない再生可能なエネルギー源が海にあると主張する人もいます。その一例は，波エネルギーです。波エネルギー変換は，波の動きから電気エネルギーを生み出します。

　世界中で海産物の生産を向上させ，維持するためにも，研究費を増やすことが必要です。人口が増加し続ける一方で，魚類資源は減り続けています。実は，多くの種の魚が乱獲のせいで絶滅に瀕しています。これに対応するため，水産養殖—養殖とも呼ばれます—は，ますます一般的になってきています。しかし，養殖の持続可能性と生態への影響に関しては，まだ研究が十分ではないのです。

【リスニングスクリプト】　　　　　　　　　　　　　　　　　　　　　　　🔘 CD 04

Now listen to part of a lecture on the topic you just read about.

　The writer of this article appears to believe that funding ocean research and exploration is just as important as funding space research and exploration… Well, there are a few flaws in his argument.

　I think we can all agree that climate change is a major global issue. And I'm sure that further funding of ocean research could lead to some promising discoveries about reducing CO_2 in the atmosphere. However, when it comes to understanding climate change, I doubt that ocean research and exploration will ever contribute as much as space programs… One of the main reasons that we are even able to measure climate change is thanks to NASA. Using monitoring devices developed by NASA, we can measure the atmospheric concentrations and emissions of greenhouse gases and a variety of other key variables.

The writer also talks about how ocean research could contribute to energy production issues… There's a reason that the government isn't funding programs like wave energy conversion —— they have a lot of problems. The scientific community still needs to agree upon the ideal types of devices for generating wave power. Adding to this, the ocean is not a friendly environment for technological devices, largely because of the damaging effects of salt water. It might be a good option for generating power eventually, but it seems unlikely in the near future.

Last, he claims that ocean research can help preserve the globe's fish stocks… But more ocean research probably won't improve aqua farming techniques. I agree that it's important to protect the oceans from the possible negative effects of aqua farming, but this research is not going to increase seafood supply. Companies developing bigger and more efficient aqua farms will be the ones to do that.

【リスニングスクリプト訳】
今読んだトピックに関する講義の一部を聞きなさい。

　この記事の筆者は，海洋の研究と探査への資金提供は，宇宙の研究と探査へのそれと同じくらい重要だと思っているようです…。彼の主張にはいくつか問題点があります。

　気候変動が世界の大きな問題であることには，誰もが同意すると思います。海洋研究への研究費を増やすことが，大気中の二酸化炭素を減らすことに関する有望な発見につながる可能性はあるでしょう。しかし，気候変動を理解するということになると，海洋の研究と探査が，宇宙プログラムと同じくらい寄与するかどうかは疑わしいと思います…。我々が気候変動を観測できる主な理由の1つは，NASAのおかげであるということです。NASAが開発した観測装置を利用することで，我々は温室効果ガスの大気中の濃度や排出量，その他さまざまな重要な数値を計測することができているのです。

　この筆者は，海洋研究がどのようにエネルギー創出の問題に寄与するかについても話しています。政府が波エネルギー変換などのプログラムに研究費を出さないのには理由があります。これらにはたくさんの問題があるのです。科学界はまだ，波力発電の理想的な装置の種類について，合意をまとめる必要があります。これに加え，海は技術装置には優しい環境ではありません。大きな理由として，海水には装置に損傷を与える作用があります。ゆくゆくは発電のよい選択肢になるのかもしれませんが，近い将来には実現しそうにありません。

　最後に，この筆者は，海洋研究は世界の魚類資源の保全に役立つだろうと主張しています…。しかし，さらなる海洋研究はおそらく，養殖技術を向上させることはありません。養殖によって起こりうる負の影響から海を守ることは重要だとは思いますが，この研究は海産物の供給量を増やすことはないでしょう。それができるのは，より広大で効率的な養殖場を開発する企業でしょう。

✅重要表現チェック

- ☐ flaw「欠点」
- ☐ contribute「寄与する，貢献する」
- ☐ measure「～を測る」
- ☐ concentration「濃度」
- ☐ promising「有望な」
- ☐ device「装置」
- ☐ variable「数値，変数」

問題2

【課題文訳】

　組み立てラインの導入は製造過程に革命を起こし，大幅なコスト削減をもたらしました。その考えは，一連の作業全体を次々にこなしていく作業員を使う代わりに，人々に素早く繰り返すことのできる個別の作業を割り当てるというものでした。作業自体が変わらないのであれば，なぜ組み立てラインの方が効率的だったのでしょうか。

　まず個々の作業員が，いろいろな場所から製品が組み立てられる場所まで部品を運んでくるのにかかる時間の損失がありませんでした。その代わり，作業員はすべての時間を部品の取り付けに使ったのです。組み立てる品物は，ベルトコンベヤーに載って作業員の所まで運ばれてきました。品物が自分たちの所へやって来るので，作業員は一つの場所にとどまることができたのです。

　また，割り当てられた作業を行うことで，各々の作業員が高い専門性を獲得することができました。同じ行為を1日に何百回，いや何千回と繰り返すことで，作業やその出来映えに関する混乱を避けることができたのです。効率を最高まで高めるために同じく重要なのは，それぞれの作業にかける割合と，組み立てラインが動く速さを決めることでした。時間と動作の研究によって，最小の努力で最高の速度を生み出すための調整が繰り返されてきました。

　最後に，製品の自動測定によって，作業員は，手作業で行う時間のかかる製品検査から解放されました。出来のよい品物と出来の悪い品物を自動的に選り分けることによって，製造工程で可能な限り費用を抑えて製品を生産することができました。これにより利益が最大化され，大量販売を可能にするのに十分な低価格を持続できるようになりました。

【リスニングスクリプト】

Now listen to part of a lecture on the topic you just read about.

　The assembly line drastically reduced manufacturing costs by efficiently using labor at high rates of speed, but what sort of problems did the assembly line create?

　First, all of the assembly work and movement of parts have to happen in a continuous flow. If there's any problem, stopping the line at any point brings work to a halt for everyone along the line. This is a huge blow to efficiency. Ways need to be found to correct mistakes without stopping the line.

　Second, reducing each worker to repeating a single task infinitely is likely to bore that worker or cause stress. It is difficult to do the same thing every day, especially when you are possibly getting sick of it. It also increases the possibility that the task might be done incorrectly, as when workers lose their ability to concentrate, they tend to make simple mistakes or even risk injury.

　Third, if workers do not have to test the items they are assembling, they lose the sense of involvement in the finished product. Workers may intend to produce a quality product but create a flaw that a more highly-skilled worker in another department would easily notice. Without an overall sense of the whole, workers may be unable to see mistakes as they are made. If mistakes or a lack of sense of the whole forces a worker to produce inferior products, then the ultimate goal of efficiency in the process is lost.

【リスニングスクリプト訳】
今読んだトピックに関する講義の一部を聞きなさい。

　組み立てラインは労働者を速いスピードで効率的に働かせることによって製造コストを劇的に減少させましたが，組み立てラインによってどんな問題が生まれてきたのでしょうか。

　まず，すべての部品の組み立て作業や移動のすべてが，一連の流れの中で行われなければいけません。もし何らかの問題があった場合，組み立てラインを止めることは，どの地点であってもライン上の全員の作業を中止させることになってしまいます。これは効率性において大きな打撃です。ラインを止めずにミスを正す方策を見つけることが必要です。

　次に，各々の作業員をただ1つの作業に限定して延々と繰り返させると，その作業員は飽きたり，ストレスを感じたりしがちです。毎日同じことをし続けることは，場合によって飽きてしまった時には特に耐え難いものです。また作業員の集中力が低下すると，単純なミスをしがちで負傷する危険さえあるため，その作業が正しく行われない可能性が高まります。

　第3に，もし作業員が，自分たちが組み立てている品物を検査する必要がないなら，最終製品に関与しているという感覚を失うことになります。作業員は質の高い製品を作ろうとするでしょうが，別の部門のもっと高度な技術を持つ作業員が簡単に気づくような欠陥品を作り出してしまうかもしれません。全体を見渡す感覚がなければ，ミスがあった時に作業員はそれに気づくことができないかもしれません。ミスや，全体を見渡す力が欠けていることが，作業員に不良品を作らせているとしたら，製造過程で最終的に目指される効率性は失われていることになります。

✓【重要表現チェック】
☐ blow「打撃」　　　　　　　　　☐ reduce ～ to …「～を無理に…の状態にする」
☐ concentrate「集中する」　　　☐ flaw「欠陥品，傷」
☐ ultimate「最終的な，究極の」

問題3

【課題文訳】

　合衆国第3代大統領であるトーマス・ジェファーソンの著書や信条は、長年論争の的になっています。彼はアメリカ独立宣言の起草者として、合衆国建国の父たちの中でも永遠に抜きん出た存在であり続けるでしょう。

　彼は外交問題に関して、1801年3月4日の就任演説の中で、「すべての国と、平和、通商、誠実な友交関係を結び、いかなる国とも煩わしい同盟関係を結ばないこと」を是認しました。合衆国の他国との関係性は本来商業的であり続けるべきだというのが彼の見解でした。これは、アメリカは「外の世界のいかなる地域とも永久的な同盟を結ぶことを避ける」べきであるというジョージ・ワシントンの見解を引き継いだものでした。事実、1789年から第二次世界大戦終戦まで、合衆国は他のどの国とも同盟条約を結びませんでした。

　国の法律を改正するかどうかという議題に関しては、彼はサミュエル・カーチェヴァルへの手紙にこう書いています。「もちろん私は、頻繁に未審理のまま法律や憲法を改正することを支持していません。」彼はまた、憲法は「単に司法の管理下で意のままになるもの、ねじ曲げ、好きなように形を変えてよいもの」であるべきではないとも言っています。彼は、法律を改正するのではなく、それらを作った人の説明に基づいて解釈すべきであると主張しました。

　そして宗教に関しては、自分はキリスト教徒だと言い、神の存在や、人間に関する事柄における神の役割を信じていると表明しました。彼は定期的に教会に通い、たまに家族が行けない時は、1人でも通いました。彼の道徳感は明らかに信仰に導かれていました。

【リスニングスクリプト】

Now listen to part of a lecture on the topic you just read about.

　There has been a great deal of attention given in recent years to Thomas Jefferson's writings and words. Much of it, as seen in this passage, seems to be somewhat misleading.

　It's true that Jefferson entered no "entangling alliances" with other countries during his term as President. However, Thomas Jefferson spent several years in France, and later wrote about their people, "Their kindness and accommodation to strangers is unparalleled, and the hospitality of Paris is beyond anything I had conceived to be practicable in a large city." So even if official policy was of non-intervention, there was a sincere appreciation for other parts of the world, at least for France.

　There's also the matter of his approach to changing laws. You have to read the rest of that letter that's quoted in the reading passage. He also wrote, "Laws and institutions must go hand in hand with the progress of the human mind. As that becomes more developed, more enlightened, as new discoveries are made, new truths disclosed, and manners and opinions change with the change of circumstances, institutions must advance also, and keep pace with the times." Clearly he was advocating for amendments to laws.

And the religious issue is something that many people try to twist around today... Jefferson almost lost the election because of what people considered his "unorthodox," or unusual, views on Christianity. He's the one who coined the phrase, "wall of separation between church and state." And he once wrote in a letter to his nephew, "Question with boldness even the existence of a God." He was truly progressive and even controversial in his religious attitudes, and while he was inspired by Jesus as a man, he did not think he was God's son, as Christians do.

【リスニングスクリプト訳】
今読んだトピックに関する講義の一部を聞きなさい。

　最近トーマス・ジェファーソンの著書や発言がおおいに着目されています。この課題文にも見られるように，その多くは少々誤解されているようです。
　ジェファーソンが，大統領の任期中，どの国とも「煩わしい同盟関係」を結ばなかったのは事実です。しかし，彼自身はフランスで数年間を過ごし，後にフランス人についてこのように書いています。「彼らの親切心や，よそから来た人に対するもてなしは並ぶものがない。また，パリでのもてなしは，私が大都市で実現されうると想像していたものをはるかに上回っていた。」だから，たとえ公的な政策が不干渉であったとしても，世界の他の地域，少なくともフランスを心から評価していたのです。
　彼の法改正への取り組み方に関する問題もあります。課題文で引用された手紙の残りの部分を読まなくてはいけません。彼はこうも書いています。「法律と制度は，人間の精神の進歩と手を取り合って進んでいかなくてはならない。人間の精神がより発達し，より啓蒙されるにつれ，新しい発見がなされ，新しい真実が明らかになり，そして情勢の変化に伴い風習や意見が変わるにつれ，制度も前進し，そして時代に歩調を合わせなければならない。」明らかに，彼は法改正を支持していました。
　それから宗教に関する論点も，今日多くの人々が曲解しようとしていることです。ジェファーソンは，人々がキリスト教に関する彼の「型破りな」，すなわち普通でない見解を考慮したために，危うく選挙に敗れるところでした。彼は「教会と国家間の分離の壁」という言葉を作った人物です。そして彼はかつて甥に宛てた手紙にこのように書いています。「大胆に疑問を持ちなさい。たとえ神の存在に対してであっても。」確かに彼は進歩的であり，彼の宗教的な態度は議論の的ですらありました。また，彼は人間としてのイエスに刺激を受けていましたが，キリスト教徒が考えるように，イエスが神の子だとは思っていなかったのです。

✓ 重要表現チェック

- ☐ misleading「誤解されやすい」
- ☐ unparalleled「並ぶものがない」
- ☐ coin「新しい言葉を作る」
- ☐ controversial「議論の的となる，賛否両論のある」
- ☐ inspire「刺激を与える，鼓舞する」
- ☐ accommodation「人をもてなすこと」
- ☐ enlightened「啓蒙された」
- ☐ boldness「大胆さ」

問題4

問題 ➡ 本体 p.60

【課題文訳】

　マイクロクレジットは，マイクロローンとも呼ばれ，大手銀行のような従来の融資機関から融資を受けることができない貧しい人々への少額融資のことを言います。それは発展途上国で貧困と闘う最も効果的で持続可能な方法の1つです。

　多くの専門的な研究で，マイクロファイナンス・プログラム，特にマイクロクレジットは，貧しい人々に恩恵をもたらすことが示されています。発展途上国の恵まれない市民は大手銀行からの融資の資格を得ることができませんが，マイクロクレジット・ローンは寛大な支払い条件で少額の融資を受ける機会を彼らに与えます。これらの融資は，ひいては彼らの財政状況を改善する助けとなります。例えば，あるマイクロファイナンス会社は，顧客の週あたりの収入が145パーセント増加したと報告しています。

　おそらく，マイクロクレジット・プログラムの最大の利点は，持続可能性の高さです。マイクロクレジット・ローンに貢献した多くの人は，これまでのような慈善の寄付金に代わる望ましい代替手段だと考えています。慈善活動では，恵まれない人々がお金を使えるようにするためにお金が与えられます。しかし，マイクロローンでは，人々がより安定したより高い収入を得られるようにするために，お金が使われます。このローンで借りたお金で，借り手は経済的な支えとなる事業を立ち上げることができます。お金が全額返済されると，貸す側は，また別の誰かにお金を貸すこともできます。

　マイクロクレジット・プログラムは，貧しい人々の起業努力を支える手段としてだけでなく，男性優位の社会にいる女性たちなど，恵まれない社会集団の地位を向上させる点でも評価されています。この最も有名な例は，バングラディシュにある，とある銀行です。その銀行は，バングラディシュで何百万人もの女性が経済的な自立を達成するのを助けてきました。その結果，ノーベル平和賞を受賞したのです。

【リスニングスクリプト】　　　　　　　　　　　　　　　　　　　　　　🔘 CD 07

Now listen to part of a lecture on the topic you just read about.

　Now don't get me wrong —— I like the idea behind microcredit programs. It sounds like a great idea, right? You lend some money to a poor person. They use it to make more money. Then they pay you back, and you have the option of lending it to another poor person... Unfortunately, microcredit programs don't really work as well as their supporters claim.

　For one thing, microloans typically have high interest rates, and as a result they tend to increase the financial burdens of the poor people borrowing money. In other words, they can make the financial situation of borrowers worse than it was before getting the loan... One reason for high interest rates is administrative costs. It takes a lot less administrative time to set up one $5,000 loan than it takes to set up 20 different $250 loans… This increased administrative burden is one factor that forces microcredit institutions to raise interest rates.

Perhaps the biggest problem with microcredit, though, is that it's not the best way to fix poverty. A more effective solution is creating jobs… For example, if I loan $100 to 1,000 different women so that they can buy sewing machines to start their own clothing businesses, then those women have to compete with each other, charge prices that are too low to be profitable, and many of them may fail… A more effective option would be to lend $100,000 to a clothing factory that provides fair wages and good working conditions, creating 1,000 new, stable, sustainable jobs.

The passage also mentions that microcredit programs empower women. Well, kind of. Yeah, these programs give women more opportunities, but they're certainly not a solution for cultural prejudices. Giving a woman a small loan won't make her closed-minded male neighbors stop discriminating against women. Only changing a culture's values gradually over time can fix gender inequalities.

【リスニングスクリプト訳】
今読んだトピックに関する講義の一部を聞きなさい。

誤解しないでくださいね。私はマイクロクレジット・プログラムの背景にある考えは好きです。素晴らしい考えに思えますよね。貧しい人にお金を貸します。借りた人はもっとお金を稼ぐためにそのお金を使います。そして、彼らがあなたに返済したら、あなたはまた別の貧しい人にお金を貸すこともできる…。でも残念ながら、マイクロクレジット・プログラムは、実際には、それを支持する人々が主張するほどうまくは機能しないのです。

1つには、マイクロローンは通常高金利になっていて、結果としてお金を借りる貧しい人々の経済的負担を増加させる傾向にあるのです。言い換えれば、借り手の財政状況が融資を受ける前よりも悪化することもあるのです…。高金利の理由の1つには、管理コストがあります。5,000ドルのローンを1件組むほうが、250ドルのローンを20件組むよりも管理時間がはるかに短くて済みます…。このような管理面での負担増が、マイクロクレジット関連機関が金利を上げざるを得ない一因となっています。

しかしおそらく、マイクロクレジットの最大の問題は、貧困を解消する最良の方法ではないということでしょう。より効果的な解決策は雇用を創出することです。例えば、もし私が1,000人の女性に、衣料品事業を始めるためのミシンが買えるように、100ドルを貸したとします。この女性たちは競合関係になり、利益が出るよりも低い価格設定をしなければならなくなって、その多くが失敗するでしょう…。より効果的な選択肢は、公正な賃金とよい勤務条件を与える縫製工場に10万ドルを融資して、1,000人分の安定した持続可能な新しい雇用を生み出すことでしょう。

課題文では、マイクロクレジット・プログラムが女性の地位を向上させるとも述べられています。

まあ，ある程度は。確かに，こうしたプログラムは女性により多くの機会を与えますが，文化的な偏見を解決するものでは決してありません。女性に少額の融資をしても，その女性の近所に住む偏狭な男性に，女性への差別をやめさせることはできないでしょう。時間をかけて徐々に文化的価値観を変えていくことでしか，男女間の不平等を是正することはできないのです。

✓ 重要表現チェック

- [ ] work「うまくいく」
- [ ] interest rate「利率」
- [ ] sewing machine「ミシン」
- [ ] empower「〜に権限を与える」
- [ ] gender inequality「男女不平等」
- [ ] supporter「支持者」
- [ ] administrative「管理の」
- [ ] clothing「衣類」
- [ ] discriminate against 〜「〜を差別する」

問題 5

【課題文訳】

　遺伝子工学は，DNA を，ある生物から，それを持たない別の生物へ付加する技術です。それはすでに魅力的かつ有益な方法で利用されています。

　カナダに，リンを消化するように遺伝子操作されている豚がいます。リンは水中に多量の藻を発生させる化学物質です。あまりにも多くの藻が生じると酸素が少なくなり，海洋生物が死滅してしまいます。遺伝子改変された豚は，排泄物に含まれるリンが通常より少なくなるようにリンを処理します。これにより環境に対する豚の影響が小さくなります。

　別の開発で，中国の大学の農業科学者がサソリ毒をキャベツへ付加しました。これはキャベツの生産を損なうイモムシを殺すためです。彼らは，イモムシは殺しても，人体には害を及ぼさないように毒を改良しています。このようなキャベツの栽培は，殺虫剤の使用の減少や，農家の出費削減，作物に使われる化学薬品の減少などをもたらすでしょう。

　最後に，アメリカの会社が，より速く成長するようにサケの遺伝子を組み換えました。そのサケを育てるため，約 7,700 万ドルを費やし，より多くの成長ホルモンを作ることができる別の種の遺伝子を混ぜました。FDA（米国食品医薬品局）は，食べても安全なようであり，環境に害を及ぼすことはなさそうだと言っていますが，まだそれを承認はしていません。もしそれがスーパーマーケットで販売されることができるようになれば，世界的に増えている魚の需要を満たすのに役立つでしょう。

【リスニングスクリプト】　　　　　　　　　　　　　　　　　　　　　CD 08

Now listen to part of a lecture on the topic you just read about.

　I don't wish to say that genetic engineering is always scary, or that scientists shouldn't be doing it. But I think we need to look at these examples a little more closely.

　The pig in Canada is called an Enviropig. It was approved for production in Canada in 2010, but it still had to be kept apart from other animals. The research stopped in 2012 and hasn't really been picked up since then. Even if the research began again, it would take years before any country would approve of using such a pig for food.

　I don't think anyone's going to be in a rush to buy cabbage with scorpion venom. They claim the venom is harmless, but they didn't test it on live humans —— only on cancer cells. Plus, when they tested the toxin, they applied it to the insects, but didn't test how effective it was if ingested. That means the caterpillars maybe won't die just by eating the cabbage, so pesticides will have to be used anyway.

　And the salmon has been in regulatory limbo for several years. Even if it is approved for sale, several supermarket chains have already said they aren't going to sell it. No matter how safe governments and scientists say that genetically modified food is, the public is largely against it and highly resistant toward eating it. So these scientists certainly have great ideas, and probably have human benefit in mind when they're doing this research, but I have to conclude that their work is probably not going to see the light of day in terms of large-scale commercialization.

【リスニングスクリプト訳】
今読んだトピックに関する講義の一部を聞きなさい。

　私は遺伝子工学がいかなる場合でも恐ろしいものだとか，科学者はそれをすべきではないなどと言いたくはありません。しかしながら，私たちはこれらの例をもう少し詳しく見る必要があると思います。

　カナダの豚はエンバイロピッグと呼ばれています。それは2010年にカナダで生産を承認されました。しかしその豚は，いまだに他の動物から隔離されなければなりません。その研究は2012年に中止され，それ以来あまり取り上げられていません。たとえその研究が再開したとしても，そのような豚を食用として使用することを許可するまでには，どの国であっても何年もかかるでしょう。

　サソリ毒入りキャベツを躍起になって買いたい人はいないと思います。彼らはその毒は無害だと主張していますが，がん細胞で試しただけで，生きた人間では試しませんでした。しかも彼らがその毒素を試した時には，虫に散布はしましたが，もし虫の体内に取り込まれたらどのような効果があるかについては試しませんでした。それは，ただキャベツを食べただけではイモムシは死なないかもしれないということを意味しています。したがって，いずれにしても殺虫剤が使用されなければならないでしょう。

　そして，サケについては，何年間も調整中で忘れられつつあります。たとえ販売が認可されても，いくつかのスーパーマーケットチェーンはそのサケを売るつもりはないとすでに表明しています。政府や科学者たちが，遺伝子組み換え食品がどんなに安全だと言ったとしても，一般の人々の大半はそれに反対で，それを食べることにかなりの抵抗を示しています。だから，これらの科学者たちは確かに素晴らしい考えを持っており，おそらくこの研究をする時には，人の役に立つということを心に留めているのでしょうが，大規模な商業化という観点から考えると，おそらく彼らの仕事が日の目を見ることはないだろうと結論づけなければなりません。

✓重要表現チェック
- □ approve「〜を承認する」
- □ regulatory「規制する，調整的な」
- □ resistant「抵抗を示す」
- □ toxin「毒（素）」
- □ limbo「忘れられた状態」
- □ in terms of 〜「〜の観点から」

問題6

【課題文訳】

　3Dプリンティングとは，電子ファイルから固体の3次元の物体を作る技術のことです。3Dプリンターが特別なものであると言えるのは，まったく同じ機械から，異なる素材でさまざまな種類の物体を作り出すことができるためです。3Dプリンティング産業は今後数十年にわたり一貫して成長し，数多くの有望な投資機会を生み出すと期待されています。

　3Dプリンティングは，世界の人々が製品を製造する方法を完全に変えるでしょう。3Dプリンティングは，消費者が自宅にいながらにして事実上何でも製造できるようにする可能性を秘めています。例えば，あるデザイナーに新作のジュエリーのアイデアがある場合，3Dプリンターを使えば，構想を抱いてから完成品を作るまで，たった数時間で済むかもしれません。

　すでに，この新しい産業を活用しているたくさんの企業があり，その多くには有望な未来があります。個人向けの3Dプリンターを製造して販売している企業もあります。デザインの設計と実装に焦点を当てている企業もあります。専門家たちは，3Dプリンティング産業は今後数年間，着実に成長を続けるだろうと予測しており，この新しくておもしろい技術を活用して成功する企業がどんどん出てくることが期待できます。

　多くの経済専門家がこの新興産業に参入しているさまざまな大企業への投資を勧めています。これらの企業は，3Dプリンティング産業が発展し続けるのと共に成長し続けるでしょう。さらに，複数の企業に分散して投資することで，かかるリスクを抑えることができます。

【リスニングスクリプト】　CD 09

Now listen to part of a lecture on the topic you just read about.

　You'll notice that in this article, the author presents a pretty convincing argument for investing in 3D printing. However, I'd like to point out some problems with both his argument and this type of investing in general.

　The article makes it sound like the world is going to be completely changed by 3D printing. There are actually quite a few experts making claims like this. The thing is ─── we still don't know how 3D printing will change the manufacturing industry… For example, most 3D printer models today can only make very simple products… Yet major factories can produce simple products at much lower costs, and some argue that 3D printing will never be able to beat the low costs of traditional manufacturing techniques for widely distributed products.

　The article also discusses the range of companies that are being created. This happens any time that a new industry emerges… A whole bunch of companies start trying to take advantage of the new opportunity… And a lot of those new companies fail. Some of the most popular companies for 3D printing are making consumer models of 3D printers, for example. However, a lot of experts are saying that 3D printers might never become widely used consumer products, which would, in turn, hurt these companies pretty badly.

   Finally, the article advises investing in multiple 3D printing-related companies. As we've seen before, though, investing in young markets can be very risky. It's almost impossible to know where the market is going. And as a result, it's very difficult to judge which companies are safe investments —— if any! The chance at a high return is certainly tempting. But high returns come with high risks, also.

【リスニングスクリプト訳】
今読んだトピックに関する講義の一部を聞きなさい。
　この記事では，著者が，3D プリンティングに投資すべきだというかなり説得力のある主張をしていることに気づくでしょう。しかし私は，著者の主張と，このような投資全般の両方について，いくつかの問題を指摘したいと思います。
　この記事は，3D プリンティングによって，世界が完全に変わろうとしているかのような印象を与えます。実際，このような主張をしている専門家はかなりいます。でも本当のところ，3D プリンティングが製造業界をどのように変えるかは，まだわからないのです…。例えば，現在 3D プリンターのほとんどのモデルは，とても単純なものしか作ることができません…。その上，多くの工場では単純なものをそれよりもずっと低いコストで製造することができ，3D プリンティングは，広く流通する製品の製造において，従来の製造技術の低コストに打ち勝つことはできないだろうと主張する人もいます。
　この記事は，生まれつつある企業の幅広さについても述べています。これは新しい産業が出現する時にはいつでも起こることです…。多くの企業がその新しい機会を利用しようとし始めます…。そして，こうした新しい企業の多くは失敗するのです。例えば，3D プリンティングで最も評判のよい企業の中には，3D プリンターの消費者向けモデルを製造しているところもあります。しかし，多くの専門家が，3D プリンターは広く普及する消費者製品にはならないかもしれないと言っています…。そうなれば，こうした企業への大きな打撃となりかねません。
　最後に，この記事では，複数の 3D プリンティング関連企業に投資するようアドバイスしています。しかし，これまでに見てきたように，日の浅い市場に投資をするのはとてもリスクが高いです。市場がどこへ向かうのか知ることはほとんど不可能です。そしてその結果，どの企業が安全な投資先なのかを判断するのは，とても難しいのです。もしそんな企業があるとしたらの話ですが！　ハイリターンのチャンスは確かにそそられます。しかし，ハイリターンにはハイリスクもつきものなのです。

✓ 重要表現チェック

- ☐ convincing「説得力のある」
- ☐ beat「〜に勝つ」
- ☐ in turn「今度は」
- ☐ quite a few「かなり多数の」
- ☐ distribute「〜を流通させる」
- ☐ return「利益, 収益」

問題 7

問題 ➡ 本体 p.73

【課題文訳】

　科学者たちは，目下大量絶滅が起こっていることを確認しています。このことが意味するのは，無数の多種多様な動植物が不自然に速いペースで消滅しているということです。実は，動物種が消滅しているこのペースは，恐竜時代以来最も速くなっています。加えて，科学者たちは，人類がこの大量絶滅の原因であると主張しています。

　おそらく，この出来事の最大の要因は気候変動でしょう。ここ千年ほどの間に起こった数多くの技術的進歩により，人口は急増しました。その負の影響の1つが地球温暖化です。地球温暖化は，気候パターンに有害な変化をもたらしています。人類の自動車や工場が気候を変化させ，その結果，何千もの生物種が絶滅しようとしています。

　これに関するもう1つの大きな原因は，海洋破壊です。言い換えると，海の生態系が破壊されており，その結果，多くの魚種が死滅しつつあります。この原因のほとんどは，人間による乱獲です。人口の増加に伴い，乱獲は主要な地球規模の問題になっています。わかりやすく言えば，人類は，海が生産できるよりも多くの魚を食べているのです。

　陸上では，生物種の消滅を招いている最大の原因は，森林破壊です。これは，森林以外の土地利用のために森林を伐採してしまうことを言います。例えば，人口が拡大すると，住宅を建設するためにしばしば森林地帯が破壊されます。森林はこうした住宅を作る材木を提供するためにも破壊されます。簡単に言えば，増加する人口が，地球の動植物を多くの点で危機的な状況に押しやっているということです。早急に何かが変わらなければ，危険な結果をもたらす可能性があります。

【リスニングスクリプト】　　　　　　　　　　　　　　　　　　⚫ CD 10

Now listen to part of a lecture on the topic you just read about.

　Even conservative estimates by scientists conclude that a mass extinction event is taking place... So this is a very real problem. However, this article gives misleading information about what's causing this global issue.

　Climate change is definitely a major cause of the disappearance of so many species. However, climate change is much more complicated than just global warming. The scientific community still doesn't totally understand everything that's causing climate change, though many agree that it's probably humans... A better way to explain this problem of disappearing species is to say that many natural ecosystems are being damaged or changed. For example, in addition to global warming, pollution also upsets the environment... Plus, humans are also responsible for introducing harmful species of animals into new environments... All of these can lead to the extinction of species.

　Overfishing is certainly a problem, too, but oceanic devastation is not only caused by overfishing. Some of the climate changes we've discussed, for example, can actually change the chemical properties of ocean water, and this can cause severe damage to ocean species. Another problem is marine pollution. As you probably know, major oil spills have occurred multiple times in human history… Serious industrial accidents like this kill large numbers of plants and animals.

Finally, the article claimed that deforestation is the most significant cause of species loss on land… Well, not really. Destroying forests is actually just one part of a bigger problem, which is changing and destroying large areas of land for human use. Experts estimate that 10 to 15 % of the earth's land surface is occupied by human buildings and farms. When humans make farms, we don't always destroy forests. Sometimes we just clear open fields to make farms. But this still changes ecosystems, and it is a major cause of disappearing species.

【リスニングスクリプト訳】
今読んだトピックに関する講義の一部を聞きなさい。

　科学者たちによる控えめな予測でさえも、大量絶滅が起こっていると結論づけています。そう、これはまさに現実に起こっている問題なのです。しかしこの記事は、何がこの地球規模の問題を引き起こしているのかについて、誤解を招く情報を与えています。

　気候変動は間違いなく、これほど多くの生物種を消滅させている大きな原因です。しかし、気候変動は単なる地球温暖化よりもずっと複雑です。科学界はまだ、気候変動を引き起こしているすべてのものを完全には把握していません。その原因はおそらく人類だろうということに、多くの人々が同意していますが…。生物種の消滅というこの問題を説明するよりよい方法は、自然の生態系の多くが破壊されている、または、変化させられていると述べることでしょう。例えば、地球温暖化に加え、汚染もまた環境を狂わせています。それに、有害な動物種を新しい環境に持ち込んでいるのも人間です…。これらはすべて、生物種の絶滅につながる可能性があります。

　魚の乱獲も確かに問題ですが、海洋破壊は乱獲だけで引き起こされているわけではありません。例えば、すでにお話しした気候変動の中にも海水の化学的性質を実際に変える可能性があるものもあり、このことは海の生物種に深刻な損害を与える可能性があります。もう1つの問題は、海洋汚染です。おそらくご存じのように、人類史上何度も大規模な石油流出が起こっています。このような深刻な産業事故も、多数の動植物を死に至らしめているのです。

　最後に、この記事は、森林破壊が陸上での生物種損失の最大の原因であると主張していました…。ところが、そうとも言えないのです。森林破壊は実際には、人間が利用するために広い範囲の土地に変化を与え破壊しているという、より大きな問題の一部でしかありません。専門家たちは、地球の地表の10パーセントから15パーセントを人間の建物や農場が占めていると推定しています。人間が農場を作る時、必ずしも森林を破壊するわけではありません。農場を作るために、開けた野原を整備するだけの場合もあります。しかし、このことはそれでも生態系に変化を与え、生物種の消滅の大きな原因になっているのです。

✓ 重要表現チェック

- scientific community「科学界」
- ecosystem「生態系」
- cause damage「損害を与える」
- upset「混乱させる」
- chemical property「化学的性質」
- oil spill「石油流出」

問題 8

問題 ➡ 本体 p.77

【課題文訳】

　過去数十年間で，インターネットはダイエットや栄養に関する記事であふれるようになり，その多くが相反する主張をしています。あまりにも多くの異なる意見があって，どれが栄養に関するまっとうなアドバイスなのか，見分けるのが難しいことがあります。そこで，きちんとした科学研究に裏づけられたダイエットのアドバイスをいくつか紹介したいと思います。

　最初のアドバイスとして，推奨される1日あたりのたんぱく質摂取量について考えてみましょう。ボディビルダーやダイエットの専門家の多くは，シェイクやプロテインパウダーといったたんぱく質を補うサプリメントなど，高たんぱく質の食事を勧めています。これを推奨する人々全体が合意しているのは，「たんぱく質は多ければ多いほどよい」ということのようです。しかし，医学研究所の委員会が発表した調査研究は，18歳以上の人が1日に摂取するたんぱく質の推奨量は，体重1ポンドにつき0.36グラムだと結論づけています。

　体重1ポンドにつき0.36グラムは，それほど多いたんぱく質ではありません。これは，体重160ポンドの人では，1日あたりたった57.6グラムにしかならないということです。この要件を満たす一番の方法は，海産物や脂肪分の少ない鶏肉，低脂肪の乳製品など，良質でたんぱく質に富む食品を食べることです。例えば，皮なしの鶏胸肉4オンスには，約30グラムのたんぱく質が含まれ，この1日に推奨される必要量の半分以上になります。

　体重を減らそうとしている方は，1日に2，3回たくさんの食事を取るよりも，少量ずつ複数回食べたほうがよい選択かもしれません。1日に複数回少量の食事をとると代謝速度が上がり，1日により多くのカロリーを消費することになると主張するダイエットの専門家もいます。また，頻繁に少ない量の食事をとれば，お腹がすきすぎず，その結果，食事の時に食べすぎなくて済むため，よい食習慣であるとも言えます。

【リスニングスクリプト】　　　　　　　　　　　　　　　　　　　　CD 11

Now listen to part of a lecture on the topic you just read about.

　These days, more and more nutrition experts and health bloggers have been claiming to give science-backed dieting advice. On the surface, this might seem like a good idea. But it also causes some problems.

　Take a look at this article, for example. It says that the ideal amount of protein for a person is .36 grams per pound per day... As nutrition scientists, we should always avoid overly simplified dietary advice like this. For example, .36 grams per pound per day might be a good amount for a normal, working individual, but other studies have shown that athletes need more than this amount of protein. Some athletes might need .8 grams per pound per day.

　Next, the article says that the best way to get that protein is by eating seafood, lean chicken, and dairy… Yes, these are protein-rich foods. However, the body does not need protein-rich foods, specifically, in order to hit daily protein requirements. The important thing is giving your body foods that it can use to make protein. This is why, for instance, some of the world's greatest athletes are vegetarians. They can build muscle on plant-based diets… For the majority of people, having a balanced diet of nutrient-rich foods is all that is needed to hit recommended intakes. Some experts even argue that counting grams of protein is usually a waste of time.

Last, the author mentions that people can avoid overeating by having multiple small meals throughout the day. I think that this is good advice…for some. But there have been many cases of people who accidentally eat too many calories using this dieting method. So while it is an option for dieting, it can sometimes be worse than eating traditionally spaced meals.

【リスニングスクリプト訳】
今読んだトピックに関する講義の一部を聞きなさい。

　最近，科学的根拠に基づくダイエットのアドバイスをしていると主張する栄養の専門家や健康ブログの著者が増えています。表面的には，これはよい考えのように思えるかもしれません。しかし，いくつかの問題も起こしているのです。

　例えば，この記事を見てください。1人の人の理想的なたんぱく質摂取量は，1日に体重1ポンドにつき 0.36 グラムと書かれています…。栄養学者として，私たちは常に，このような過度に単純化した食事のアドバイスを避けるべきです。例えば，1日あたり体重1ポンドにつき 0.36 グラムという量は，標準的な働く人々には適度な量かもしれませんが，スポーツ選手はこの量よりももっと多くのたんぱく質を必要とすることを示す研究もあります。スポーツ選手によっては，1日あたり体重1ポンドにつき 0.8 グラムを必要とする人もいるかもしれません。

　次に，この記事は，この量のたんぱく質を摂取する一番の方法は，海産物，脂肪分の少ない鶏肉，乳製品を食べることだと述べています…。確かに，これらはたんぱく質に富んだ食品です。しかし，1日あたりのたんぱく質摂取量を満たすために，身体はたんぱく質に富んだ食品を特に必要とはしていません。重要なのは，あなたの身体にたんぱく質を作るために使うことのできる食品を与えることです。例えば，世界最高のスポーツ選手の中には菜食主義者もいるのはこのためです。菜食を基本とした食事から筋肉を作ることができるのです…。大半の人々にとって，推奨摂取量を満たすために必要なのは，栄養の豊富な食品をバランスよく食べること，それだけです。たんぱく質の量を測ることはたいてい時間の無駄だと主張する専門家さえいます。

　最後に，この著者は，1日に複数回少量の食事をとることによって，食べすぎを防ぐことができると述べています。これはよいアドバイスだと思います…一部の人にとってはね。でも，この食事法をとることで，カロリーを多くとりすぎてしまうケースも多々あるのです。ですから，これはダイエットの1つの選択肢ではあるものの，時には従来の間隔をおいた食事と比べて悪い影響を及ぼす可能性もあります。

✓ **重要表現チェック**
□ simplify「〜を単純化する」　　□ hit「(特定の水準) に達する」
□ accidentally「偶然に」

問題9

【課題文訳】

社会の他の分野に比べ，高等教育は過去数百年間でほとんど変化していません。しかし，21世紀の技術的発展の進行に伴い，大学教育はより多くの問題に直面するようになっており，かなりの数の大学が今後20年間で破産するだろうと推定する評論家もいます。

少なくともアメリカでの主な問題は，大学が財政危機に陥っていることです。世界クラスの大学を経営するコストは上昇し続けていますが，政府からの資金は減り続けています。例えば，2012年までの5年間で公立大学の学費は27パーセント増加しました。ほぼすべての大学がこの費用を学生に負担させています。その結果，アメリカの学生の借金は1兆ドル以上にまで膨れ上がっています。

未来の学生たちは高額な大学教育に代わるものを探し始めています。その1つにオンライン学習があります。このよく知られた例は，大規模公開オンライン講座で，よくMOOCsと呼ばれます。学生はウェブを通じてこれらの講座を受講します。つまり，多数の学生が同じ講座を取ることができるということです。これにより，学生にかかる費用は大学で学ぶ場合よりも劇的に減ります。その中には，公式の学位を提供し始めているものまであり，大学に代わる実効性のあるものとなっています。

しかし，大学には，大きな変化はまったく起こっていないのです。旧来の大学教育を擁護する人々は，それでも，大学で学ぶことには，学生や教員とのネットワークを持つ機会があるという利点があると指摘します。しかし，オンラインスクールは，すぐにこれらの弱点に対応するようになるでしょう。いくつかのオンライン教育の企業は，学生が，クラスメイトの少人数のグループや高いスキルを持つ大学教授と，高度なやりとりをすることができるオンラインのセミナーを提供し始めています。これは，どれだけオンラインスクールが急速に発達しているかを示す一例です。

【リスニングスクリプト】　●CD 12

Now listen to part of a lecture on the topic you just read about.

These days, I hear a lot of people talking about how online education is going to destroy universities... But many universities are actually embracing changes to education and experimenting with new approaches to teaching.

Let's look at funding issues first. I think we can all agree that college education is too expensive, right? But many universities are working to develop new financial models that make university education cheaper. For example, some universities are beginning to experiment with these online learning options. The idea is that their students can simultaneously study online courses and also study at their university. This way they can get a solid education but also spend less money on student fees.

Many universities are realizing that online learning is not a threat. Online learning is easy to start, but it is difficult to complete. In fact, only around 10% of students complete online courses after enrolling. Maintaining motivation is a huge problem with online learning. In contrast, the resources that universities offer to students, such as fellow classmates, free tutors, teaching assistants, and highly engaged professors are highly beneficial. Although online learning can be utilized in university education, it is unlikely to completely replace universities.

Finally, the article makes it sound like universities are not changing or innovating at all, but that's simply not true… I already mentioned how many universities are experimenting with online courses… Also, a large number of universities are experimenting with new and interesting study programs. For example, a university in the U.S. recently developed a special building where students can work together to launch businesses. The building has 3D printers, power tools, office spaces, and lounge areas. This is a great example of how universities are adapting to modern trends.

【リスニングスクリプト訳】
今読んだトピックに関する講義の一部を聞きなさい。

　最近，オンライン教育が大学を破壊しようとしていると多くの人々が話しているのを耳にします…。しかし，多くの大学は実際には教育への変化を受け入れ，新しい教育法を試しています。

　まず，資金の問題を考えてみましょう。大学教育はあまりにも高額すぎるということには皆さん，同意見ですよね。しかし，多くの大学は，大学教育をより安くする新しい財政モデルを開発しようと取り組んでいます。例えば，こうしたオンライン学習の選択肢を試し始めている大学もあります。これは，学生がオンライン講座を学び，同時に大学でも勉強をするという考え方です。こうすれば，学生はしっかりとした教育を受けることができ，かつ，学費は少なくて済みます。

　多くの大学は，オンライン学習は脅威ではないと考えています。オンライン学習は手軽に始めることができますが，修了することは難しいのです。実は，登録した学生のうち，ほんの10パーセントほどしか講座を修了していません。オンライン教育においてモチベーションの維持は大きな課題です。これに対し，仲間のクラスメイト，無料のチューター，ティーチング・アシスタント，熱心な教授といった従来の大学が学生に提供する資産は，非常に有益なものです。オンライン学習は，大学教育の中で活用していくことができますが，従来の大学に完全に取って代わる可能性は低いでしょう。

　最後に，この記事は大学がまったく変化していない，もしくは変革していないと思わせるような書き方をしていますが，まったく真実ではありません…。いかに多くの大学がオンライン講座を試しているかについては，すでに述べましたね。また，たくさんの大学がおもしろい新型の学習プログラムを試しています。例えば，アメリカにあるとある大学は最近，学生が共同で事業を立ち上げることができる特別な建物を開発しました。この建物には，3Dプリンター，電動工具，オフィススペース，ラウンジエリアがあります。これは，いかに大学が現代の潮流に適応してい

るかを示す好例です。

✓ 重要表現チェック
- embrace「〜に喜んで応じる，〜を採用する」
- solid「堅実な，確かな」
- engaged「熱心な，積極的に関わる」
- power tool「電動工具」
- simultaneously「同時に」
- enroll「登録する」
- launch「(事業など) を始める」

問題 10

【課題文訳】

　アメリカ政府は，世界の他のどの国よりも多額の軍事予算を組んでおり，このため，多くの評論家が軍事支出を減らすように求めています。しかし，軍事支出の増加を支持する多くの人々は，軍事支出によって技術的発見が推進され，アメリカ国民の雇用が創出され，国家の安全保障が強化されると主張しています。

　21世紀において，技術革新以上に経済を動かすものはなく，軍事支出は技術のさらに大きな発展につながります。ほとんどのアメリカ国民にとって，インターネットや衛星通信，高速ジェットエンジンのない世界を想像することは難しいでしょう。というのも，これらは皆，現代の経済に欠かせないものだからです。これらの技術はすべて，軍事から始まりました。論理的な観点から見て，軍事支出を継続することは，さらなる技術的な発見につながるでしょう。

　軍事支出のもう1つの大きな利点は，アメリカの国民にとって多くの雇用を創出することです。専門家らは，10億ドルの軍事支出は約11,000件の雇用を生むと推定しています。防衛予算を削ると，多くのアメリカ人が職を失うことになります。この記事を書いている時点で，アメリカの軍事支出に依存する職に就いているアメリカ国民はおよそ1,000万人いると推定されています。予算が削減されることで危機にさらされる仕事の数は，これほど大きなものなのです。

　最後に，国家の安全保障以上に重要なことはありません。世界はもう，従来のような戦争をしません。国民はむしろ，21世紀において，別の形の脅威に直面しています。つまり，サイバー攻撃，テロ行為，大量破壊兵器や気候変動といった脅威です。多額の防衛予算を組むことで，政府は，こうした脅威から国民を守ることができるようになります。

【リスニングスクリプト】　　　　　　　　　　　　　　　　　　　CD 13

Now listen to part of a lecture on the topic you just read about.

　While I'm not going to give my own personal opinion about US military spending, I would like to point out some serious flaws in this article's arguments.

　First, let's look at this claim that military spending improves technology. This is totally true. However, if the goal of spending is to improve technology, then military spending is not the answer. Commercial companies make equally impressive technological discoveries using a tiny fraction of the military's budget. To give just a few examples, these companies are building cars that drive themselves, faster and safer airplanes, contact lenses that help diabetes patients, and renewable power sources. Obviously, if the government wanted to improve technology, there are more efficient ways to spend money than on the military.

　Also, the article argues that the military creates jobs. Again, this is true. It does create jobs. But other government sectors create more jobs. The example in the article was that $1 billion to military spending creates about 11,000 jobs. But if we gave the same amount of money to education, it would create around 29,000 jobs. If we gave the same amount of money to healthcare, it would create around 19,000 jobs.

Last, the article's author emphasizes the importance of national security. I think we can all agree that this is pretty important. However, critics of military spending claim that budget cuts would actually increase national security. Part of national security is having a strong economy, good healthcare, and high-quality education. To give one example, many experts agree that decreasing military spending would improve the economy. A strong economy means that more people have jobs, which means that they can feed and house their families.

【リスニングスクリプト訳】
今読んだトピックに関する講義の一部を聞きなさい。

　アメリカの軍事支出に関して，私の個人的な意見を述べるつもりはありませんが，この記事の主張に見られる重大な問題点をいくつか指摘したいと思います。

　まず，軍事支出が技術を向上させるという主張について考えてみましょう。これは完全なる事実です。しかし，支出の目的が技術の向上であるのなら，軍事支出はその解決策ではありません。民間企業は，軍事予算額のほんのわずかの資金を使って，同様の目覚ましい技術的発見を生み出します。少し例を挙げると，こうした企業は，自動運転する車，より速く安全な航空機，糖尿病患者の助けとなるコンタクトレンズ，再生可能なエネルギー源を開発しています。明らかに，政府が技術の向上を望むのなら，軍事にかけるよりももっと有効なお金の使い方があります。

　また，この記事は，軍事が雇用を創出すると主張しています。これも事実です。確かに，雇用は創出します。しかし，政府の他の部門はもっと多くの雇用を生み出します。この記事の事例には，10億ドルの軍事支出が約11,000件の雇用を生むとありました。しかし，同じ額を教育にかけたなら，約29,000件の雇用を生むのです。同じ額を医療にかけたなら，約19,000件の雇用が創出されます。

　最後に，この記事の著者は国家の安全保障の重要性を強調しています。安全保障がとても重要だということには，私たち誰もが同意できるでしょう。しかし，軍事支出を批判する人々は，実際には軍事予算の削減こそが国家の安全保障を強化するのだと主張しています。国家の安全保障を成すものには，好調な経済，充実した医療，質の高い教育があります。1つ例を挙げると，多くの専門家たちが，軍事支出の減少は経済を上向かせるということに同意しています。経済が好調であるということは，より多くの人々に職があるということを意味します。そして，このことはつまり，より多くの人々が家族に食と住を提供できるということなのです。

✓ 重要表現チェック
- □ a tiny fraction of ～「ほんのわずかな～」
- □ diabetes「糖尿病」
- □ power source「エネルギー源」
- □ emphasize「～を強調する」

問題 11

【課題文訳】

　コアラは、彼らの母国オーストラリアのシンボルである、短い毛で覆われたクマのような生き物です。彼らはほとんどの時間を木々の中で過ごし、ユーカリの葉を食べます。そして、その生物学上の科を代表する唯一の動物です。しかしこの独特な生き物は、農業用や宅地用の土地の過剰な開発、乱獲、病気、地球温暖化による森林破壊などのさまざまな要因のために、絶滅の危機に瀕しています。彼らの生息地は著しく減少し、生息地となっている地域では残っているコアラが過密状態になっています。

　野生のコアラは4つの州、クイーンズランド州、ニューサウスウェールズ州、ヴィクトリア州、南オーストラリア州に生息しています。各州は環境を守るための法律を施行しています。これらの法律は、国によるコアラの保護を強化しており、コアラの個体数に著しく影響を与える可能性のある開発計画はどれも評価を実施するよう要求しています。

　いくつかの環境保護団体もまた、コアラの生息地を改善し、コアラを保護するための植林事業に従事しています。これらのうちの1つは、木の植え方や、植林事業への寄付の仕方についての情報を提供する有益なウェブサイトを立ち上げています。民間企業もまた役割を果たしています。ある日本の自動車メーカーはオーストラリアで植林事業を始め、それによりパースとメルボルンの近くに1763ヘクタールのユーカリの木が植えられました。

　最後に、世界中の動物園が、オーストラリアからコアラを受け入れることで保護活動を助けることができます。日本、シンガポール、アメリカ、その他の地域の動物園で、コアラの世話がされています。コアラはかわいらしく、来園者に人気があるので、動物園にとっても利益になります。こうした努力が続く限り、コアラは絶滅の危機から救われるはずです。

【リスニングスクリプト】　　　　　　　　　　　　　　　　　　　　　CD 14

Now listen to part of a lecture on the topic you just read about.

　It's true that there are efforts under way, including those by the Australian government, to protect koalas. However, there have been numerous challenges in implementing these efforts, and much more needs to be done overall.

　First, legislative efforts in Australia have only been at the state and local levels. The national government declared the koalas "Vulnerable," meaning they are at risk but at a lower level than "Endangered." However, the government has not put forth any enforceable legislation. Numerous journalists and environmental groups have said that the government's "vulnerable species" designation does not go far enough to save the species. What is more, developers can easily get around the state governments' existing rules. Stronger national laws are required for the rules to have any real effect.

　Second, the deforestation problem will not be solved simply by planting more eucalyptus trees. Koalas are very picky about the eucalyptus they eat. Some of their favorite species of trees are dying out due to human-made threats. Creating a suitable habitat in which koalas can thrive requires careful planning and a high level of knowledge. Ensuring that reforestation is happening in a way that allows koalas to live comfortably will require much greater awareness-raising efforts.

Finally, shipping the koalas to other countries raises a whole new set of problems. It's very expensive to provide the eucalyptus species they like to eat. Moreover, koalas live in societies and are most comfortable in their natural habitats. And most of all, zoos abroad will only accept a limited number of koalas, usually just a few. Moving the koalas abroad is not a feasible solution. The only real solution is for the Australian government to fully recognize the threat to koalas and take decisive action to address it.

【リスニングスクリプト訳】
今読んだトピックに関する講義の一部を聞きなさい。

　オーストラリア政府による取り組みを含め，コアラを保護する取り組みが行われているのは事実です。しかしこれらの取り組みを実施するにあたり，多くの問題を抱えており，全体としてはさらに多くのことがなされる必要があります。

　第1に，オーストラリアにおける立法上の取り組みは，州または地域レベルで行われているにすぎません。中央政府はコアラを，危険な状況であるが "Endengerd"（絶滅危惧ⅠB類）より低いレベルの "Vulnerable"（絶滅危惧Ⅱ類）にあたると言明しました。しかし政府は，強制力のある法律を何も提案していません。多くのジャーナリストや環境保護団体は，政府の "Vulnerable種" への指定は，その種を救うのに十分な役割を果たさないと主張しています。その上，土地開発業者は簡単に州政府の現存の規則をかいくぐることができます。それらの規則が実際の効力を持つには，より強力な国の法律が必要です。

　第2に，森林破壊の問題は，単により多くのユーカリの木を植えるだけでは解決されないでしょう。コアラは自分たちが食べるユーカリに強い好き嫌いがあります。彼らの大好きな種の木々の中には，人間による脅威のために絶滅しかかっているものもあります。コアラが繁栄するのに適した生息地を作るには，慎重な計画と高いレベルの知識が必要とされます。森林の再生を，コアラが快適に暮らせる形で進めるには，さらに大きな意識改革の努力が必要とされるでしょう。

　最後に，コアラを他国へ輸送することで，まったく新しい一連の問題が生じます。コアラが食べるのに好むユーカリの種を供給するのには，とても費用がかかります。さらにコアラは社会の中で生きており，自然のままの生育地がもっとも居心地がよいのです。そして何より，海外の動物園は限られた数のコアラを受け入れるだけで，たいていはほんの2, 3頭でしょう。コアラを海外へ移すのは，実現可能な解決方法ではありません。唯一の現実的な解決法は，オーストラリア政府がコアラへの脅威を十分に認識し，それに対処する決定的な行動をとることです。

✓ 重要表現チェック

- [ ] under way「進行中で」
- [ ] legislative「立法の，法律による」
- [ ] vulnerable「傷つきやすい，絶滅危惧Ⅱ類の」
- [ ] endangered「絶滅寸前の，絶滅危惧ⅠB類の」
- [ ] put forth ~「(意見・案など)を提出する，~を発案する」
- [ ] enforceable「強制力のある」
- [ ] designation「指定，指名」
- [ ] go far「役に立つ，うまくいく」
- [ ] what is more「その上」
- [ ] developer「宅地造成業者，開発者」
- [ ] get around ~「(法律など)を逃れる」
- [ ] picky「えり好みする，神経質な」
- [ ] die out「絶滅する」
- [ ] thrive「うまく育つ，繁栄する」
- [ ] feasible「実行できる，実現可能な」
- [ ] decisive「決定的な，明確な結果をもたらす」
- [ ] address「~に取り組む」

問題 12

【課題文訳】

　大企業の大半が，階層的な経営構造をしています。これはつまり，企業の経営がピラミッドのように組織されているということです。社員はゼネラルマネジャーの管理下にあり，ゼネラルマネジャーはエリアマネジャーの管理下にあり，といった具合です。最終的に，組織の頂点には，最高経営責任者（CEO）や最高財務責任者（CFO）といったエグゼクティブマネジャーがいます。ほとんどの人は，これが大規模な事業を取り仕切る最善の方法だと思っています。

　1つには，階層的な経営構造をとることで意思伝達が向上します。管理職は，彼らの部下がきちんとコミュニケーションをとり，協働しているかを確かめることができます。また，経営管理者から入社したての社員のレベルまで降りていく明確な伝達系統があります。このことは，重要な経営管理レベルの決定や方針を全社員に簡単に伝達できるということです。

　明確に定義された経営構造は，下層レベルの社員にモチベーションを与えるものでもあります。それは，社員の社内における未来像を理解しやすいものにするからです。企業内での昇進の可能性は，大きな動機づけとなり，努力が昇進につながることが見えていれば，社員はより熱心に働くでしょう。

　最も重要なのは，管理職は，自分たちのチームが会社の目標を確実に達成できるようにする責任があるということです。このことはある面から言えば，仕事を割り当て，各社員に期待される働きを伝えるということです。加えて，難しい状況において助言を与え，下層の社員がスキルを高められるように助けるのも管理職の仕事です。管理職は厳密には上司のことであり，作業や担当業務を指示する一方で，よき助言者としての役割も担い，精神的観点・専門的観点の両方から支援します。

　概して，階層的な経営構造は，数百人規模の，時には数千人規模の従業員を抱える企業を経営する上で非常に効果的です。

【リスニングスクリプト】

Now listen to part of a lecture on the topic you just read about.

　Today I'd like to tell you a story about a company... It has around 400 employees, and they generate over $100 million in sales per year. This company operates with a very unique management structure —— there are no bosses... No promotions... Nothing like a traditionally structured organization... Perhaps surprisingly, this is working very well for them.

　While they don't have managers that act as bosses, they do have project managers that help make sure that employees are completing projects. Since there are no levels to the organization, important decisions can be made without getting approval from upper-level managers. Members of the company say that this has sped up decision-making and actually improved communication, because teams can work independently and not waste time in unnecessary meetings.

In this company, no one "works their way to the top." Rather, as employees improve their skills and take on more responsibilities, their salaries increase. As a result, employees are more motivated to improve and work hard, because it leads to higher pay... Also, the company gives large bonuses for exceptional performance... Ninety-five percent (95 %) of the company's employees reported that they prefer this type of pay structure to traditional, hierarchical structures, because they feel that they are rewarded for the quality and value of their work.

Since all employees are jointly responsible for achieving company goals, there is better teamwork overall. Newer employees often seek help from more experienced coworkers, because they want to take on more responsibility. Senior team members are motivated to help newer employees to improve, because they want their teams to work together better, as this is more likely to lead to the successful completion of their shared goals.

【リスニングスクリプト訳】
今読んだトピックに関する講義の一部を聞きなさい。

　今日は、皆さんにある企業についてのお話をしたいと思います…。この会社には400人ほどの社員がいて、年間1億ドル以上の売上を生み出しています。この会社はとてもユニークな経営構造をしています。上司がいないのです…。昇進もありません…。従来の構造を持った組織にあるようなものは何もありません…。意外かもしれませんが、このことがこの会社の人々にとって非常にうまく機能しているのです。

　この会社には、上司として振る舞うマネジャーはいませんが、社員が確実にプロジェクトを完了できるようにするプロジェクトマネジャーがいます。この組織にはまったく階層がないため、上層部の管理職からの承認を得なくても重要な決定をすることができます。会社のメンバーは、チームが独立して働くことができ、不必要な会議で時間を無駄にせずに済むため、このことで意思決定の速度が上がり、実際には意思疎通の向上になっていると話しています。

　この会社には、「トップの座に上り詰める」人が誰もいません。そうではなく、社員はスキルを高め、より多くの責任を負うことで、給与が増えます。その結果、社員は技能に磨きをかけ、熱心に働く意欲がより高まります。それが、賃金の上昇につながるからです…。また、この会社は、非常に優れた仕事ぶりに対して、多額の賞与を与えています。同社の社員の95パーセントが、こうした賃金の構造のほうが、自分たちの仕事の質と価値が報われていると感じられるので、従来の階層的な構造よりも好ましいと報告しています。

　全社員が会社の目標の達成に共同で責任を負うので、全体的にチームワークがよくなります。新入社員はより大きな責任を負いたいという気持ちから、しばしば経験を積んだ先輩社員からのサポートを求めます。チームが一丸となってよりうまく機能することが、共有している目標の達

成をより導きやすくするため，チーム内の先輩社員は，新入社員の向上のために手助けすること
に意欲的になります。

☑ **重要表現チェック**
- ☐ approval「承認」
- ☐ exceptional「非常に優れた」
- ☐ take on 〜「〜を引き受ける」
- ☐ reward「〜に報いる，〜に報酬を与える」

問題 13

【課題文訳】

　印象主義は，画家が自身の作品を照らすのに自然な方法を用い，色鮮やかな太い線で絵を描くようになった頃に始まりました。その名前は1873年に描かれたクロード・モネの絵画『印象・日の出』に由来します。そしてその翌年には，独立した最初の印象派展が，パリにある写真家ナダールのスタジオで開かれました。

　印象派の絵画の特徴の1つは，彼らが昼間の非常に短い時間だけ作業をしたということです。彼らは描く場面や風景のある場所へ行き，素早く絵を描きました。そして光が変化すると描くのをやめたのです。そして描き始めた時と同じような光の時に，その場に戻ってきました。それにもかかわらず，彼らの絵の完成までにかかった時間はより伝統的な方法よりもはるかに少なかったのです。

　色使いと太い筆さばきは彼らの絵画のもう1つの特徴です。彼らが注目したのは色調や色彩で，細部にはあまり関心がありませんでした。彼らはそれまでより色彩豊かな色や飽和色を使い，影にさえ色を塗りました。それが彼らの絵画を全体的に明るくしたのです。彼らは補色を混ぜ合わせることで灰色や暗色を作り，黒色の使用を避けようとしました。

　最後に，彼らの題材はよく見られる風景や普通の人々でした。彼らは近代的なものや娯楽の光景，例えばカフェやホテルや海辺などを描きました。1世紀以上もの間，それまでの画家もありふれた光景を描いてきましたが，印象派の画家は，どんな特定の要素にも焦点を置くことはなく，こっそり撮られたスナップ写真のように，風景全体がその絵を表すようにしていたのです。当時彼らの作品は伝統主義者に疑問視されましたが，すぐに一般大衆の間に根づき，今日まで非常に高い人気を維持しています。何十万人もの人々が最近行われたシカゴやボストンでの展示会を訪れました。

【リスニングスクリプト】　　　CD 16

Now listen to part of a lecture on the topic you just read about.

　We are so accustomed to seeing the Impressionists' paintings among the great historical works of art, as well as on people's walls as posters and even on T-shirts and neckties. However, while their work may seem lovely to people of today, at the time it was considered totally radical. They broke so many of the rules of painting in the 19th century that the Salon in France refused to exhibit their works.

　One example of their radicalism was the way they painted so quickly. Real art was supposed to be a laborious process that took time, and artists were supposed to spend weeks on a single work. You don't just go somewhere and paint whatever you see, the traditionalists thought.

　Another criticism was their thick brush strokes and lack of detail. To the critics of the time, paintings were supposed to be about composition. To them, the Impressionists' works were just dots of paint on a canvas. They even said they used too much paint on their shadows! Some art collectors asked Impressionist painters to "tone down" their colors so their paintings would not stand out so much among other, more classical paintings.

And the subjects of the paintings, which we now consider quite pleasant, were thought to be ugly and dirty. People wondered why anyone would appreciate paintings of such boring scenes. The critic Louis Leroy, writing in the magazine Le Charivari, was particularly brutal in his criticism. In his review of the first exhibition, he wrote that the first Impressionists' works were "commonplace" and even "vulgar." He slammed Monet's Sunrise painting by saying that more work had probably gone into the wallpaper than the painting! Those paintings that got so much criticism are now hanging in the world's best museums and they're worth millions of dollars, so that shows you how much tastes change over even a short period of time.

【リスニングスクリプト訳】
今読んだトピックに関する講義の一部を聞きなさい。

　私たちは印象派の絵画を見ることに慣れています。偉大な歴史的芸術作品の中で目にするだけでなく、ポスターとして壁にかかっていたり、Tシャツやネクタイにも描かれていることさえあります。しかし、現代人にとって彼らの作品は素晴らしいものに思えるかもしれませんが、当時は非常に急進的だとみなされていたのです。それらは19世紀の絵画の数多くのルールを破ったので、フランスのサロンは彼らの作品を展示することを拒みました。

　急進主義の1つの例は、素早く描く方法でした。真の芸術とは時間を要し骨の折れる作業であると考えられていました。そして芸術家は1つの作品に何週間もの時間を費やすものだと考えられていたのです。ただどこかへ行き、見えるものを何でも描くようなものではない、と伝統主義者は考えました。

　もう1つの批判は、彼らが太い筆で描いたことと、詳細が欠けていることでした。その当時の批評家にとって、絵画とは構図そのものだと考えられていました。彼らにとっては、印象派の作品はキャンバス上にただの絵の具の点をのせたにすぎなかったのです。影に多くの絵の具を使いすぎているとさえ言いました！　美術品収集家の中には、印象派の画家に、彼らの絵画がその他のより古典的な絵画より目立ちすぎることがないよう、色彩を「抑える」ように頼んだ人もいました。

　そして絵画の題材は、今ではとても心地よいと感じるのですが、当時は不快で卑しいと考えられました。人々は、なぜあのような退屈な場面の絵画を評価する人がいるのかと不思議に思いました。ル・シャリヴァリという雑誌に記事を書いた評論家のルイ・ルロワはとりわけ容赦ない批判を繰り広げました。彼は第1回展示会に関する評論の中で、印象派の作品は「ありきたり」で「下品」でさえあると書きました。彼は、おそらくその絵より壁紙の方が多くの労力が費やされただろうと言って、モネの『日の出』の絵を酷評しました！　大変多くの批判を受けたそれらの絵画は、

今では世界の最高の美術館に飾られ，何百万ドルもの価値があります。だから，そのことは短い間にさえ人の好みは変わるものだということを示しています。

☑重要表現チェック
- ☐ radical「急進的な，過激な」
- ☐ radicalism「急進主義，過激主義」
- ☐ vulgar「下品な，粗野な」
- ☐ slam「〜を酷評する」

問題 14

【課題文訳】

　南極大陸は，地球上の7つの大陸の1つですが，ほとんど無人のままになっています。その理由はそこに人が暮らしていける永久的な生活共同体を築くことが極めて難しいからです。冬の間，100人以上の人々が生活する観測基地があり，この人数は夏には数千人に増えます。しかしこれらの基地は研究目的のためだけのものであり，子供やお年寄りのいる生活共同体ではありません。

　その1つの理由は，南極大陸は人間が定住するにはあまりに寒すぎるということです。南極半島の最も温暖な地域の冬の平均気温は摂氏マイナス40度，内陸奥地の最も寒い地域の冬の平均気温は摂氏マイナス70度です。このような環境で屋外で過ごすことは，いくらかの時間でも耐えられるものではないでしょう。

　もう1つの理由は南極の環境では植物を育てるのが非常に難しいことです。南極大陸で見られるわずかばかりの植物はすべて南極半島に生息しています。その他の場所ではどこも，大きな氷のかたまりが，植物が育つのを妨げています。

　最後に，植物がないために生態系が存続するのが不可能になっています。これは，特に海から離れた内陸ではほとんど動物がいないことを意味します。食物を集めるための狩猟と漁獲は，人間にとって欠かせない活動です。生態系を構築する植物なしでは人間は社会を構築することができません。これらの理由で，南極地方には事実上生物はいないのです。

【リスニングスクリプト】　　　　　　　　　　　　　　🔘 CD 17

Now listen to part of a lecture on the topic you just read about.

　Compared to the Arctic, the Antarctic is a much harsher environment for life. Although the Arctic and Antarctic regions are both remarkably cold, the distinctions between the two are striking.

　First, the Antarctic is significantly colder and has far more ice. This affects everything. The thickness of the ice is a huge factor. The ice at the Arctic is about 10 meters thick at most, but at the Antarctic it averages about 2,500 meters. Also, in the Arctic the ocean covers much of the area, so it stays relatively warm. But inland Antarctica is nothing but ice, with no ocean to mitigate the coldness.

　With respect to plants, the plant life of the Arctic is relatively complex compared to that of the Antarctic. Areas north of the Arctic Circle on three continents have an abundance of hardy plants. Grasses, mosses, lichens, flowering plants and small shrubs grow throughout large areas north of the Arctic Circle. In contrast, the Antarctic Peninsula has what little life can be found on the continent. Interior Antarctica is virtually lifeless.

　With respect to animals on Antarctica, no species has evolved to live on the land there. The ocean life of the two regions has some similarities as they both support whales and seals. However, the major difference is in the animals living on land. The Arctic supports one of the largest land mammals, the polar bear. It spends much of its time in the water but is equipped with legs that work well on land. The Antarctic has no advanced animal life living entirely on land. Its largest land animal is a kind of mosquito.

【リスニングスクリプト訳】
今読んだトピックに関する講義の一部を聞きなさい。

　北極に比べて，南極は生命にとってはるかに過酷な環境です。北極地方と南極地方はいずれも著しく寒いですが，両者の違いは際立っています。

　第1に，南極の方が相当に寒く，氷の量がはるかに多いです。このことがすべてに影響を及ぼしています。氷の厚さが大きな要因です。北極の氷の厚さは最大で約10メートルですが，南極では平均約2,500メートルです。また，北極では，海がほとんどを占めているので，比較的暖かく保たれています。しかし南極の内陸部では，寒さを緩和する海がなく，氷しかありません。

　植物に関しては，北極の植物は南極の植物に比べて，比較的多くの種類で成り立っています。3つの大陸上に位置する北極圏の北部の地方では耐寒性の植物が豊富です。草，苔，地衣類，花をつける植物や低木が北極圏の北部の広い地域で育っています。対照的に，南極半島にはその大陸で見られるわずかばかりの生物が見られ，南極の内陸の奥地には生物はほぼいません。

　南極の動物に関しては，そこで生きるべく進化した種は1つもありません。2つの地域の海洋生物には，いずれもクジラやアザラシが生息しているように，いくつかの類似点があります。しかし最も大きな違いは陸に住む動物にあります。北極には最大の陸の哺乳類の1つ，ホッキョクグマが生息しています。ホッキョクグマはほとんどの時間を水の中で過ごしますが陸の上でうまく機能する足を持っています。南極にはもっぱら陸の上で暮らすように進化した動物はいません。南極の最も大きな陸の動物は蚊の一種なのです。

✓ 重要表現チェック

- □ the Arctic「北極（地方）」
- □ distinction「区別，相違」
- □ mitigate「〜を緩和する」
- □ the Arctic Circle「北極圏」
- □ hardy「耐寒性の」
- □ shrub「低木，灌木」
- □ evolve「進化する」
- □ seal「アザラシ，アシカ」
- □ harsh「厳しい，過酷な」
- □ striking「著しい，目立つ，際立った」
- □ plant life「植物」
- □ abundance「豊富」
- □ lichen「地衣（菌類と藻類の共生体）」
- □ interior「内陸の，奥地の」
- □ support「〜を生息させる」

問題 15

【課題文訳】

　脳は、その研究に人生をささげている科学者にとってさえも、常に謎のままです。最近の研究では、脳に関する多くの謎、特に記憶の仕組みに関するものを解明してきました。

　最初は、忘却の仕組みについてです。人はある種の記憶は忘れることができないと、長い間考えられていました。強い否定的な反応を引き起こすような記憶は特にそうです。最近の研究で、実はそれらの記憶を消すことができるということがわかりました。研究者たちは、ある遺伝子を持っていないマウスは、ある檻の中で電気ショックを与えられるとその檻を怖がりましたが、その遺伝子を持っているマウスは、新しい記憶を形成し、その檻を怖がることはなくなったということを発見しました。

　次に、睡眠の役割についてです。別の研究で、研究者たちは、睡眠が記憶や学習を向上させる仕組みについて、多くの知見を得ました。科学者たちは長い間、睡眠が記憶に関して重要な役割を果たしているということは理解していましたが、その理由について確かなことはわからなかったのです。アメリカと中国で行われたこの研究では、新しい技術を学んだ後、睡眠中のマウスは、脳内で神経細胞間のやりとりがより多くなされたことが判明しました。

　最後に、最近の研究により、記憶がどのように形成されるかの理解が進んでいます。以前科学者たちは、記憶を形成するために何が必要なのか、限定的にしか理解していませんでした。たんぱく質合成や神経細胞の構造の変化が関わっていることは知っていましたが、その他の仕組みは謎でした。今では研究者たちは、脳の中でも感情記憶に関わる部分にある分子群の一部が、たんぱく質合成を促進している可能性があるという知見を得ています。学習が行われると、この分子の量が減少することがわかりました。

【リスニングスクリプト】　　　　　　　　　　　●CD 18

Now listen to part of a lecture on the topic you just read about.

　The knowledge we have gained about the brain comes from some amazing advancements in technology and research. None of this would have been possible many years ago.

　In the first study, it's actually a gene called Tet1 that was found to be involved in retaining or replacing memories. It's part of the DNA. And once a bad memory forms, the researchers found, in order to get rid of that bad memory, a new memory has to form. That new memory will eventually take the place of the old memory, and the person will forget her fear. A drug could be developed that would alter the body chemistry to combat fear and anxiety. This could really be beneficial for people who have had some kind of trauma, such as soldiers coming back from wars or people who have suffered abuse.

　The role of sleep is interesting, too. The study showed that even if the subjects trained intensely while they were awake, they could not make up for lost sleep in terms of memory formation. That's how vital sleep is. Researchers used some of the most advanced microscopes in the world to look inside the brain and see what the brain was doing during deep sleep.

The study about memory formation, that's a little more complicated. But it was interesting to see how that one molecule, called miR-182, is actually suppressed when learning takes place. There's less of it. So for older people and those suffering from loss of memory, there may be some hope that regulating the level of this molecule with drugs could help restore memory function.

【リスニングスクリプト訳】
今読んだトピックに関する講義の一部を聞きなさい。

　私たちが脳について得てきた知識は，技術や研究における驚くべき進歩のおかげです。何年も前には，そのどの知識も得ることは不可能でした。

　最初の研究で，実はTet1と呼ばれる遺伝子こそが，記憶をとどめておいたり置き換えたりすることに関わっていることがわかりました。それはDNAの一部です。一度悪い記憶が形成されると，その悪い記憶を取り除くために新しい記憶を形成する必要があるということを，研究者は確認しました。その新しい記憶は，最終的には古い記憶に取って代わり，やがてその人は恐怖を忘れます。恐怖や不安と闘えるように生体の化学反応を変化させるような薬が開発されることもあり得るでしょう。このことは，戦争から戻ってきた兵士や虐待に苦しんでいる人のように，ある種のトラウマを抱えている人にとって大変有益でしょう。

　睡眠の役割も興味深いです。研究によると，起きている間に被験者がどんなに熱心に訓練したとしても，記憶の形成において不眠を補うことはできませんでした。それほど睡眠は重要なのです。研究者は，脳の中を見て，熟睡している間に脳が何をしているのかを理解するために，世界で最も進んだ顕微鏡を使いました。

　記憶の形成についての研究，それはもう少し複雑です。しかし，学習が行われている時に，miR-182と呼ばれる分子が実際にどのように抑制されるかを見るのは興味深かったです。この分子は減少するのです。すなわち，お年寄りや記憶喪失に苦しんでいる人にとっては，この分子の量を薬で調整することが，記憶機能を修復する助けになるかもしれないという希望が，いくらかあるかもしれないのです。

✓ 重要表現チェック

- [ ] retain「〜を覚えている」
- [ ] take the place of 〜「〜に取って代わる」
- [ ] body chemistry「生体の化学反応」
- [ ] anxiety「不安，心配」
- [ ] trauma「トラウマ，心的外傷」
- [ ] subject「被験者」
- [ ] make up for 〜「〜を補う」
- [ ] advanced「進歩した」
- [ ] suppress「〜を抑制する」
- [ ] eventually「最終的には」
- [ ] beneficial「有益な」
- [ ] abuse「虐待」
- [ ] intensely「熱烈に，猛烈に」
- [ ] vital「きわめて重要な」
- [ ] microscope「顕微鏡」
- [ ] restore「〜を修復する」

MEMO

MEMO

MEMO

MEMO

MEMO

MEMO